nympho
mania

OTHER WORKS BY CAROL GRONEMAN

Corporate Ph.D.: The Humanities Outside the Academy
(coauthor with Robert Lear)

To Toil the Livelong Day: America's Women at Work, 1780–1980
(coeditor with Mary Beth Norton)

nympho *mania*

A History

Carol Groneman

W. W. Norton & Company

New York   London

Some of the material from chapter 1 appeared in different form as
"Nymphomania: The Historical Construction of Female Sexuality"
in *Signs: Journal of Women in Culture and Society* 19. Copyright © 1994
by The University of Chicago. All rights reserved.

For information about permission to reproduce selections from
this book, write to Permissions, W. W. Norton & Company, Inc.,
500 Fifth Avenue, New York, NY 10110

The text of this book is composed in Perpetua.
Composition by Chelsea Dippel
Manufacturing by Quebecor Fairfield
Book design by Ellen Sasahara

Library of Congress Cataloging-in-Publication Data

Groneman, Carol.
    Nymphomania : a history / Carol Groneman.
        p.   cm.
    Includes bibliographical references and index.
    ISBN 0-393-04838-1
    1. Nymphomania. I. Title.

    RC560.N9 G76 2000
    616.85'833'009—dc21   00-027257

W. W. Norton & Company, Inc., 500 Fifth Avenue, New York, N.Y. 10110
www.wwnorton.com

W. W. Norton & Company Ltd., 10 Coptic Street, London WC1A 1PU

1 2 3 4 5 6 7 8 9 0

To Steve,
love of my life

contents

acknowledgments

Like the proverbial offhand comment dropped by a waiter at Sardi's that metamorphoses into a Broadway play, this book was born at a Little Berks Conference of Women Historians, when Susan Reverby jokingly said that a history of nymphomania would be a hoot. Intrigued by the idea of what nymphomania might reveal about attitudes toward female sexuality, I spent a decade doing research in such areas as medicine and the law, in which I had little expertise. Consequently, this book owes more than the usual debt to the kindness of friends and colleagues.

My thanks start with my writing group, Betty Boyd Caroli and Deborah Gardner, who met regularly for three years and critiqued every draft, sometimes several times. Their intelligent reading never let me settle for easy answers.

I called on many people to read and comment on various drafts and to help me turn vague ideas into words and chapters. My thanks to Joan Jacobs Brumberg, Faye Dudden, Max Gitter, Dorothy Helly, Jacqueline Jaffe, Judith Levine, Richard Lieberman, Mary Ann Mason, Ralph Norgren, Mary Beth Norton, Ruth Rosen, David Rosner, Shirley Sarna, Nancy Tomes, Hannah Waldman, Lynne Zeavin, and Judith Zinsser. I am especially grateful to Elisabeth Gitter, whose rare combination of intellectual insight and good cheer helped me in so many ways.

Leonore Tiefer, psychologist, sex therapist, and friend extraordinaire, listened patiently to every intellectual doubt that this book raised, responding with tough criticism, good ideas, and unfailing support. She also introduced me to a world of sex researchers, including an invitation to present a paper to the International Academy of Sex Research in 1995, and to participate in the Women's Sexuality Study Group, which she founded. I learned much from this interdisciplinary group of psychologists, psychiatrists, and sex researchers, which includes Cydelle Berlin, Peggy Brick, Betty Dodson, Marian Dunn, Clare Holzman, Suzanne Iasenza, Meg Kaplan, Brunhild Kring, Sandra Leiblum, June Reinisch, Pat Schreiner-Engel, and Sharon Thompson.

Thoughtful comments of papers given at the Berkshire Conference on the History of Women, the Columbia Seminar on Women and Society, the John Jay College of Criminal Justice Women's Studies Seminar, the Women's Studies Program of the Graduate Center of the City University of New York, and New York University Institute for the Humanities' Seminar sharpened the analysis. I was especially lucky to have wonderful research assistants from the CUNY Graduate Center, including Page Delano, Tracy Morgan, and especially Kathy Feeley, who contributed so much to the research of this project.

An American Council of Learned Societies' Fellowship and a sabbatical year provided me with time to write. The Professional Staff Congress and the Board of Higher Education of the City University of New York funded several faculty research grants, which provided funds for research at the Kinsey Institute in Bloomington,

Indiana; the Institute for Advanced Study of Human Sexuality in San Francisco; and the National Library of Medicine in Bethesda, Maryland. I would also like to thank the University Seminars at Columbia University for assistance in the preparation of the manuscript for production.

My editor, Amy Cherry, believed in this project almost before I did. Her willingness to read each chapter individually without waiting for the entire manuscript, together with her very thoughtful suggestions, smoothed the writing process immeasurably. My thanks go as well to my agent, Georges Borchardt, who was enthusiastic about the book from the start.

I am fortunate to have a very supportive administration at John Jay College of Criminal Justice. I would like to thank President Gerald R. Lynch, Provost Basil Wilson, and especially the grants officer, Jacob Marini, who was very helpful in guiding me in the intricacies of writing successful grant proposals. My colleagues in the History Department, and especially in the Thematic Studies Program, the interdisciplinary program in which I teach, deserve many thanks for their willingness over the years to remain enthusiastic while listening to endless discussions of this topic. In particular, Thematic Studies former chair Gerald Markowitz, and the present chair, Michael Blitz, colleagues Rudy Gray, Dan Juda, the much-missed Billie Kotlowitz, Sondra Leftoff, Jane Mushabac, Jill Norgren, Dennis Sherman, and Abby Stein all offered insight, comments, suggestions, and support. Also, thanks to my colleagues at the American Social History Project for their support and encouragement.

I also owe a debt of gratitude to New York University Law School Librarian Ron Brown, who helped me through the mysteries of legal research, and to David Garcia, who regularly rescued me from the vicissitudes of having changed computer programs in the middle of this project. Many thanks to the former Dean of the School of Continuing and Professional Studies at New York University, Gerald Heeger, who provided me with access to NYU's libraries.

My sister, Lorraine Hayne, and my stepdaughter, Joanna Curry, generously nurtured me over the long haul. My most important reader and critic, Steve Curry, participated in countless dinner conversations about nymphomania with his usual keen insight and unfailing good humor, despite the fact that even stories about nymphomaniacs become tedious on the zillionth telling. I could not have written the book without him.

introduction

A S I BEGAN to do research on the history of nymphomania in 1991, I asked my students at the urban university where I teach what they thought the term nymphomania meant. After the embarrassed giggles subsided, I took an informal, anonymous survey. About one-third answered that nymphomania meant an oversexed or sex-crazed woman; about one-third believed it was the same as sexual addiction, including a few students who thought the label applied to both men and women; and about one-third had never heard of nymphomania or did not know how to define it.[1]

My colleagues were equally uncertain about nymphomania's meaning, and many asked whether it still existed. Had the sexual revolution eliminated the concept altogether? An acquaintance remarked that her hip, twentysomething son and his crowd used "nympho" as a positive comment about girls who liked sex. Other people offered their thoughts unbidden: a dealer in used books who helped me find some rare sources asked me to introduce him to a nymphomaniac because he felt he had missed out on the swinging sixties.

My feminist friends wanted to know whether it was just another sexist stereotype. And many asked if there was a male equivalent. Yes, and revealingly none of us had ever heard of the term, "satyriasis."

As research so often does, my study evoked an incident from my past that crystallized the importance of understanding a concept like nymphomania. At the midwestern, Catholic high school I attended in the late 1950s, my circle of friends greatly admired and also envied a pretty, smart sophomore whom I will call Martha. Carefully walking the good girl–bad girl tightrope, she managed to be both popular with the boys and regularly attend Mass on Sundays.

In the spring of her junior year, however, Martha abruptly left school. Word went around that she had gone "to visit an aunt in Indiana," code in those days for going to the Elizabeth Crittenton Home for Unwed Mothers. Martha, so the story went, had attended a party where she was given "Spanish fly"—which everybody knew made you "want it so bad you couldn't stop." A rumor spread that Martha "did it on the pool table" with all the guys. We were shocked: Martha had seemed so cool—we wanted to be just like her—but now we tried to distance ourselves from her by labeling her loose, a slut, a nympho. To our teenage minds, Martha's offense was much worse than being raped and "ruined." She was the aggressor; she wanted it, or so the boys said. Nobody asked Martha. We talked about her endlessly, then forgot her.

Since then, this country has witnessed extraordinary changes in sexual attitudes and behaviors. The sexual revolution we have lived through, while not eliminating a double standard of sexual conduct for women and men, has significantly reduced the gap. Virginity has lost its singular importance: young women today have more sex partners than dreamed of by their liberated mothers' generation. In addition, a new understanding in the last twenty years of what constitutes rape suggests that our assumptions about Martha's sexual experience on the pool table might be recognized today for what it was: gang rape. Given today's mores, Martha would either have an abortion or keep her baby, maybe stay in high school, graduate, and even go to college.

But the sexual revolution and equal access to sex—like votes for women—did not change the world as much as, or in all the ways, women expected. Female sexual desire has become more acceptable, less rulebound, in the post-sexual revolution, but just as fraught with uncertainty. Moreover, in recent years the pendulum has swung the other way, fueled by fear of AIDS and by the religious right's campaign to "just say no" to sex. Fierce debate has reemerged over where to draw the line—virginity, no premarital sex, sex only with a future marriage partner, or only with someone you love.

As new sexual rules develop in the twenty-first century, anxieties persist: How much is too much? How much is not enough? Is there a healthy, normal, natural amount of sex? And who decides? These are exactly the questions that a study of nymphomania addresses. Over two hundred years, its shifting and uncertain definition suggests just how much culture shapes our understanding of female sexual desire and behavior, now and in the past.[2]

A history of nymphomania even helps explain the terrible judgment we meted out on Martha. No doctor ever diagnosed Martha with nymphomania. And yet her devastating experience, the way the boys treated her, and our denunciation of her all reflected a long history of Western ideas about female sexuality, about madonnas and whores, and about holding women responsible for controlling male sexuality.

As a disease, nymphomania is a relatively modern concept, but its roots are ancient. The second-century Greek physician Galen, for example, believed that uterine fury occurred particularly among young widows whose loss of sexual fulfillment could drive them to madness. Based on a theory that the bodily humors must be kept in balance, early Greek medical writing assumed that because women's humors were cool and wet, they required sexual intercourse to open the womb, and to heat and drain the blood. This led to women's insatiable desire for semen and, given their lesser ability to control those desires, resulted in the belief that women were more carnal than men.[3]

Medical ideas of women's sexual insatiability combined with a religious legacy that viewed Eve as a temptress remained essentially intact until the eighteenth century. At that time, a dramatic change in the understanding of female sexuality began to unfold. Consequently, modern notions of nymphomania, as uterine fury gradually came to be called, reflected very different premises about female sexual desire.[4]

This extraordinary transformation of assumptions about female sexuality occurred, to varying degrees, throughout the Western world. To understand this shift, we need to look briefly at the sweeping political, economic, scientific, and social changes that shaped a new conception of women.

Specifically, in the newly created United States, the American Revolution's egalitarian promise seemed to hold forth the possibility of a new role for women. If all human beings had certain inalienable rights, as revolutionary and Enlightenment doctrine proclaimed, why then was half the population excluded? Over the next decades, natural law, science, and medicine would provide answers that maintained the traditional hierarchy: women's biology determined them unfit to participate with men in the newly acquired political and social rights.[5]

Reinforcing this period of great change, a wave of moral fervor swept the country in the early nineteenth century. Evangelical ministers called upon women to provide a model of purity for both sexes. The ideal of female "passionlessness" allowed women to claim the moral high ground. At the same time, the new feminine ideal also firmly ensconced women on a pedestal. From this exalted position, her unique role in the new republic would be to tame men's passions and maintain the purity of the home, not to participate in the public world of work and politics.[6]

Over the next century, medicine increasingly supported this articulation of men's and women's inherent differences. Consider the following illustration: Renaissance anatomical drawings had pictured women's reproductive organs as an interior version of men's—the vagina an inverted penis that had not descended because of women's lesser heat. By the nineteenth century, these images had given way to a new model of male and female generative organs as totally different, one of many examples of the profound shift that reconceived men and women as completely dissimilar, not only in body but in mind and morals as well.[7]

Of course, doctors did not decree how the majority of women actually behaved in the bedroom. In fact, the medical profession was in flux during this period and society had not yet awarded doctors the status they would eventually achieve. Nevertheless, medical men—and the overwhelming majority of physicians were men—helped to legitimate a code of sexual behavior based on rigid distinctions between feminine and masculine activity.[8] They weighed in with their understanding that women's too delicate nervous system, monthly "illness," and smaller brain, as well as their reproductive organs, all made it unhealthy for them to vote, work outside the home, write books, go to college, or participate in the public arena.

This idea of femininity developed at the same time that the older side-by-side world of farmwork and home manufacturing was changing. Men's work was beginning to move from the home to the factory and the office. Assumed to be ill equipped for this rough-and-tumble, competitive public world, middle-class women could still play an important role as wife, mother, and helpmate to men.[9]

Significantly, the increased emphasis on the domestic and maternal role came at a time when both society and women themselves expressed growing concern about threats to women's virtue. Rising illegitimacy rates and an increase in lawsuits brought against men for seduction attested to women's sexual vulnerability. A more mobile society in the early part of the nineteenth century weakened traditional community and family controls, which had ensured that young men and pregnant women would marry.[10]

At the same time, the emerging middle class began to adopt romantic love as an important ingredient in the choice of marriage partner. In doing so, they would find that sexual attraction, which now played a greater role in establishing intimacy, also became more problematic. Concern came from many quarters: writers, ministers, and physicians all emphasized the consequences of the slippery slope of passion, especially for women. In an earlier time, parents, courts, church, and village life itself had provided external control. Now it was up to individual morality.[11]

Of course, sexuality was not just a problem for women. Nineteenth-century medical theory understood the body to be a closed energy system. Danger lurked in the depletion of the male body's limited resources through ejaculation, fears that created a masturbation panic lasting into the early twentieth century. Nevertheless, medical as well as popular beliefs considered lustfulness—although needing to be controlled—a natural state for men as it presumably no longer was for women. Consequently, the male equivalent of nymphomania, satyriasis, was diagnosed far less frequently and treated quite differently. Specifically, the symptoms of flirting, seductive glances, and other behavior sometimes labeled nymphomania in women did not constitute a disease in men: Don Juan, after all, was celebrated as a hero. When diagnosed, satyriasis was rarely treated by castration, the equivalent of clitoridectomy and ovariotomy recommended by a few doctors for the nymphomaniac.[12]

In the nineteenth century, women's innate character—formerly lustful—was recreated as modest and submissive. This did not mean that women were thought to be devoid of sexual desire; only a few medical men actually proselytized that extreme view. In fact, medical attention focused on the potential for sexual desire to overwhelm women. By nature less passionate than men, women were also thought to be less rational. This meant that they were particularly vulnerable to nymphomania and to other "sexual" diseases, especially during the "critical periods" of puberty, menstruation, childbirth, and menopause. In contradictory fashion, medical theory, as well as sermons and advice literature, elaborated a new *ideal* of womanhood: more virtuous and chaste than men, their desires linked to their maternal rather than to their sexual role, women were now expected to be the moral arbiter of relationships between the sexes.[13]

The new, sexually passive "angel in the house" defined by this set of beliefs was decidedly middle class and genteel. Reflecting prevalent class and racial stereotypes, most Victorian observers assumed that only the better classes could live up to this idealized image. Dominant theories held that the more primitive, animal-like nature of lower-class women, whether poor, immigrant, or black, made them sexually promiscuous. Consequently, while the new ideal referred to "Woman" as a universal category, in reality it included only white, middle-class women.[14]

WITHIN THIS SOCIAL and political context, nymphomania was a disease in the making.[15] Over the course of the nineteenth century, the discussion intensified in medical literature, even though relatively few women were diagnosed with the disease. Ranging from brief references about a particular patient to full-scale examinations of the disease, the cases I shall be discussing reveal attempts by doctors—and sometimes their patients—to determine the meaning of nymphomania. Here were middle-class women who actively pursued sexual intercourse, experienced heightened sexual desire, masturbated, even dreamed of sex. In a world that believed women to be sexually passive, the nymphomaniac's out-of-control, insatiable sexual desires exposed all the contradictions in this model.[16]

I am not questioning that some of these women might have been mentally or physically ill. Nor am I claiming that misogynistic doctors created these diagnoses simply to oppress women. What I believe these cases do capture is the multiple ways, at particular moments in time, in which doctors and their patients understood certain expressions of sexual desire as disease or disorder.[17]

Medicine is the starting point for this study of nymphomania, but the story goes beyond medicine, to the law, psychology, and popular culture, and to the interaction between them. Since nymphomania as seen through legal, medical, psychological, and popular lenses is such an ambiguous concept, I present its history not as a straightforward narrative but in multilayered chapters organized around two overlapping themes.

Nymphomania is a metaphor, which embodies the fantasies and fears, the anxieties and dangers connected to female sexuality through the ages. By tracing its many meanings over two hundred years, we see how clearly it is reflected in the eye of the beholder. One of the twentieth century's best-known sex experts, Alfred Kinsey, captured this idea in his definition of a nymphomaniac: "someone who has more sex than you do." Exploring the medical, legal, psychological, and popular portrayals of "oversexed" women as diseased, we see how much they reflect the culture that produced them.[18]

Over time, experts of all stripes—doctors, psychologists, psychoanalysts, lawyers, biochemists, sexologists, criminologists—have claimed to speak the truth about female sexuality. Under the mantle of objectivity, they have taken for granted that sexuality is universal, innate, and biologically determined. But the many guises which nymphomania has assumed suggest the opposite: there is no unchanging, inner essence that is free from external influences. Sex is not just in the body; many forces, including what is thought to be "normal" or "natural" at the time, shape its meaning. Examining the experts' theories and pronouncements reminds us just how much these supposedly scientific notions are themselves a reworking of older stereotypes of women. In a world increasingly focused on science as the basis of truth, these ideas profoundly influence attitudes not only in medicine, psychology, and the law, but in popular culture as well.

Nymphomania used to be an organic disease, then it became a psychological disorder, and now it seems to have taken on a somewhat humorous tone, although a darker side still lingers. In the following pages, medical cases, trial records, psychology texts, and popular sources reveal the many twists and turns in the rise and not-quite-fall of the nymphomaniac in the United States over the past two centuries.

nympho
mania

I

nymphomania in the body

N 1841, MISS T., the twenty-nine-year-old daughter of a Massachusetts farmer, was diagnosed with nymphomania. According to the physicians who described the case in the *Boston Medical and Surgical Journal*, her conversation and actions left no doubt that she suffered from the disease: she uttered the "most disgusting obscenities" and moved her body in ways that expressed her uncontrolled "libidinous feelings." Although in good health, she had been restless and morose, exhibiting a "paroxysm of hysteria" when the doctors arrived. After a vaginal examination, they determined that her uterus was enlarged, her vagina over-abundantly moist, but her long and "tumid" clitoris was the telltale sign of nymphomania. They applied various caustics to her genitals to cool her ardor and tried other traditional remedies, such as bleeding and cold-water douches. After several weeks, the doctors pronounced her greatly improved, with "not a symptom remaining referable to nymphomania." This time when she was examined vaginally, she exhibited "every appearance of modesty," including a retracted and very diminutive clitoris.[1]

Nymphomania

At the time, the doctors' treatment of Miss T., particularly the use of bleeding and caustics, was a typical medical approach to most illnesses.[2] Physicians did not understand much about the causes of disease and still relied on traditional remedies based on ancient Greek notions: disease meant that the body's system was out of balance. Consequently, bloodletting or purging restored the necessary equilibrium in the body. Blistering and caustics created a counterirritant, which drew poisons to the surface, and stimulated the body to return to its natural balance. Cooling baths, moderate diet, and sedatives calmed overstimulated nerves. This belief system was widely shared by both lay people and physicians.[3] Doctors and patients alike looked to the results of strong emetics or bleeding as tangible evidence that the physician was resolutely treating the disease.

In diagnosing Miss T., the doctors understood her to have a disease connected to her genitals. Men, too, would have been bled, purged, and blistered for a variety of conditions; but physicians were less likely to connect men's ailments to their genitalia, while assuming that women's reproductive organs caused both physical and mental disease. At a time when many women were overworked and undernourished, and further burdened by numerous pregnancies, it is not surprising that they experienced a variety of physical maladies. Consequently, debilitating conditions related to the ovaries and uterus were not that unusual.

But ideological beliefs played a crucial role as well. It was widely accepted that women's reproductive capacity—from puberty to menopause—dominated their entire being. Wombs (and by the middle of the nineteenth century, ovaries) shaped and determined women's nature far more than testes affected men's lives. As a result, not only doctors but average citizens as well believed that gynecological problems lay at the root of many female diseases, including nervous and mental conditions.

4

Since all parts of the body were thought to be interrelated, an upset stomach or an inflamed organ could lead to a disordered mind, and vice versa. In particular, a theory of "reflex action" posited that a disease in the genitals caused a sympathetic response in other organs of the body, particularly the brain. Reflex action presumably affected men as well, but women's more delicate nerves and monthly "crises" increased their vulnerability to potential maladies. Much more frequently than men, women faced the potential danger of reestablishing an internal equilibrium following the monthly loss of menstrual blood.[4]

These theories shaped medical notions of ill-defined diseases such as nymphomania. In the case of Miss T., the physicians tell us nothing more about what happened to her, other than to pronounce her cured, but if she had not responded to their medical therapy, she might have been placed in one of the newly created mental institutions. There doctors observed firsthand the most extreme forms of the female behavior which they diagnosed as nymphomania: indecent attacks on asylum attendants, lewd and obscene language, violent tearing off of clothes, and incessant, public masturbation.[5] The women described in these accounts may have been psychotic or suffering from brain disease. On the other hand, they may have been rebelling against the institution's strictures, while asylum doctors and attendants understood their unladylike behavior to be a symptom of a sexual disease.[6]

In any case, medical men who wrote about nymphomania made a connection between inappropriate behavior observed among patients in mental hospitals and women who came to them to express concern about their sexual desires. As a result, physicians saw the potential for nymphomania in a wide range of behavior. Nymphomania was diagnosed in behavior as diverse as lascivious glances, on the one hand, and sexually attacking a man, on the other.

Nymphomania

In the Victorian period, both doctors and the patients who sought medical help believed that strong sexual desire in a woman was a symptom of disease. Self-control and moderation were central to the health of both men and women, but women's presumably milder sexual appetite meant that any signs of excess might signal that she was dangerously close to the edge of sexual madness. Not surprisingly, physicians registered the greatest concern when the disease appeared in "refined and virtuous" women.

Many different medical theories attempted to account for the causes of nymphomania: overwrought nerves, brain inflammation, spinal lesions, misshapen heads, as well as irritated genitals and enlarged clitorises.[7] But the physicians' concern was also a moral one. They understood nymphomania to be about sexual indulgence and excess, about sexual desire uncontrolled by the will, about succumbing to temptation. While attempting to define excessive sexual desire as a disease, physicians continued to identify the patient's lack of moral restraint and willpower as central to the malady. The first full-length study of the disease, *Nymphomania, or a Dissertation Concerning the Furor Uterinus*, written by an obscure French doctor, M. D. T. Bienville, and translated into English in 1775, emphasized that particular connection. Eating rich food, consuming too much chocolate, dwelling on impure thoughts, reading novels, or performing "secret pollutions" (masturbating), according to Bienville, overstimulated women's delicate nerve fibers and led to nymphomania.[8]

Bienville's successors continued to repeat these same concerns, and exhortations to virtuous behavior intensified throughout the nineteenth century. Without any medical breakthrough or discovery concerning "excessive" or "ungovernable" sexuality, and with very few cures for nervous and mental diseases in general, the physician's best weapon remained a combination of common sense and moral proclamations, administered along with traditional remedies. In the last quarter of the century, as we will see, some gynecologists thought they had finally found the answer to curing nervous and mental disorders by surgically removing female reproductive organs.

Brain or Genitals?

THE DEVELOPMENT OF medical specialties such as gynecology, neurology, and psychiatry over the course of the nineteenth century led to turf wars in which each specialty promoted its own physiological explanation and treatment for women's diseases. Yet nymphomania remained elusive, despite attempts to classify its symptoms and to categorize its causes on sound scientific principles. Some medical specialists, such as neurologists and alienists (the earlier name for psychiatrists), looked for a physiological cause of nymphomania in cerebral lesions, changes in the brain's blood vessels, thickening of the cranial bones, or overexcited nerve fibers. They generally took issue with the "uterine theory," which argued that diseased genitals caused the malady. By doing so, they hoped to be able to diagnose, treat, and perhaps cure nymphomania, staking out their particular medical specialty's claim to expertise.[9]

Neurologists looked to the relationship between the brain and the nervous system to explain cases of oversexed men and women. Through postmortem examinations of spinal fluid, for example, they hoped to find some evidence that might help them sustain their claim to treat these disorders. But autopsies that showed no significant alteration in the brains of those defined as nymphomaniacs critically challenged the nerve doctors' theories.[10] Neurological research found little organic evidence linking nymphomania to the brain. Even so, for lack of alternatives, neurologists continued to recommend treating the disease with cold compresses, long periods of enforced inactivity, and other remedies directed at the brain and the nervous system.

Nymphomania

Alienists, while identifying suppressed or disordered menstruation and similar symptoms as connected to female nervous and mental illness, also looked to the brain and the nervous system as the location of the disorder. As superintendents of newly opened mental asylums, they espoused the then modern idea that mental illness was curable. The most progressive advocated that it be dealt with by "moral treatment" : maniacs and others diagnosed insane were no longer to be restrained in basements and attics, but placed in institutions and treated with a pleasant environment, simple work, and a "regular mode of living." Although uncertain of the causes of female disorders, such as hysteria, hysteromania, and nymphomania, alienists remained confident, until later in the century, that positive change could be brought about through this new, humane approach.[11]

During the early part of the century, phrenology—at the time thought to be a serious science—took another approach to the question of sexual excess. Phrenologists believed that mental faculties could be determined by measuring the shape of the skull: an enlarged cerebellum (the part of the brain located at the back of the head, which controls muscle coordination and bodily equilibrium) indicated inordinate sexual appetite. But a particularly sensational case, mentioned in the 1840s in both the American *Journal of Psychological Medicine and Mental Pathology* and the British medical journal, *Lancet*—whose tantalizingly few details were cited throughout the nineteenth century—dramatically refuted this claim: an autopsy report on a twelve-year-old girl diagnosed as a nymphomaniac declared that she had *no* cerebellum. No further details were given, and we do not know why she was diagnosed with nymphomania, but without a cerebellum the girl would presumably not have been able to walk.[12]

If some nineteenth-century doctors located women's diseases in as-yet-undiscovered lesions in the brain or in too highly strung nervous systems, gynecologists emphasized the central role played by the reproductive organs, not only in diseases of the body but in those of the mind as well.[13] Gynecology, not yet a respected medical specialty in the first half of the nineteenth century, had to fight to establish its professional status and to counter the unseemliness of male doctors examining female genitalia. Social mores combined with female modesty to limit what a doctor could see or touch. In the early part of the century the physician generally viewed the patient fully clothed, asked probing questions, looked at her face, hands, and feet, then made a diagnosis without ever physically examining her genitals.[14]

By midcentury, gynecologists very tentatively began to use the speculum (forerunner to today's instrument, which is inserted into the vagina) and to undertake more elaborate physical examinations, although moralists of all stripes protested this invasion of women's bodies. One critic even feared that the use of the speculum itself might so excite a woman's passions that it could cause nymphomania.[15]

Medicine was not a monolith in the nineteenth century and doctors did not speak with one voice about women's diseases. In addition, patients and their families had treatment alternatives from which to choose: homeopathy, hypnosis, hydrotherapy (water cure), and folk remedies. Various medical specialties developed competing theories, definitions, and treatments, especially for uncertain diagnoses such as nymphomania. As we will see, women patients also influenced the concept of nymphomania by the way they described their symptoms to the physician.[16]

In the following case, discussed by Dr. Homer Bostwick, author of *A Treatise on the Nature and Treatment of Seminal Diseases, Impotency and Other Kindred Affections*, in its eighth edition in 1855, we meet such a woman, who presents herself as so inflamed by passion she fears she might go crazy.

A Case of Nymphomania

MRS. R., DESCRIBED as a short, stout, recently widowed twenty-year-old woman with a lively disposition, came to Dr. Bostwick out of desperation. She explained, "If I can't be relieved of this agonizing condition, I am certain that the struggle between my moral sense and lascivious longings must soon send me to the grave." She blamed reading novels and attending gay parties in her youth as the cause of "my imagination [being] wrought up to the highest point." She appeared to be familiar with the assumption that women's reason was thought to be inferior to men's. As a result, she understood that stimulating the imagination in these ways was very dangerous. Her passions were so strong, she told Dr. Bostwick, that "it was with the greatest difficulty that I could conduct myself in a decorous and lady-like manner in the presence of the other sex." Even after her marriage, her "inordinate desire" was not entirely subdued and she continued to practice "self-abuse" (masturbation). Since her husband's death, "my passion has been more inflamed than ever, and I fear that, unless something can be done to relieve me, I shall go crazy." [17]

This case, presented in Mrs. R.'s words, reads like one of the cases Bienville described in his classic study of nymphomania. It contains all the elements that shaped the eighteenth-century understanding of the disease: inflamed imagination, uncontrollable desire, novel reading, moral struggle, and an inevitable downward slide into madness. Mrs. R.'s assertion that "I am sure my lascivious feelings cannot be natural— they must be the effect of disease," suggests the influence of "medicalized" notions about female sexual desire and women's sense of proper conduct.[18] It is unlikely that Mrs. R. read Bienville or other medical texts, and yet she was obviously affected by the ideas they contained, including the notion that sexual improprieties required a doctor's help.

Dr. Bostwick used a speculum to examine the "irritated" and "inflamed" genitals, including an elongated clitoris. He treated Mrs. R. with various remedies: hip baths, spare diet, douches, bags of pounded ice applied to the genital region, and leeches to the uterus, presumably to draw off the noxious blood. After several weeks, Dr. Bostwick declared that he had completely cured this "highly respectable" Boston widow. She even married again.[19]

Here, as in several other cases Dr. Bostwick described, defining nymphomania was not simply the physician's prerogative. Patients shared similar ideas about the body and the passions. They, too, were highly suspicious and fearful of "unnatural" feelings and interpreted them to mean sexual disease.

Nymphomania vs. Satyriasis

NINETEENTH-CENTURY PROFESSIONAL JOURNALS, medical textbooks, and encyclopedias often declared that satyriasis was the equivalent of nymphomania. Yet, in keeping with their belief that women were less highly sexed than men, many doctors took for granted that the male disease occurred far less frequently. Medical men also assumed that nymphomania, as a disease, was much more severe than satyriasis. The consequences predicted for the nymphomaniac were generally worse than those for the satyriasist; a nymphomaniac's fate was prostitution or the insane asylum, while at least some physicians thought that a satyriasist might go through life without getting into trouble if he learned to control himself.[20]

Further, many doctors recognized—although they publicly criticized the fact—that it was easier for men to fulfill their sexual desires in "illicit indulgences." According to an influential English psychiatrist and editor of the *Journal of Mental Science*, Henry Maudsley, such liaisons were "openly condemned, secretly practiced, and tacitly condoned."[21]

Nymphomania

The case studies of satyriasis, both in mental institutions and in private treatment, vary enormously. Like nymphomania, cases of satyriasis included men who openly masturbated, exhibited their genitals, and sexually attacked women, children, and mental institution attendants. Similarly, the causes of satyriasis were varied: genital inflammation, lesions of the "cerebro-spinal system," brain tumors, use of opium, and extreme sexual abstinence or overindulgence. Some medical authorities confused satyriasis with "priapism," an extremely painful condition in which a man's penis remains erect for hours and even days. Castration was sometimes used as a treatment for satyriasis, but this drastic procedure does not appear to have been a routine treatment for mental disorders in men.[22] Moreover, none of the satyriasis cases presented male behavior equivalent to the flirting, lascivious glances, or wearing of perfume, which was sometimes called "mild nymphomania."

The standards of behavior for women were, of course, much stricter than those for men. And some doctors recognized the role that social strictures played in limiting women's sexual expression. At an 1869 meeting of the Boston Gynecological Society, a woman diagnosed with nymphomania was brought before the gathered doctors. Typical of these medical presentations, the patient wore a mask, presumably to protect her identity. Even so, we can assume that exposure to a roomful of physicians must have been excruciating for this unnamed Victorian woman. One doctor responded to her in a patronizing, but possibly sympathetic manner: "If this woman could go … to a house of prostitution, and spend every night for a fortnight at sexual labor, it might prove her salvation." He hastily concluded that, of course, no physician could recommend such a course of treatment.[23]

In the nineteenth century, sex had become fraught for both men and women; bourgeois respectability demanded increased control, moderation, and self-discipline. Middle-class women in particular were expected to be a model of purity, to control men's lusts by the strength of their example. Although we do not know how the great majority of women coped with these moral pressures, some at least—like Mrs. B. in the following case—internalized contemporary notions of illness and consulted doctors with their sexual fears and concerns.

Mrs. B.'s Lascivious Dreams

IN 1856, MRS. B., a twenty-four-year-old, middle-class married woman, went to the Boston office of gynecologist Dr. Horatio R. Storer, future vice president of the American Medical Association. Described by Dr. Storer in his published case notes as small and pale, Mrs. B. sought the doctor's help for decidedly un-Victorian feelings. Excessively lascivious images of sexual intercourse with men not her husband, she told Dr. Storer, filled her dreams. Recently, whenever she met and talked to a man, she dreamed about having intercourse with him. Even during the daytime, if she conversed with a man, erotic feelings overwhelmed her. Up to that moment, she had resisted any actual sexual encounters, but she greatly feared that if the malady increased, she might not be able to restrain herself in the future.[24]

We can only surmise how difficult it must have been for a mid-Victorian woman to speak of these very private matters to a male physician. What we do know is that she understood these feelings to be a medical issue, which should be discussed with a gynecologist, not a clergyman. Whether or not she knew what nymphomania was, she interpreted her dreams as dangerous, laden with sexuality, and a warning that she was losing control.

Encouraged by the doctor to tell her story, Mrs. B. revealed that although she had never masturbated, from a young age she had felt strong, undefined desire. She assumed that she had inherited these feelings from her mother, who had experienced similar, intense desire as a young woman. This strong sexual need had driven Mrs. B. to marry at a relatively youthful seventeen years of age. She was happily married, she assured Storer, and greatly enjoyed intercourse with her husband, a wine merchant and much older man. In fact, during the seven years of their marriage, she and her husband had engaged in intercourse every night. She admitted that even when her husband restrained himself, she could not keep away from him. Recently, however, her husband complained that she had an obstruction that made intercourse difficult. She disagreed; the problem, she believed, was that her husband was having difficulty sustaining an erection.

Mrs. B. came to Dr. Storer not because she was concerned about the strong sexual desire she felt for her husband, the frequency of their marital intercourse, or her husband's possible impotence, but because she was afraid she was not going to be able to limit her sexual desire solely to her husband in the future. At a time when women were supposed to be innately less passionate than men, and during a period when Victorian modesty prevented many women from speaking about sexual matters to their physicians, Mrs. B.'s revelations to Dr. Storer suggest just how worried she must have been by her potentially adulterous feelings.

Interestingly, in this pre-Freudian time, Dr. Storer probed further into the meaning of her erotic dreams: Mrs. B. thought they arose because she and her husband longed for but had not yet conceived a child. Of all the possible explanations for her nymphomania—including the timing of her husband's presumed impotence—Mrs. B. chose the one which reflected her understanding of her role as a woman in the mid-nineteenth century. At least in what she reported to Dr. Storer, Mrs. B. determined that barrenness, not lack of sexual satisfaction, had caused her sexual dreams and daytime desires. For a Victorian middle-class woman, this conclusion is not surprising. It reflected prevalent assumptions that having children was not only a woman's major function in life but also the focus of her sexuality.

Dr. Storer, like most nineteenth-century doctors, looked to Mrs. B.'s body to explain her disorder and interpreted her libidinous dreams about a man other than her husband as a symptom of nymphomania. After a general physical examination, the physician pronounced her in tolerably good health: normal heart and lungs; regular but scanty menstrual flow; daily bowel movement; and good appetite.

He then turned his attention to her genitals. Like most gynecologists of the time, he undoubtedly was extremely careful in examining Mrs. B. Deciding that a speculum was unnecessary in this case, Storer reported on his examination: Mrs. B.'s clitoris was normal-sized, her vagina slightly overheated, and her uterus somewhat enlarged. According to Mrs. B., her clitoris constantly itched. In order to determine the seriousness of her condition, Dr. Storer gently touched it, at which point she shrieked, not with pain, but with excitement. Shocked and concerned about the extent of her disorder, Storer warned her that if she continued without treatment, she would most likely end up in an asylum.

The recommended course of therapy involved her whole family. First, Mrs. B. must totally abstain from intercourse with her husband. Because she was "unable to restrain herself," her husband was required to leave home temporarily. Her sister moved in and oversaw that Mrs. B. restricted her intake of meat, brandy, and all other stimulants that might excite her animal desire. The patient was ordered to replace her feather mattress and pillows with ones made of hair to limit the sensual quality of her sleep. To cool her passions, she was to take a cold sponge bath morning and night, a cold enema once a day, and swab her vagina with borax solution. Finally, she had to give up working on the novel she was writing. We learn nothing more about Mrs. B.'s literary output, but Dr. Storer was obviously concerned that dwelling on romance and passion was dangerous to her highly excitable mind.

Because medical cases—this one included—are usually published to illustrate a diagnosis and treatment, the narrative abruptly ends after the prescription is determined. We have no way of knowing whether Mrs. B.'s lascivious desires subsided, whether she and her husband had a child, or whether her husband's erection returned. Dr. Storer had only a brief, but hopeful, final comment about the case: Mr. B. remained absent and Mrs. B.'s lewd dreams had not reappeared.

A Young Working-Class Nymphomaniac

THE MEDICAL UNDERSTANDING of female sexuality shared by both Mrs. B. and Dr. Storer affected more than just the middle class. Poor and working-class girls generally did not go to private physicians in the nineteenth century, but in the mid-1850s, the mother of a seventeen-year-old girl contacted Dr. John Tompkins Walton because her daughter was having a "fit." In his discussion of this case in the *American Journal of Medical Science*, Walton described what he saw when he came to Catherine's house: her face was disfigured and her body contorted by a "peculiar and revolting paroxysm," marked by a "lascivious leer" and an "insanity of lust."[25]

Walton feared that as the only male present, he was contributing to Catherine's agitation; he proceeded to calm the girl by mesmerizing (hypnotizing) her. Then, borrowing from a technique he remembered described in medical school—farm wives who had difficulty getting their laying hens to give up their eggs would plunge the chickens' posteriors in cold water—Walton forced Catherine to sit in a tub filled directly from the tap. Quieted, Catherine was able to submit to his examination. He concluded that she was suffering from nymphomania because her attacks of ungovernable sexual excitement always occurred when she was alone or with lewd acquaintances.

In what appeared to be a contradiction of his initial statement, Walton commented that a lay person would see in Catherine an "ingenuous countenance" and "pleasing deportment." But because of his professional training, he claimed that he was able to see beyond these superficial observations to the primary cause of her affliction. Catherine's well-proportioned body and her "animal organization"— small, drooping eyes, large, broad nose and chin, thick lips—were the keys to her overdeveloped sensuality, and ultimately to her nymphomania. Reading Dr. Walton's reading of Catherine, we can see how contemporary racial and class theories influenced him. He "saw" Catherine's face and body in the categories available to him: pseudo-scientific theories that claimed those physical features revealed her character. According to these theories, proof of the primitive races' and the lower classes' licentiousness could be found in the shape of their lips, the look on their faces.

Looking for additional signs of Catherine's character, Dr. Walton determined that she was not a virgin, based on the "flaccidity of the nymphae" (the inner lips of the vagina) and the "distension of the vagina." The extreme sensitiveness of Catherine's clitoris proved to the physician that she was addicted to masturbation as well. At first he found her unwilling to confess to him, but under his unrelenting cross-examination, Catherine admitted that she was "a wanton" and that her appetite for masturbation was "insatiable."

Dr. Walton deplored the corrupting effects of Catherine's environment: she lived in a house with several families, shared a water closet with the whole courtyard, and associated with the young men lounging about the place. Some contemporary physicians would have recognized these conditions as signs of poverty, not moral failing. They believed that social and environmental factors contributed to disease—whether cholera or nymphomania—and advocated solutions such as cleaning up the slums. Dr. Walton did not share those reformers' sentiments.

Walton tried various medical remedies: inserting cool water into the vagina, putting leeches on the perineum (the area between the anus and the vaginal opening) to draw off the excess blood, and placing caustics on the vagina's mucous membrane, which was supposed to lessen its sensitiveness. In addition, the physician enlisted both her mother and her mother's clergyman to try to correct Catherine's moral "lesions." He entreated her mother to watch Catherine at all times. She diligently followed his orders; Catherine complained that her mother watched her so closely "as to prevent sexual fruition save at rare intervals." With typical Victorian moralistic fervor, Walton entreated Catherine to obey his strict regimen or else face the terror of an early and horrible death.

Catherine apparently rejected the physician's advice and was soon intercepted "in coitu," which presumably meant sexual intercourse. Outspoken and assertive over the months of treatment, she repeatedly denounced Walton for having destroyed her "virility." Because of the seriousness of her "insanity of venereal desire," Dr. Walton says he "rendered her emasculate" for a time (although he did not describe his method). He continued to control her "with threats of exposure on the one part, if she destroyed my work, and, on the other, promised to render her sexually fit to assume the duties of a wife whenever such services were needed." After six months of treatment, Walton claimed that "though she now occasionally experiences a slight venereal orgasm," Catherine was no longer inclined to resume her old habits.

These two cases—Mrs. B. and Catherine—reveal striking similarities. Even though Mrs. B. is married, middle class, and seeks medical help, and Catherine is working class, unmarried, and struggles mightily against medical interference, both cases define female sexuality as diseased. Nymphomania in Mrs. B.'s case consists of lascivious dreams, overwhelming sexual desire, and fear of losing control; in Catherine's case, nymphomania involves masturbation, and sexual intercourse—presumably with the young men in the courtyard. Physical causes are assigned in both cases, but nymphomania is still interpreted as a moral issue: inappropriate, problematic, out-of-control female sexuality, which requires watching, restricting, and taming.

A New Cure for Nymphomania: Gynecological Surgery

PERHAPS BECAUSE CATHERINE'S MOTHER had sought Walton out and expressed obvious concern about her daughter's behavior, the doctor did not simply write Catherine off as part of the innately immoral lower classes. Other physicians might have. Over the next few decades, physicians, as well as politicians, clergymen, and civic leaders—the middle and upper classes in general—grew ever more fearful as hundreds of thousands of immigrants and rural poor crowded into America's cities. In the eyes of those who saw themselves as the "respectable classes," these "teeming masses" spread moral depravity as well as disease.

New theories about heredity made this festering cancer within even more frightening. No theory of inheritance or evolution was universally accepted and much contemporary foolishness masqueraded as scientific truth. One widely held theory, for example, claimed that immoral traits acquired in one generation passed to the next generation and became innate from then on. Supposedly, daughters and granddaughters could inherit—much like blue eyes or brown hair—a nymphomaniac's abnormally carnal traits. To understand a patient's present condition, doctors began examining family histories, looking for an alcoholic grandfather, an epileptic brother, or a nymphomaniacal aunt. An inherited constitution which predisposed a woman to nymphomania or other female diseases meant that her condition would be that much more difficult to treat.[26]

Drastic measures were required. Since gynecologists linked women's diseases and complaints to disorders of the reproductive organs, a new radical "cure"—gynecological surgery—captured the hopes of doctors and sufferers alike.[27] Over the decades, surgeons had made enormous progress since Dr. Ephraim McDowell, in the Kentucky backcountry in 1809, had successfully removed a woman's twenty-pound diseased ovary. The lives of many women who suffered from fibroids, cysts, and cancer of the reproductive organs would be saved through surgery. In addition, some gynecologists hoped that removing ovaries might also relieve patients of their previously incurable nervous prostration, epilepticlike menstrual convulsions, and uncontrollable sexual desires as well. An ovariotomy provided additional benefits: the taint and perversion of diseases like nymphomania would not be passed on to the next generation.[28]

Surgeons removed thousands of non-diseased ovaries in the last three decades of the nineteenth century. Like many other physicians, one of the chief American proponents of this operation, Dr. Robert Battey of Rome, Georgia, founder and future president of the American Gynecological Society, believed he was ridding women of otherwise debilitating maladies. Affected deeply by the death of a young patient "in the bloom of early womanhood"—a woman whom he thought might have been saved if he had removed her ovaries and stopped the violent spasms she suffered during her menstrual periods—Battey advocated the operation in cases where the patient was "utterly miserable and without remedy."[29]

Operations were performed on both sides of the Atlantic for nymphomania, hysteria, dysmenorrhea (painful menstruation), epilepsy, ovarian insanity, and all manner of ill-defined female diseases. With little to offer in the way of a cure, many surgeons and their patients assumed that surgery might relieve a woman's suffering.[30] Excessive sexual desire—one of the amorphous, indeterminate symptoms for which gynecological surgery was recommended —also led to clitoridectomies (removal of the clitoris). Performed relatively infrequently, this operation suggested the extremes to which some doctors would go—and as we will see later in the chapter some patients would demand—in order to control what was perceived as sexual disease.[31]

The sexual response of very young girls or of older women particularly upset notions of appropriate sexuality. Too young or too old to reproduce, little girls' and post-menopausal women's sexual desires appeared to be unnatural, a likely sign of disease. In a case published in the *New Orleans Medical and Surgical Journal* in 1894, the gynecologist A. J. Block reported that a mother brought her nine-year-old daughter to him because she suspected the girl of masturbating. Fearful that the "taint" of sexual perversion had spread to this refined family, Block attempted to determine if it were true by putting the child to a "practical test." First, he touched the vagina and labia minora, but got no response. "As soon as I reached the clitoris," he reported, "the legs were thrown widely open, the face became pale, the breathing short and rapid, the body twitched from excitement, slight groans came from the patient." The child's violent response, according to the physician, proved that the clitoris alone was responsible for her "disease." He performed a clitoridectomy.[32]

Gynecological surgery became something of a panacea for a time, but it was by no means universally accepted. Attacks came from all quarters of the medical profession, including a sarcastic critique by an eminent British surgeon, T. Spencer Wells. Consider how outrageous it would be, he argued, if a society of female physicians proclaimed that "Most of the unmanageable maladies of men were to be traced to some morbid change in their genitals . . . one of them sitting in her consultation chair, with her little stove by her side and her irons all hot, searing every man as he passed before her."[33]

Wells was not alone in recognizing the essential misogyny of removing non-diseased ovaries; many gynecologists objected and used terms like "spaying" and "unsexing" for the operation. Nevertheless, although men also underwent extreme medical procedures for alleged sexual disorders, removal of the gonads was never a routine treatment.[34]

Autobiography of a Nymphomaniac

GYNECOLOGISTS CLAIMED THAT SURGERY—made much safer by the increasing use in the post–Civil War period of antisepsis and anesthesia—provided one answer to the problematic nature of women's sexuality. But because medical cases were presented in the doctor's words, very little firsthand knowledge of this operation from a woman's point of view exists. The following "patient's history as told by herself," although published in a medical journal, partially fills in this gap. The case graphically reveals one woman's horrific ordeal, but it also suggests how female patients themselves both incorporated and influenced medical notions about the meaning of sexuality.[35]

In 1885, "The Patient," as she was called, appeared briefly before a group of physicians at the Philadelphia General Hospital. Dr. Charles K. Mills, a famous neurologist, presented the twenty-nine-year-old woman's "pathetic and almost dramatic" case with some hesitation, presumably because of the delicacy of the sexual matters to be discussed. The gravity of this case of nymphomania overrode his misgivings.

The Patient came to see him, Mills recounted, desperate after many years of unsuccessful treatment, to implore him to sign a certificate of insanity committing her to an asylum. Instead, Mills convinced her to enter his hospital's nervous disease wards. While there, he encouraged her—as he did all his intelligent patients—to write her history in detail. This self-proclaimed nymphomaniac recounted the following story:[36]

"I inherited a morbid disposition from my mother, and the opposite temperament from my father, giving me a contradictory nature. Before I was six years old my sexual feelings were aroused by sexual play with other children and at twelve I was told by one who taught me to do wrong, that if any man knew of it he wouldn't marry me. I did not understand what that meant, knew little about my body, about the menstrual periods that began soon thereafter, and did not know that an orgasm could be produced by masturbation: I handled myself to quiet the excitement.

"Gradually, my nervous system became affected. The orgasms took place without my volition. Getting into a bath or merely washing the parts would often bring it on.

"At first my doctor gave me medicine to try to strengthen my nerves and induced me to exert my will, but my mind and body seemed to separate and the latter would act independently.

"Next, a clitoridectomy was tried but the relief was brief. Perhaps because of the particular manner in which the operation was performed—sewing the parts together—the clitoris grew again, so that other doctors scarcely believed it had been cut. The second time it was done the parts were stretched apart until they healed. The relief only lasted six weeks. At times I felt tempted to seek the company of men to gratify my passion, but was too modest and proud to do so. I

23

held myself above anything that looked 'fast' and never soiled my lips with unclean conversation.

"In 1881 I entered a hospital. I tormented the doctors to operate again but instead I was given treatment to strengthen the nerves. While in the hospital, I decided that my vocation was to take care of the sick. I had not been educated as I wanted and had earned my living by labor that occupied my hands. In the seven months that I spent in the hospital, happy and living up to my highest intelligence, I was not once troubled with the nymphomania; but when I left, and had to spend my days in work that held no interest for me, the disease came back.

"I again went for an examination and both ovaries were found to be enlarged. It was decided that the only thing practicable was to remove them, as a questionable experiment.

"Since the removal of the ovaries I have been able to control the desire when awake. But at times in my sleep I can feel something like an orgasm taking place. There is no diminution of sexual feeling. If my will gave way I would be as bad as ever."

This remarkable account captures one woman's dramatic and tragic response to her sexual fears and desires. To the patient, masturbation, orgasm, and overwhelming sexual desire meant disease. Calling her disease "nymphomania," the autobiographer herself understood her sexual feelings to be excessive and linked these emotions to mental illness.[37] She envisioned her mind and body in a terrific struggle that her will no longer controlled. As a respectable Victorian woman, the thought that she might give in to these desires terrified her. Believing that the overpowering sexual excitement she felt came from her genitals and affected her brain, she went from doctor to doctor trying to cure the nymphomania—like a cancerous growth—by having parts of her body cut away.

The autobiography also describes the contradictory approaches among the various doctors who treated her for nymphomania. Uncertain about the nature of the disease, gynecologists, neurologists, psychologists, and general practitioners considered a panoply of treatments, from nerve tonics to clitoridectomy, willpower to institutionalization. As a neurologist, Dr. Mills was convinced that nymphomania's cause lay, not in the genitals, but in a defect of the nervous system, and therefore could not be cured by genital surgery.

Although most women diagnosed with nymphomania did not undergo surgery, Mills was concerned enough about the prevalence of this treatment to condemn the contemporary tendency "to operate on everything and anything for the relief of nervous conditions."[38] He relented a bit on his criticism of surgery in the case of his tormented patient because it had achieved what he believed to be a laudable goal: she no longer masturbated. In his eyes, ending this unseemly behavior did not justify surgery, but it was a significant enough outcome for him to mention it with approval.[39]

In an interesting insight, the patient herself believed that meaningful work was the cure for her disease. She treasured caring for the sick not for the reasons we might expect from a woman of her time—selflessness and altruism—but because nursing called upon her "highest intelligence." Compared to other kinds of manual work she had been required to do, she preferred the still-to-be professionalized job of nursing, which in the 1880s included much mopping of floors and removing of bedpans. Even though Victorian mores pronounced marriage and motherhood as women's highest aspiration, this woman articulated what probably was not a unique desire: "work that I would have to climb to." When she had to spend her days in "work that held no interest," nymphomania reclaimed her.[40]

The autobiography of a nymphomaniac pointed to another major medical concern in the late nineteenth century, sexual excitement in children. When the patient revealed her own childhood sexual experiences to Dr. Mills, he became increasingly pessimistic about the potential to cure her nymphomania. To him as to many other medical men, evidence of sexual excitement in young children—Dr. Mills reported his concern upon observing it in two year olds—suggested abnormal, unhealthy sexuality. The assumed difference between male and female sexuality also shaped his observations: a four-year-old girl who was so sexually excited she would "get into all sorts of extraordinary positions to accomplish a species of abnormal masturbation" particularly upset him.[41] Even though the neurologist had earlier railed against too many operations, in cases of childhood masturbation he suggested that removal of the local genital irritation by circumcision for boys—he did not specify a procedure for girls—might be beneficial.

Deceitful Temptresses

AT THE SAME TIME that Mills presented this relatively sympathetic account, warnings appeared about another kind of sexually dangerous nymphomaniac. According to the British gynecologist C. H. F. Routh, and echoed in American medical journals, physicians should beware of a certain type of female patient who appeared outwardly modest, but in reality was a manipulative seductress. Recognizable by their "languishing looks" and "frequent sighs," these nymphomaniacs attempted to entice unsuspecting physicians to examine their genitals and to insert a speculum as a means of sexual excitement. According to Routh, the fact that some of these women then sued their doctors for sexual assault proved that they were mentally unbalanced. He warned his colleagues that several "members of our profession at least have been rendered insane by the mental stress from [these] false charges."[42]

Dr. Routh attempted to bolster his argument about the deceitfulness of these nymphomaniacal seductresses by pointing to the extraordinary stories they told. One seventeen-year-old girl claimed that her father had taken her to the seaside and forced her to live with him as his wife. Another young woman declared "that her own brother had ravished her in her bed at night." Years before Freud changed his mind about the reality of women's sexual revelations, Routh dismissed them as delusions or fantasies and proof that women lied about sexual attacks. "If they can invent such terrible stories about those whom they ought most to love and revere," Routh concluded, "they seem very apt to invent and believe other and more terrible stories about their medical attendants."[43]

In his eyes, no other explanation was possible: these women had invented the scenes of seducing fathers and ravishing brothers. Over the next decades, this assumption that women's sexual desire can so twist their minds that they fantasize sexual attacks became institutionalized in the law. (In chapter 4, we will meet more of these supposed nymphomaniacal liars.)

Physicians also claimed that women patients resorted to other remarkable subterfuges to induce handling of their sexual organs. Dr. Joseph Howe—who believed that nymphomania was most likely to occur between the ages of sixteen and twenty-five, and more frequently to blondes than brunettes—described a thin, highly nervous eighteen-year-old nymphomaniac who came to New York City's Bellevue Hospital, where he was house physician. According to Howe, because she complained of urine retention, "I introduced the catheter and found only a few ounces of urine. While doing so I noticed by a series of peculiar convulsive movements that she was under the influence of strong excitement." In his eyes, this was a better explanation than an alternate theory, such as infection or injury. He gave orders to watch her carefully. After thirty-six hours, she had refused to urinate. Dr. Howe told her that he would not use the catheter again and she left the hospital. When last he heard about her, she had consulted another doctor, who advised her to get married. Dr. Howe did not know what finally became of her.[44]

Many doctors assumed that women used the insertion of such objects as "hair pins, pencils, crochet needles, small keys, bits of bone, of tobacco pipes, of glass tubing, etc. etc." into the vagina, bladder, and urethra, and the subsequent gynecological examination, as a means of sexual gratification.[45] They understood the various insertions—of objects or speculums—as a form of masturbation, a desperate attempt at sexual satisfaction. The physical evidence they described might have led to multiple explanations, including sexual abuse or attempted abortion. Instead, many physicians saw these women as temptresses, not victims.

Once again, the nature of female sexuality is at issue here. Female orgasm was known and described in the medical literature—although with much debate over its nature—and many doctors recognized that the clitoris contributed to that excitement.[46] Nevertheless, the ideological assumptions of the period imagined that female desire was passive and latent, connected to true love, marriage, and motherhood. Thus, physicians expressed shock at the violent excitement, "loss of control," and "very evident delight" they witnessed in the doctors' offices during gynecological examinations.[47]

A lengthy article in the *American Journal of Obstetrics* in 1883, for example, suggested that female masturbators were easily detectable because "the clitoris will usually be found erect, and on touching it, the patient will almost invariably show her want of self control." [48] A woman's strong physical response to a doctor's touching her clitoris or labia—mentioned often enough in the medical journals to suggest that doctors "tested" women's reactions—or her vaginal contractions upon insertion of a speculum, were interpreted as signs of excessive sexuality, indicative of a masturbator or a nymphomaniac.

Perverse Sexualities

IN THE LATE nineteenth century, diseases that were intimately linked with moral character, such as nymphomania, defied medical attempts at definition, categorization, or cure. Increasingly pessimistic theories claimed that depraved behavior in one generation was passed on and became innate in the next generation. This fueled growing fears about the human capacity for progress and improvement. If a daughter could inherit nymphomania from her mother or aunt, what good would moral admonitions to resist sexual desires do?

Sexual behavior of all kinds came under new scrutiny: abortion was criminalized, venereal disease attacked, prostitution assailed, and pornography regulated. Previously unmentioned sexual behavior began to be widely discussed in the medical literature, creating ever finer distinctions between so-called normal and abnormal sex. Concern, both moral and hygienic, focused particularly on sex that was neither procreative nor heterosexual. Anecdotal case studies luridly detailed a hodgepodge of equally distressing "perversions," including cunnilingus, fellatio, fetishism, homosexuality, masochism, necrophilia, nymphomania, pederasty, sadism, satyriasis, and voyeurism.[49]

Rather than focus on the sexually deviant act itself, those who studied sex began to look instead to the very character of the sexually perverted. According to the Austrian sexologist Richard von Krafft-Ebing, in his soon-to-be-classic study, *Psychologia Sexualis* (1886), disease and pathology marked the individual identity of nymphomaniacs, homosexuals, and other perverts. No longer did a woman have nymphomania; instead, she was a nymphomaniac—dangerous, unnatural, and sexually out of control.

All sexualized women—nymphomaniacs, prostitutes, and lesbians—began to be grouped together. Supposedly, nymphomaniacs were driven to prostitution in order to satisfy their desires; prostitutes were often lesbians.[50] Carlton Frederick, surgeon in chief at Buffalo, New York, Woman's Hospital, commented that "All sorts of degenerate practices are followed by some [nymphomaniacs]. One of the most frequent is tribadism—the so-called 'Lesbian Love,' which consists in various degenerate acts between two women in order to stimulate the sexual orgasm." Conjuring up a monstrous image of lesbians, Frederick pictured them fondling the genitals of small boys and babies. These often-titillating pseudo-medical discussions included condemnations of literature describing lesbian love. Reading about lesbians was thought to arouse uncontrollable sensations in young girls and highly excitable women. They became nymphomaniacs and, driven by their insatiable need, prostitutes, who then completed the perverse circle by becoming lesbians. [51]

These groups of sexualized women challenged conventional notions in different but related ways. Too much sexual desire and excessive sexual activity in women was not natural, thus nymphomaniacs and prostitutes were abnormal and perverted. Since sexologists recognized heterosexuality as the model of normal sexual relations, they also labeled sexual relations between two women as perverse. They assumed that one of the female partners in a lesbian relationship must have "inverted" her role and taken on the active pursuit of sexual satisfaction reserved for men. It was this role, rather than what sexologists assumed to be the "passive" part supposedly played by her partner, which marked her as a sexual pervert. In fact, the "passive" female in a lesbian relationship was often not considered to be a "real" lesbian.[52]

All these women defied late nineteenth-century norms, which required both sexual restraint and adherence to highly differentiated gender roles. Lesbians, nymphomaniacs, prostitutes, and, as we will see in the next chapter, other women who refused to accept their assigned place, such as suffragists, feminists, and working women, were represented not only as diseased but dangerous as well. Determined upholders of the status quo labeled a whole range of women who stepped outside the rigid boundaries of femininity as a threat to the family, the moral order, even civilization itself.

Mrs. L.'s Sexual Pyrotechnics

IN THE SPIRIT of the new scientific inquiry into sexual perversity, Dr. L. M. Phillips, a general practitioner in a small upstate New York town, Penn Yan, attempted to answer a provocative moral question put to him by a colleague. In a case study published in the *Cincinnati Medical Journal* in 1895, Phillips first mused upon the following question: "What influence does the nude statuary, exposed in our public museums and the *fin-de-siècle* theater, have on susceptible minds?"[53] His answer was an attempt to clarify the mystery of this particular sexual perversity by quantifying it. Except for artists who were taught that nudity was not lewd, and the 1 percent of the population who never experienced sexual excitement, all the rest of the population, Dr. Phillips believed, felt heightened sexual desire when confronted with these images. For the sexually healthy 60 percent of the population, nothing abnormal occurred. For the other 39 percent— including Mrs. L., whose case he would use to illustrate his theory— the impression formed by these statues was so extraordinary that it lingered long afterward. In fact, viewing this nudity caused such mental upheaval that it might lead to nymphomania.

Phillips did not attempt to explain or to indicate the source of his sexual statistics. He was not alone in conjuring up numbers: at this time, the scientific study of sex was still in its infancy, and wildly divergent figures were bandied about as authoritative assessments of sexual behavior. Nevertheless, Phillips was certain that these percentages helped to explain the case of Mrs. L., who came to see him in 1895 complaining that for the past seven years she had been unable to control her sexual desires. She told the doctor that she was thirty-five years old, married for thirteen years, and although her erotic appetite had once been quite strong, after the birth of her third child she had lost all interest in sexual intercourse. So indifferent had she become to her husband that for the next two years she urged him to seek pleasure elsewhere. As quickly as the desire was quenched, Mrs. L. declared, it subsequently flared up and burned again with such intensity that it almost destroyed the couple's health. Consumed by lust, at times she shut herself into her room for fear that otherwise she would sacrifice her honor. Once again, desire disappeared; but eighteen months later it blazed anew, reprising her earlier "sexual pyrotechnics." She begged the doctor to help her master these overpowering fluctuations in sexual feelings.[54]

Like most other doctors of the era, Phillips was concerned about whether Mrs. L. had inherited her condition. But according to his patient, no diseases or mental abnormalities existed in her family. After examining her physically, Dr. Phillips declared her to be a "perfect woman" and ruled out organic causes, such as an inflamed ovary, lacerated cervix, or early menopause. Instead, without further elaboration, Phillips declared that a disturbance to the "psycho-sexual center of her brain" was causing her nymphomaniacal state.[55] With his prompting, Mrs. L. recounted how the condition had begun.

Some years earlier, before the nymphomania had taken hold, she had attended a fashionable New York City theater party. A *tableau vivant*—beautiful women, draped in diaphanous gowns, posing as living statues—had provided the evening's entertainment. Repelled by this display, she had fled the scene. But she had also been fascinated, and returned for several nights in a row to view what in her eyes was a disgusting yet compelling public display of the divine female form.

In his diagnosis, Phillips borrowed from the psycho-pathological classifications recently created by Krafft-Ebing. Mrs. L., the doctor believed, "was a case of *acquired anaesthesia sexualis episodiac*." This Latin mumbo-jumbo meant that Mrs. L. had developed—not inherited—these intermittent episodes when her libido disappeared. These interludes were interspersed with *paranoia erotisa episodiac*, the nymphomaniacal manifestations of the illness. Although no brain disease existed, gazing at the *tableau vivant* had seared an indelible impression upon the psycho-sexual sphere of her brain. The hypnotic, fetishlike quality of the imprint had impelled her eroticized mind to dwell on the forbidden image: constantly available to stimulate her desires, but never attainable. Without treatment, the exquisite torture of contemplating the object of desire would eventually induce brain disorder.[56]

Interestingly, in interpreting this case, both Dr. Phillips and Mrs. L. focused on the fetishistic allure of the living statues, but did not appear concerned that the object of Mrs. L.'s sexual excitement was the nude display of *women's* bodies. Krafft-Ebing had identified female homosexuality as a sexual perversion, but discussion of lesbianism was only beginning in the late nineteenth century. Also, Mrs. L. did not fit the image of female homosexuality most feared at that time: a woman "invert" who assumed the masculine role and actively pursued other women.

Contemporary medical notions shaped both Mrs. L.'s description of her ailment and Dr. Phillips's interpretation. She believed that she was sexually out of control and presumed that meant disease. Phillips asked the typical medical questions: Had she inherited her nymphomania? Had diseased reproductive organs caused it? But the psychopathological lens with which Phillips viewed Mrs. L.'s nymphomaniacal condition also shifted the focus of his diagnosis. Concerned with the presumed twisted and deviant nature of her sexual desires, Dr. Phillips understood these feelings to well up from some inner place. The "psycho-sexual center of the brain"—perceived as a physiological, not a psychological site—provided Phillips with a presumed location for the disease, but not a cure. He confessed that he was "at his wits end to provide relief" for Mrs. L. and the 39 percent of people for whom viewing nude statues was likely to lead to sexual perversion.[57]

In the same year that Dr. Phillips struggled over a treatment for Mrs. L., Sigmund Freud began publication of a series of works that would revolutionize the understanding and interpretation of sexuality. Freudian theory opened the way for an explanation of nymphomania as a symptom of a disordered psyche rather than as a physiological disease. Biological models of nymphomania were not discarded, but psychological explanations pointing to nymphomania as a personality disorder began to take precedence. Nymphomania took on dramatic new guises: explanations now included an inadequate sense of self, repressed homosexuality, and incomplete psychological development, all of which will be examined in the next chapter. Most surprisingly, frigidity—which at first glance appears to be nymphomania's opposite—became a clear indicator of the disease.

A mere decade or two after Mrs. L. walked into Dr. Phillips's office, neither of them would have recognized this new Freudian-inspired world. In the early twentieth century, these new psychologically based diagnoses encouraged fresh readings of the women we will meet in the next chapter: the semi-nymphomaniac, eroticized wife, encouraged by modern notions to expect marital sexual satisfaction, but often left unfulfilled; the "new" working-class girl, sexually precocious, "hypersexual," and delinquent; and the masculinized, sexually deviant "New Woman"—reformers, suffragists, educated professionals demanding their place in the public arena.

2

nymphomania's new guises

FROM ALL SIDES in the first decades of the twentieth century came the cry that a major "revolt from old standards, unlike any other" was taking place. "For the first time in history . . . women can gratify the sex instinct without the risk of pregnancy," proclaimed the progressive author of *What Women Want*, Beatrice Forbes-Robinson Hale. Women, she continued, were now able to earn a living without getting married, divorce almost at will, and voluntarily limit the number of children they had. These decidedly exaggerated notions of the availability of birth control, divorce, and free love captured both the desires and the fears of her contemporaries.[1]

At the same time, new ways of thinking about sex itself emerged. Starting with the late nineteenth-century works of the founder of sexology, Richard von Krafft-Ebing, through the prolific writings of the pioneering British sexual reformer, Havelock Ellis, to Sigmund Freud's elaboration of the role of the unconscious in sexual desire, sex was understood to be a driving force, not just in the body but in the psyche as well. These new psychological theories stressed that sexuality was central to fully developed human beings, to their identity, personality, and sense of self. By the 1960s, these ideas would eventually lead to a much greater emphasis on sexual exploration and expression.

A seismic shift was taking place as the sexual act assumed even greater importance, becoming responsible for everything from cementing marriage bonds to providing better mental health.[2] These sexual shock waves affected both men and women, but as we will see, the move away from idealized Victorian notions of female sexuality called forth the biggest changes.

Momentous shifts accompanied the new century in more areas than psychology. Across the land, women workers poured into urban factories, shops, and offices in unparalleled numbers. Female clerical workers more than doubled as women took the first, tentative steps in a long-term move away from domestic service to eventually taking their place in sales, service, and other expanding occupations. In higher education, women increased from under one-fifth to over one-third of all college graduates during the first two decades of the century. Campaigning for the vote, marching on picket lines, demanding that the city clean up slums and red light districts, the "New Woman" assumed an increasingly public role during a period energized by reform movements of all kinds.

Public spaces also drew working-class, and eventually middle-class, women to newly popular dance halls, amusement parks, and nickelodeons. From turkey trots to roller coasters, a rowdier, more sexually stimulating kind of commercialized leisure attracted young men and women. Women's appearance as workers and consumers in these various public arenas challenged an earlier generation's idealized notion of separate spheres for women and men: hers in the home, kitchen, and nursery, his in the world of work and public life. Depending on their point of view, contemporaries saw this unprecedented mingling of the sexes as leading either to long-overdue personal fulfillment or to potential societal breakdown. [3]

In what more than one commentator called a "freedom-intoxicated" age, where everything from hemlines to hairstyles was in flux, the concept of nymphomania too would assume new guises. Nymphomania, now understood to reside in the psyche as well as in the body, expanded as a construct in paradoxical ways. Not only too much sex, but too aggressive sex, the wrong kind of orgasm, and a catchall category of "masculinized" women all became indicators of mental disorder. No more scientific than earlier organically based definitions, the broader meanings of nymphomania reflected both fears and anxieties raised by women's changing roles, as well as new psychological explanations of sexuality. New categories of nymphomania appeared, which mirrored those groups of women struggling to achieve greater personal freedom. Nymphomania now threatened wives seeking erotic satisfaction in the bedrooms of America, sexually active working girls out for a night on the town, and career women whose independent lives challenged traditional notions of femininity.

Eroticized Wives

AT THE START of the twentieth century, anti-vice crusaders marched on red light districts, social hygiene advocates sounded the alarm against syphilis and gonorrhea, and reformers called for sex education in the schools. Spurred by a variety of motives, predominantly a desire to curb immorality, these campaigns had one common outcome—a dramatic increase in the public discussion of sex.

Witness the early twentieth-century battle for birth control. Margaret Sanger's astute and newsworthy challenges to the federal restrictions on disseminating contraceptive information through the mail opened a broad debate on birth control. Though limiting conception was not new—in fact, white women's fertility rate had fallen over the previous century from over seven children per woman to fewer than four—sexual abstinence or withdrawal had accounted for much of the decline in the birth rate. Now increased emphasis on the importance of sexual expression in marriage would lead to a rejection of the sexual denial these techniques entailed.[4]

These methods of birth control had been useful to an earlier generation of feminists determined to curb what they saw as the lustful desires of men, but a younger generation of women and men would interpret their sexual role quite differently. In recent decades, but particularly by the 1920s, they turned to marriage manuals and sexual experts who stressed the need for female sexual pleasure in marriage. Successful marriages, according to the gynecologist Theodore Van de Velde's enormously popular advice book, *Ideal Marriage* (1926), depended on mutual sexual satisfaction: women, too, must experience "a fully equal and reciprocal share in love making."[5] Marital sexual pleasure was not invented in the twentieth century, of course, but greater attention was paid to women's sexual enjoyment than in previous decades.[6]

With the genie of female sexuality now out of the bottle, contemporaries hoped that "companionate marriages," unions that stressed much greater equality between the partners, would transform modern marriage. To some, the institution appeared to need shoring up against women's increased—although still very limited—autonomy and economic opportunity. The newly eroticized wife created a modern ideal and signaled a rejection of what many assumed had been the sexually repressed marriages of their parents and grandparents.[7]

While marriage manuals now recognized and encouraged women's sexual response, they also created new standards. Women who exhibited more sexual desire than their husbands—or not enough desire—raised fears of abnormality and deviance. Consequently, women were cautioned, on the one hand, about lack of orgasm, and on the other, about excessive desire. Both generally repelled a husband, either because his manhood was tied to "giving" his wife an orgasm or because he feared that his wife's sexual desire indicated that she was the more potent partner.

This new middle-class ideal of marriage also subsumed what might once have been a source of power for women. No longer the "sexless angel" in charge of controlling men's more insistent desires, women were now expected to participate fully in marital sex. In a major turnaround from the previous century, modern notions of marriage stressed that the well-adjusted woman was orgasmic— preferably simultaneously—in intercourse with her husband.

But the insistence on female sexual satisfaction raised the specter of millions of sexually unsatisfied wives haunting the bedrooms of America. In contrast to the glowing ideal of sexually harmonious companionate marriages, medical authorities expressed increasing concern about female frigidity. Based only on anecdotal evidence and observations of individual cases, doctors claimed wildly disparate percentages—anywhere from 10 to 75 percent—of women were "frigid." White, middle-class, married women were the focus of these concerns. Immigrant or African American women were often ignored or simply written off as innately more sensual and less sexually inhibited.[8]

Frigidity was generally understood to mean a woman's lack of sexual desire or failure to have an orgasm in sexual intercourse; orgasm itself had many meanings. For thousands of years the clitoris had been recognized as the seat of women's sexual pleasure. Even in the nineteenth century, despite assumptions about female "passionlessness," the connection between the clitoris and female sexual satisfaction was not totally ignored. Freud's introduction of a new and startling dichotomy between vaginal and clitoral orgasms changed all that. In *Three Essays on the Theory of Sexuality* (1905), he argued that although the clitoris is the principal erotogenic zone in female children, at puberty, following a period of sexual anesthesia, libidinal excitement must be transferred to the vagina. In the process, "a little girl turns into a woman" and adopts "a new leading zone for the purposes of her later sexual activity." The pre-pubertal period of anesthesia "may become permanent if the clitoridal zone refuses to abandon its excitability," a condition which Freud considered to be so common as to be typical.[9]

Nevertheless, in the mature woman, the vagina—passive receptor of the active male penis—was supposed to take over as the center of erotic sensibility. Thus, not having the *right* kind of orgasm, that is, a vaginal orgasm, as well as having no orgasm, came to be defined as frigidity and interpreted as a rejection of femininity. Although relatively few people actually underwent psychoanalysis, Freudian theories greatly influenced medical, psychological, and popular writings from then on. Not until the popular dissemination of the sex research of William Masters and Virginia Johnson in the 1960s would this theory finally be laid to rest.

The frigid woman elicited both sympathy and suspicion. Some contemporaries blamed an unenlightened childhood for creating the sexually repressed woman. Psychologists, sex reformers, and marriage counselors called for sex education and a husband's sympathetic understanding of a wife's sexual needs. Others blamed husbands. America's most famous birth control crusader, Margaret Sanger, author of *Happiness in Marriage* (1926), compared the average man's sexual technique to "an orangoutang trying to play a violin." In the popular medical advice book, *The Doctor Looks at Love and Life* (1926), the eminent neurologist Dr. Joseph Collins echoed similar concerns: "It has often been said that American husbands are the best providers and the poorest lovers."[10]

But the Freudian psychoanalyst Wilhelm Stekel, whose ideas reached a broad audience through his influence on such popular writers as Theodore Van de Velde, saw something much more frightening in the "anesthetic woman who plays the harlot in order to triumph over the male and to give herself the appearance of being a 'modern' woman." Stekel's description of the frigid nymphomaniac conjured up a nightmare image of oversexed women whose sexual activity really masked hostile feelings. Either by coldness or by lasciviousness, she sapped the male's sexual strength.[11]

In this remarkable transformation, frigidity—whose meaning was anything but scientific—came to be identified with nymphomania. Neither frigid women nor nymphomaniacs had vaginal orgasms; both were unable to discharge sexual tension completely. Accordingly, the nymphomaniac, driven by her failure to have an orgasm, became sexually insatiable.[12]

Freudian theorists explained that the nymphomaniac's sexual need was like an infant's need for nourishment: always desirous and never fully satiated. Nymphomaniacs had not made the necessary transference of sexual excitement from the clitoris to the vagina. According to the Freudian psychoanalyst Otto Fenichel, the nymphomaniac was stuck in an early, oral stage of psychosexual development; her "vagina remains essentially a mouth."[13]

As in other psychosexual disorders, Freudians traced the causes of nymphomania to infancy. To illustrate, Fenichel analyzed the early childhood of a woman whom he diagnosed as a nymphomaniac. The outline of this case—much simplified in this retelling—described his patient's infancy, during which she "had a severe gastro-intestinal illness, because of which she had been starved. The result was a huge oral desire ... correlative with her oral fixation the patient developed an intense fear of losing love, and clung closely to her mother. Hence when she was three years old and her mother became pregnant, she was much embittered." When her mother unexpectedly died, the girl displaced her attitude toward her mother onto her father. Her "love tie" to her father was unconsciously formed by the "displacement of her pregenital relationship with the mother to the genital relationship with the father." She wanted "to become her father's penis in order to have a share in his maleness. All subsequent relationships with men were made after this infantile pattern." [14]

According to Fenichel, this nymphomaniacal patient endlessly sought sexual intercourse but was never satisfied. She was frigid, never having progressed through the oral, anal, and phallic stages to become a normal, mature woman sexually stirred by sensations arising not just from the clitoris. [15]

The unlikely pairing of nymphomania and frigidity in this and other cases reflected new psychoanalytic theories about the nature of female sexuality. The linkage also captured contemporary anxieties about the modern emphasis placed on female sexual satisfaction in marriage. On the one hand, medical writers touted female sexual pleasure as the keystone to marital success. On the other, they recognized the potential danger of unleashing what until then had been rigidly controlled.

Gynecologists, as well psychoanalysts, found the dividing line between normal and pathological increases of libido not easy to determine. Many of them still clung to the nineteenth-century notion that women were naturally coy and modest. "Excessive" female sexual desire continued to arouse suspicions of disease and disorder. Wives were encouraged to participate fully in marital sex, and yet too sexually demanding wives might sap their husband's vital energy. In the words of one of the most influential contemporary gynecologists, Bernard S. Talmey, "the weakest, most delicate woman is able to tire out the strongest man." Increasing numbers of women, not satisfied by "normal" marital coitus, Talmey believed, remained in a constant state of excitement. In a book directed to physicians, he claimed that these women suffered from *orgasmus retardatus*, similar to nymphomania in that they were sexually almost inexhaustible.[16]

Women on the verge of nymphomania might be left unsatisfied because of inconsiderate or ignorant husbands, but female masturbation was also considered to be a cause.[17] No longer totally demonized as it had been in the past, female masturbation's focus on the clitoris supposedly increased the excitement of that organ at the expense of the vagina. Companionate marriage supporters feared that this would lessen the sexual satisfaction of intercourse. According to the conservative critic Walter Gallichan, female masturbation "tends to blunt the finer sensibilities for coitus in wedlock, and the practice is often preferred to the normal gratification."[18]

Women's sexuality presumably had no life of its own, and was discussed mainly in relation to the role it played in marriage. Female masturbation was thought to resemble intercourse far less than male masturbation did, because it "involves very frequently the special excitation of parts that are not the chief focus of excitement in coitus." "Normal" heterosexual intercourse, it was feared, might be insufficient to produce an orgasm in women who masturbated. Reflecting increased concerns about women's sexual role in marriage, these critics discouraged female masturbation, not because they thought it was a sin, but because it might cause frigidity or nymphomania.[19]

Medical case studies featured these masturbating nymphomaniacal and frigid women. Revealing hidden details of women's sex lives, these cases also show how physicians, influenced by cultural notions of appropriate female sexuality, interpreted the symptoms presented to them. In what he called a typical case of masturbation leading to "retarded orgasm," Dr. Talmey discussed Mrs. G., a forty-one-year-old married schoolteacher who consulted him in 1908. In the case history that he asked her to write, Mrs. G. revealed that she had learned to masturbate when she was nearing puberty. She stopped when she went to college because she was absorbed in her studies. At the age of twenty-three, she met her husband-to-be, and although she enjoyed his caresses, she remained a virgin until they married. At present, she wrote, "I exceedingly enjoy the act, yet experience no orgasm save in the position face downward—the male underneath. . . . My husband prefers every other position to the one in which I have orgasm; they give him more pleasure."[20]

In a similar case, Talmey described Mrs. H., who told him that she also enjoyed the act, calling out endearing words to her husband, "begging him not to let it come so soon." But she was always dissatisfied when the frictions ceased or her husband withdrew his penis.[21]

Talmey diagnosed both women as "partially impotent." In his view, masturbation caused their frigidity and continuous desire. Talmey believed that women like Mrs. G. and Mrs. H. sought intercourse oftener than normal women did because their desire was seldom really satisfied. Without explaining how they differed, the gynecologist declared that this partial frigidity should not be confounded with nymphomania; in particular, it should not be treated with amputation of the clitoris. That operation would simply impede the inducement of the orgasm to a greater extent than before.[22]

Mrs. G. and Mrs. H. personified two problems which increased expectations in marital sex had created: Mrs. H. wanted the sexual act to last longer and Mrs. G. had an orgasm only when she was on top. These women's sexual desires ran counter to still-existing notions of women's innate nature reminiscent of the previous century. Slower, more passive, not aroused except by a lover's caress, wives were expected to be responsive but not demanding and aggressive. Seeing his patient's sexual experience through this lens, Talmey diagnosed Mrs. H.'s orgasm to be "retarded," not her husband's ejaculation to be "premature." Talmey understood Mrs. H.'s demands to continue the act, which her husband refused, to be signs of her sexual disorder.

Similarly, some contemporary writers interpreted Mrs. G.'s problem—only having an orgasm in the so-called female superior position—as usurpation of the male role. The "woman-on-top" was seen to be taking on masculine sexuality: too active and too demanding to be feminine. Potentially nymphomaniacal, women's commandeering of the "male" sexual position countered the belief that nature made her the passive receptor of male penetration.

As with all medical ideas, these attitudes were not monolithic. Van de Velde's marital advice book, in fact, encouraged what he called the "equestrian attitude"—woman astride the man—as contributing to female sexual pleasure and thus to marital success.[23] Yet, coupled with the remnants of Victorian attitudes, there were enough mixed messages being sent to lead some wives to seek out medical help for what they perceived to be their sexual problem.

Hypersexual Working-Class Girls

DURING THIS PERIOD, the guise most closely resembling traditional stereotypes of nymphomania was that of "hypersexual girls." This term was applied to a particular group of young women, in their teens and early twenties, who filled the new dance halls, skating rinks, theaters, and nickelodeons springing up in American cities. Concerned social commentators railed against these "coquettes" who promenaded along city streets and mingled freely with young men, flaunting their independence and sexuality. Earlier reformers had also worried about young girls, fearing that predatory men might victimize them. But now the tables had turned. Many professionals interpreted young working girls' sexual boldness as a serious social problem, an indicator of innate immorality. William Healy, founder of the first court-created juvenile psychopathic institute, ranted: "They are the temptresses of the opposite sex, purveyors of disease, and spreaders of vicious knowledge among other girls."[24]

From the point of view of many middle-class health professionals, the assertive sexuality of unmarried working girls appeared pathological. Still convinced that women's sexuality was basically passive and only awakened in marriage, many psychiatrists labeled these girls "hypersexual." Allegedly a more scientific term than "nymphomaniac," "hypersexual" and such similar terms as "sexual delinquent" and "sexual psychopath" embodied traits long associated with nymphomania. Uncontrollable sexual desire and aggressive sexual behavior remained central to the diagnosis. Exhibiting so-called hypersexual traits brought women into confrontation with the criminal justice system, which joined forces with medicine to confront potential threats, such as venereal disease, illegitimate births, and shockingly unconventional sexual behavior.[25]

Not surprisingly, the young women saw their experience very differently. In Chicago, New York, and smaller cities across the country, thousands of young women experimented with independence unknown to their mothers or grandmothers, trying on new identities, which ranged from adventuress to pal. Neither demure nor modest, these working girls were sometimes mistaken for prostitutes by reformers and the police. Dressed "dead swell," in high-heeled shoes, colorful hats, and low-cut dresses, these "tough girls" challenged the simple middle-class dichotomy between "bad" and "good" girls. The young women had their own code of morality. As a twenty-one-year-old waitress proclaimed, "A new generation of women has arrived and the wrong of Grandma's day is the right of today."[26]

These new mores also placed young women at risk. Living away from their families, in their own rented rooms or in boardinghouses, turn-of-the-century young women faced sexual exploitation, venereal disease, and unwanted pregnancy. Even those who lived at home encountered sexual risks. Emboldened by their contribution to the family income, many flaunted their parents' rules and went unchaperoned to dance halls, flirted, and stayed out all night.[27]

Progressive Era vice investigators, such as New York City's nationally known George Kneeland, expressed shock at these girls' disturbingly frank avowals of sexual desire and pleasure. He railed against "charity girls" who "offer themselves to strangers, not for money, but for presents, attention and pleasure, and most important, a yielding to sexual desire."[28] Breaking with Victorian notions of female gentility and modesty, working-class girls dismayed social workers who heard stories such as that of eighteen-year-old Helen Perkins. She wrote to a friend about falling in love with the furnace repairman: "Of course you know what that means. I was so God Dam hot that I didn't know weather [sic] I was going home or to hell. I suppose you got yours from Fred. I hope so."[29]

A long lineup of professionals attempted to understand—and also to control—these adolescent girls' unconventional sexual behavior. However, not all of them condemned it. Influenced by newer psychoanalytic notions that assumed the normalcy of young girls' sexual feelings, some reformers advocated a shift away from the sexually restrictive notions of an earlier period. Psychologist Phyllis Blanchard, head of the Philadelphia Child Guidance Clinic and author of *The Adolescent Girl* (1920), worried that over-repressive parental restrictions might turn girls toward promiscuity. Moreover, given the violent crushes young girls developed on other girls, she feared that overcautious parents might drive a daughter "to fixate on members of the same sex." By the 1920s, Blanchard and other mental health experts were staffing hundreds of clinics and child guidance centers. One of their main concerns was to help "maladjusted," sexually precocious girls to avoid the criminal justice system.[30]

These more permissive, liberal ideas had little impact on the state agencies, courts, and institutions where the great majority of girls who were deemed hypersexual and delinquent wound up. At the turn of the century, newly established juvenile courts had assumed jurisdiction for young people's behavior, creating both social services and correctional institutions.[31] Reflecting their belief that "wayward girls" presented a dangerous threat to the social order, the criminal justice system arrested and incarcerated young women for a bad reputation alone, for being "on the road to ruin," if not already arrived. Hanging out with a tough crowd, staying out all night, going to notorious dance halls, getting caught in a hotel with a man, all could lead to arrest, conviction, and a long stay in a state institution.[32]

"Delinquency" was a malleable term, different for boys than for girls. While juvenile authorities actually arrested many more delinquent boys than girls—for pickpocketing, fighting, breaking into empty houses—judges often dismissed them or put them on probation as merely mischievous but harmless youths. Yet social workers believed that rebellious behavior threatened to ruin a girl's whole life.[33] According to one Chicago social investigator, charges of being "incorrigible" or exhibiting "disorderly conduct" disguised the fact that "more than 80 percent of delinquent girls are brought to court because their virtue is in peril, if it has not already been lost."

Continuing to link women's mental condition to their bodies' periodic cycles, experts declared it was not surprising that the delinquent girls who got hauled into court presented a different problem from the boys. In *The Individual Delinquent*, Dr. William Healy maintained that menstrual cycles greatly heightened women's sexual impulses. These desires dominated the lives of hypersexual girls and shaped their activities more insistently than sex drives influenced male delinquency.[34]

Because many reformers assumed that a normal girl would give

up her virginity only in the marital bed, they simply could not understand why waitresses, domestic servants, and female factory workers
granted sexual favors in return for "a good time." To many of the
newly created juvenile experts, this "delinquent" behavior indicated
that the girls were more than merely rowdy or sexually assertive.
Their sexual delinquency meant mental disease. As one Harvard
Medical School neuropathologist, Dr. E. E. Southard, declared, "perhaps more than half of all sex delinquents . . . are in one way or other
psychopathic." A relatively new, catchall diagnosis, psychopathy suggested that some kind of mental disorder, although one without identifiable neurological basis, afflicted these girls. Delinquency defined
as disease also legitimized the psychiatrists' professional claim to
treat the problem of hypersexual girls.[35]

Rose Talbot was one such hypersexual delinquent, diagnosed at
the Boston Psychopathic Hospital in 1915 as an "emotional and un-
stable girl with a strong sex desire." According to the hospital's published case notes, at seventeen, she married a young man afflicted
with syphilis who died soon after their marriage. Untrained and un-
dereducated, Rose bore a syphilitic child, named Betty, then married
a "respectable man" at the age of twenty-two. Headstrong, she left her
husband after a quarrel in which he suggested they live with his
mother. She tried to support herself and her child as a waitress, but
unable to make it, she applied to the "charity authorities." Now under
the watchful eye of social agencies, Rose was arrested for adultery after a social worker tipped off the police. Put on probation, placed in
a home for "wayward girls," Rose's violent outbursts there convinced
the social workers that her case was hopeless: they would have to wait
for an "'overt act' which would eventually allow her commitment
and internment in some receptacle for delinquents." Meanwhile,
Betty, now a toddler, became a ward of the state.[36]

Rose was sent to the Boston Psychopathic Hospital for evaluation

49

and for treatment for syphilis. At first, she struck the medical experts as a "hopelessly undependable, probably incorrigible instance of an oversexed woman." One physician—although he reviewed only the clinical data and did not interview Rose—thought she might be "feeble-minded." He believed that her history of promiscuous sexual behavior before she came to the hospital suggested as much. But IQ tests indicated that Rose was of high intelligence, a quality thought rare among sex delinquents.[37]

One social worker who specialized in managing psychopathic cases expressed hope in Rose Talbot's future. Miss Carroll, to whom Rose would write a series of remarkable, confessional letters after leaving the hospital, noted Rose's considerable intelligence, well-developed self-respect, and good judgment in most matters, except in the "sex sphere." For more than a year, Rose poured out her heart to her trusted confidante. Remarkably frank about her struggle with sexual desire, Rose wrote: "I'm trying so hard to be good. Course it's lots easier than at first, but I want so much to be bad." She struggled with temptation and with "passions . . . the most unruly I ever encountered." For a while she placed her trust in God and asked plaintively: "He will keep me good, won't He?" She swore to God never to commit adultery or fornication again. "But at times," she cried, "I ache all over, I feel if I could be bad just once, awfully bad, I'd be quite happy and satisfied."[38]

Capturing the struggle young women were experiencing in defining new sexual ways different from "Grandma's day," Rose proclaimed, "it was too confounded mean that one can't have free love, or at least until the children come." She broke off a relationship with an "awfully decent" young man because she did not want to marry him, even though "we were, two perfectly mated, physically and mentally—human beings, each desiring one of the opposite sex. . . ."[39]

The notion of free love, promoted a half century earlier by sex radicals such as the first woman candidate for president, Victoria Woodhull, became pervasive in the popular imagination in the early part of the twentieth century, and was discussed frequently in newspapers, movies, and novels. Sex outside marriage, while still condemned by most upstanding citizens, was no longer unthinkable or undiscussable. Rose Talbot, after reading some of Havelock Ellis's *Studies in the Psychology of Sex*, and a popular book called *The Truth About Woman*, declared that these books "quite knocked all my good resolutions to smash." From these sexologists she determined that "it is not wicked to have sexual intercourse with other men than your husband. It is merely not the fashion." She confronted Miss Carroll with the double bind in which she felt trapped: "Now with you saying to be good and this book to give free rein to any and all impulses and passion, what is one to do?"[40]

With these words, Rose challenged the good girls–bad girls' dichotomy. She also captured a modern notion of the self. In ways foreign to all but a few nineteenth-century women, Rose claimed her sexual desire as central to her identity. And yet, she felt guilty when she acted upon these passions. The desire to satisfy her "own natural cravings" continued to war with the belief that something "bad" in her made her give in to these sexual feelings.

Rose's caseworker also expressed ambivalence, but of a different kind: Was Rose sexually delinquent or did she simply lack education and information? On the one hand, Miss Carroll thought that Rose's moral defects could be abolished with suitable training, but on the other hand that disease caused a good deal of her difficulties. The social worker's confusion attested to the subjective and moralistic, rather than scientific, quality of the psychopathological diagnosis. The muddled explanation notwithstanding, "social-psychiatric treatment"—which even the case analysis recognized was not easy to define—supposedly led to Rose's remarkable improvement. At the time of the report, the young woman was working as a telegrapher earning what was then a very substantial sum of seventy-five dollars a month, living again with her ex-husband, and paying a relative to care for her child. Her syphilis was in remission.[41]

Rose, the former "sex delinquent," appears to have made a success of her life, at least temporarily; but what about other nymphomaniacal girls? Concern about their behavior became part of a much larger discussion about immigration and assimilation taking place at the turn of the century. As over twelve million immigrants flooded into America between 1900 and World War I, many influential members of society feared that the "huddled masses" from Southern and Eastern Europe would overwhelm cities with venereal disease, depravity, but most of all, inferior genes. The popular and pseudo-scientific eugenics movement denounced the "unfit races" who passed their tainted genes—not only physical characteristics, but also character traits such as sexual immorality—from generation to generation. Many eugenicists blamed immigrants, especially young immigrant women, for being unable to restrain their "instinctively emotional" sexual nature. In the most overheated of these discussions, swarms of feckless, delinquent children threatened to overwhelm America. The lethal theories which linked hypersexuality with racial inferiority conjured up fears that the Anglo-Saxon "race" was committing mass suicide.

Stimulated by this concern, advocates of a more "scientific" approach to breeding, such as the physician who evaluated Rose Talbot, attempted to define some measure of this inferiority in the notion of "feeblemindedness." This concept had come into existence in the 1850s, but attained new importance following the 1908 introduction of a test to measure IQ. Physicians and psychologists now believed they had a surefire way of determining mental defect: an individual who scored below his or her "chronological mental age."[42]

For several decades in the early twentieth century, measurements of feeblemindedness—much like measuring clitorises to determine sexual disorder in the nineteenth century—were touted as surefire methods of determining female sexual delinquency. Labeling many teenagers in trouble, especially immigrants, "feebleminded," experts administered these would-be scientific tests to tens of thousands of young people picked up by child investigators. According to their theories, gross immorality in girls went hand in hand with feeblemindedness; the mentally defective girl simply could not control her sexual urges. So surprised were they by the numbers of immigrant girls engaged in a wide variety of "delinquent" behaviors, such as staying out all night or picking up sailors, that they assumed the girls were feebleminded. Particularly worrisome, mentally defective delinquent girls supposedly greatly outnumbered similarly affected boys.[43]

Feeblemindedness, innate sexual defect, and sexual delinquency: the nymphomaniac or hypersexual girl personified all these categories. Inheriting from her ancestors an "unchecked taint flowing in her veins," she would pass these immoral qualities on to her children. Some mental health experts advocated putting these young women into institutions for the feebleminded—at least for their fertile years—to keep them from producing feebleminded offspring. The eugenicist and Los Angeles juvenile court psychiatrist Ernest Hoag called for "segregation or sterilization or both to prevent transmission of mental defects leading to crime."[44]

In a much more sympathetic vein, the supervisor of the Texas Training School for Girls, Dr. Carrie Weaver Smith, suggested that the delinquent girl was not so different from her more fortunate college-educated sisters. Smith, along with many other settlement house and social workers, recognized that both groups of young women sought adventure, getting picked up by boys and taken to dances and shows—only the working girl faced institutionalization for her escapades. Other, more patronizing voices recommended that the delinquent girl "should never be censored by society, but should be protected because of the child that she is." Some of these "children," like Rose, were in their early twenties.[45]

Concerned reformers incarcerated or institutionalized girls to protect them from the dangers of the streets. Parents, too, brought daughters they feared would get into trouble to the juvenile agencies. But another, less sympathetic theme—of evil temptresses and potential purveyors of disease—can also be found in the early twentieth-century stories of hypersexual, feebleminded girls. From around the country came near-hysterical warnings of overdeveloped, man-crazy, defective girls with enlarged hips and busts and unusual amounts of sexual feeling preying on unsuspecting young men. From the Southwest came the story of the girl who "had for her lovers all the desperadoes of Texas." From big cities came tales of feebleminded prostitutes roaming the streets. But feeblemindedness was not always easy to determine. Indeed, a California psychologist commented with some surprise that the "subnormal," institutionalized delinquent girls she studied exhibited "few signs of subnormality, and many are vivacious and of bright appearance."[46]

Heredity, if not feeblemindedness, played a major role in the case of one intelligent, sixteen-year-old immigrant girl in "tremendously good condition" who was examined by the Chicago Psychopathic Institute at the behest of the juvenile court. Very strong and physically fit, with a mature face, decidedly good features, and a firm chin, she had been referred to the juvenile authorities for staying away from home, going to work when and where she pleased, threatening physical violence, and indulging in what was labeled "sex delinquency." For her part, the daughter didn't think of herself as bad or weak-willed: "I just do as I want to." Exemplifying the feistiness that had gotten her into trouble, the teenager refused to take the mental tests proposed to determine whether she was feebleminded, declaring that she would purposely do the tests incorrectly.[47]

The social workers became interested in the issue of heredity after meeting the girl's mother, noting that "she and her daughter were both cast from exactly the same mold." After fifteen pregnancies, followed by the death of her husband, this hardworking forty-year-old woman was still remarkably "strong, healthy, fiery and emphatic." Even though the mother strongly disapproved of the daughter's behavior and had severely disciplined her, the social workers were most concerned that she had passed on her sexual vigor to the teenager. The daughter's obvious determination to continue on this same path persuaded the authorities to send her to an institution because "ordinary treatment could hardly be expected to succeed in this type of individual, when even fifteen pregnancies and much hard work had not worn out just the same sort of vigor in the mother."[48]

The fecundity of foreigners, such as this woman, and the falling birth rate of the native-born, enflamed eugenicists' fears that lack of sexual energy was sapping the "respectable" classes, and contributed to rumblings about restricting immigration. In 1914, one young woman, a nineteen-year-old Bohemian immigrant, Esther Lorenz, felt the wrath of these nativist hostilities.[49]

Together with her friend Lillian—waitresses thrown out of work when their employer went out of business—Esther was arrested for stealing two pairs of stockings, a belt, and some cheap manicure materials. According to the description of the case, reported in a Supplement to the *Journal of the American Institute of Criminal Law and Criminology*, "Her offense was slight and casual. It might have been passed over with a reprimand or as in the juvenile court, with a period of probation; but she was nineteen—above the juvenile court age." She and Lillian were committed to the New York State Refor-

matory for Women at Bedford Hills, then paroled after suitable training as domestic servants. Employed in a home outside New York City,
Esther corresponded with Lillian, who worked elsewhere as a domestic servant. Sent over a period of fifteen months, Esther's letters
eventually reached the hands of Miss R., her parole officer. It seems
that Lillian's employer was reading the letters and forwarding them
to Bedford Hills.[50]

Filled with intimate details, the mood of the letters alternated between worry about being sent back to the reformatory and excitement in retelling her exploits of going to the moving pictures and
flirting with nice young gentlemen on the train. "When I think I have
three years [of parole], I start to cry, I don't know what to do. But
when I think of nice mens [sic], I start to jump in the kitchen and [be-
gin] singing." Those "nice mens" included the egg man, whose deliv-
eries she eagerly awaited: "We kiss each other . . . when you get a kiss
from a man, its nice, isn't it? I have always a good time with him."
Once in a while, she fooled her employer into thinking she was going
to school but was actually going to a dance: "I leave my skirt and my
books in my friends house and I go to the dance. . . . I have there lots
of nice young boys and the man who brings me the eggs and lots of
other nice young men, so I['m] going to have a nice time." Esther also
complained that after going with one young fellow to have a good
time, he had given her only two dollars. "For that I bought stockings
and what I needed and the $2 were gone." With more bravado than
substance, Esther claimed, "I'm now such a devil that you wouldn't
believe it."[51]

In June 1915, Esther was taken back to Bedford Hills. In one of
her intercepted letters to Lillian, she had discussed a visit to a doctor
of women's diseases. In another letter, she had recounted how she
had borrowed and then returned four dollars from her employer's
purse. "So they read that I [was] getting [a] disease that I stole $4 and

one young man gave me $2, so they make me very dirty. . . ."[52]

Miss R. wrote to the superintendent of Bedford Hills to defend her charge. Not convinced that Esther had actually broken her parole, Miss R. argued that the immigrant girl's worst offense was relatively minor, borrowing four dollars from her employer's purse with the fullest intention of returning it. Sympathetically, the parole officer recognized the "frightful strain" Esther was under trying to win her freedom from parole, and "the conflict of what may be merely normal and natural sex interests." In fact, she thought that Esther had a "boastful desire to appear bad." Probably she had not done much more than flirt with men on the train, kiss the egg man, and possibly have sexual relations with a man in Philadelphia for two dollars, an accusation that Esther vehemently denied. Even though Miss R. doubted Esther's account, she was adamant that her charge was not a prostitute. She also called attention to what the prison authorities had learned when they examined Esther: she did not have venereal disease.[53]

Given these compassionate responses, Miss R.'s solution to the problem of Esther comes as a shock: "I think much of [the] subject's suspiciousness and deceitfulness is racial and there is small chance of her adjusting to American customs." Miss R. recommended that Esther be deported.[54]

Esther's "deceit" stemmed from both her sex and her race. Central European and Jewish, Esther embodied prevalent stereotypes of dark-eyed, dark-skinned temptresses. In addition, like other Southern and Eastern Europeans, as well as African Americans, she was considered to be a member of an inferior race.[55] Pseudo-scientific theories of the time claimed the evolutionary superiority of the Anglo-Saxon race, marking all other groups as more primitive and sensual. Esther's sexual behavior proved she was genetically and racially inferior.[56]

In Esther's case, we see how destructive the theories linking sexual and racial prejudices with new notions of psychopathology could be. We do not know whether Esther was deported, but Miss R.'s recommendation to do so suggests the level of fear and anxiety raised by this highly inflammatory mix.[57]

A Generation of "New Women"

MORE THAN PROFESSIONAL INTEREST connected Miss R. and Miss Carroll to Esther Lorenz and Rose Talbot. Both social workers and "hypersexual" girls defied conventional gender and sex roles: Esther and Rose by their active sexual pursuits; the social workers because they chose to get an education, pursue careers, and, in many cases, to remain single. While the Esthers and Roses were labeled hypersexual and delinquent, professional women faced their own stigma. Influenced by emerging psychological theories, many medical and popular writers explained the New Woman in terms of her sexual nature: allegedly aggressive, masculine, and hostile.[58]

Consternation about "uppity" women was nothing new, of course, but middle-class women's greater opportunity in this period to live independently from husbands or fathers added a new shrillness to the attack. A particularly strident formulation of what was wrong with the "New Woman" came from one New York psychiatrist and well-published author, John F. W. Meagher, who, in a sweeping generalization, linked lesbianism, nymphomania, and women's demand for equality. According to Meagher, many "so-called nymphomaniacs," women "with a reputation of being passionate, are not really potent in the adult heterosexual sense." Unsatisfied homosexual impulses, the physician contended, drove them to want a career and to agitate for equal rights: "Married women with a completely satisfied libido rarely take an active interest in militant movements."

Dismissing women's desire for equality by linking it to sexual "perversion," writers like Meagher cast suspicion on the psychological normality of the New Woman.[59]

More traditional stereotypes of old maids still retained their sting, and popular writers such as the well-known critic and misogynist H. L. Mencken continued to trivialize "the majority of inflammatory suffragettes" as "those who have done their best to snare a man and failed."[60] But these older jibes had far less power than the new, pseudo-scientific categories that linked activist women to sexual deviancy. Marshaling modern psychological theories in the service of the status quo, many physicians, psychiatrists, psychologists, and mental health professionals "pathologized" the women who demanded social and political change, as well as career women in general.

The "characteristic sterile glint, part boldness, part antagonistic" which critics such as William J. Robinson—editor of two medical journals and many books on sexuality—claimed to see in the eyes of professional women signaled the New Woman's rejection of her feminine nature. But what constituted women's nature in the early twentieth century? No longer explained only in the biological terms of an earlier era, the key to women's nature was now also thought to reside in the psyche. Revealingly, such new notions of a woman's nature proved strikingly similar to older biologically determined images. Havelock Ellis's monumental seven-volume *Studies in the Psychology of Sex*, while sexually progressive in many respects, still understood the sexual act in terms of the *active* male and the *passive* female. "In a very large number of women the sexual impulse remains latent until aroused by a lover's caresses," Ellis claimed. "The youth spontaneously becomes a man; but the maiden—as it has been said—'must be kissed into a woman.'"[61]

This difference, according to Ellis, was not simply biological: a woman's innermost self—not just her allegedly weaker, more submissive body, as in earlier theories—was more passive than a man's. This passivity seeped into all areas of women's lives. Both biological and psychological forces shaped women's character and personality, her very role in the world, according to Ellis and others. Thus, men's more aggressive, active, and creative natures rightly placed them in positions of leadership and authority. Early twentieth-century theories, which sounded much like those from centuries past, argued that women who refused to accept their innate feminine psyches— understood by these theorists to be modest, maternal, and inherently passive—were oversexed, potentially pathological, and sexually deviant.[62]

Ellis and his colleagues did not go unchallenged. Critics such as the feminist Alice Beals Parsons, author of *Woman's Dilemma* (1926), attacked Ellis's theories about profound differences between men and women's nature as "Alice-in-Wonderland" science, citing scientific evidence from psychological researchers such as Dr. Leta Hollingworth and Dr. Helen Bradford Thompson that refuted Ellis's theories.[63] But the voices were louder on the other side.

The most influential new theories, the groundbreaking work of Freud and his followers, would shape modern assumptions about the relationship between a woman's psychosexual self and her rightful role in the world for decades to come. Freudian theory, progressive and liberating because it acknowledged that women were sexual beings, at the same time created a different set of restrictions.[64] The crux of the Freudian argument was a brand-new notion of feminine and masculine. To assume proper grown-up selves, according to Freud, girls and boys had to maneuver successfully through a series of psychosexual stages. The young girl's experience was particularly fraught because at some point she realized that she lacked what Freud considered a boy's most treasured part, a penis. Unless she was able to complete the essential feminine task of transferring her envy of the penis to a desire for a child, she might wind up with a masculinity complex—sexually immature, neurotic, and hostile to men.

When applied to the New Woman, Freud's theories added fuel to the decades-long attack on women's demand for higher education, for professional opportunity, for the right to vote. Women's demands could now be denigrated as the ranting of an immature psyche. According to Ernest Jones, Freud's disciple and biographer, the "familiar type of women who ceaselessly complain of the unfairness of women's lot," who claim to be the equals of men, actually want to be men themselves. Unable to accept their inferiority—their "penisless" selves—these women attempt to pursue male roles. Some sexual deviants become erotically involved with women, others aspire to careers, to intellectual studies, and to public life—all indicators, Jones claimed, of their rejection of femininity.[65]

This, of course, did not stop women from demanding—and achieving—the right to vote, access to higher education, and wider professional opportunities. But women, too, imbibed the lessons of psychology. By the 1920s, many younger feminists supported the notion that women's fulfillment came predominantly from love and marriage, rather than from work. In a 1927 *Nation* magazine portrayal of the "Feminist—New Style," Dorothy Dunbar Bromley, future author of *Youth and Sex: A Study of 1300 College Students* (1938), described the feminist as "a good dresser, a good sport, and a pal" for whom marriage and children, not work, provided the fullest satisfaction. Even though the feminist desired to "express herself" in some kind of work, she accepted the fact that her contribution was inferior to the work of men.[66] Whereas an earlier generation of feminists had chosen to forego marriage in order to pursue a career, this generation faced the onslaught of psychological theories, which defined their desires for autonomy as masculine and sexually deviant.

The most damning critique of the New Woman was saved for the

lesbian.[67] Women had always participated in intimate female friendships, some presumably romantic and passionate. According to
Katherine B. Davis's pioneering sexual study of several generations of
female college graduates (1929), late nineteenth-century women
moved easily "between homosexual and heterosexual relationships
without necessary consequence."[68] At the turn of the century, however, with greater numbers of middle-class educated women now
able to earn a living, those choosing to share their lives with other
women came under heightened suspicion. In *The Doctor Looks at Love
and Life*, Joseph Collins remarked: "Lesbianism flows from idleness,
boredom, and loneliness and its victims are either under- or oversexed."[69] Mistrust of lesbian relationships did not stop women from
sharing their lives, but these new notions of deviance cast increasing
shadows on the single women who lived outside traditional family
arrangements.

Choice of sexual partner was not the sexologists' major concern.
Instead, they attacked the "mannish" lesbian for her rejection of femininity. The stereotyped lesbian—man-hating and cross-dressing—
threatened cherished notions of innate sexual difference. In Havelock
Ellis's terms: "The brusque energetic movements, the attitude of the
arms, the direct speech, the inflexions of the voice, the masculine
straight-forwardness and sense of honor . . . will often suggest the
underlying psychic abnormality." The New Woman was dangerous
because she challenged the social order in her demand for equality,
and by linking her with aggressive, deviant sexuality, Ellis and others
did their best to discredit her.[70]

MEDICAL AUTHORITIES and sexual experts often wrote as if they
knew the truth about sexuality, but much confusion and uncertainty
existed in the early decades of the twentieth century as modern psy-

chological theories encouraged new ways of seeing women's sexual nature. The opening of a Pandora's box of female sexuality had led to an expansion of the idea of nymphomania to include a profusion of equally imprecise sexual terms. Hypersexual, sexual deviant, and sexual delinquent joined nymphomania in masquerading as scientific certainties. As nymphomania expanded to meet the times, castrating, frigid, and masculinized women joined traditional images of excessively sexed females. The Roman Empire had had its Messalina, the "oversexed" wife of Claudius I. But the twentieth century created a pathological Everywoman: the frigid, insatiable housewife, the hypersexual working-class girl, and the masculinized New Woman. In the next decades, sex experts would search for new ways to understand female sexuality by measuring hormones, probing the psyche, and quantifying the sex lives of over 6,000 American women.

3

the sex experts

N THE SECOND QUARTER of the twentieth century, sex
research—like flappers' short skirts and bobbed hair—
sent a bold message. By tearing away the Victorian veil of
ignorance and misinformation, research promised to uncover the
"truth" about sex. But like their Victorian ancestors, the scientists investigating sex also reflected the social anxieties of their day. Would
women's newfound independence shake up traditional gender roles?
Were sexually unsatisfied wives adding to the already-rising divorce
rate? Claiming scientific objectivity, researchers nevertheless brought
their own value judgments to the task of understanding these issues.

During this period, three types of sex experts explored issues of
female sexuality, including nymphomania. Trained in different scientific methods, one measured sex hormones in the laboratory, the second probed psyches in the analyst's office, and the last quantified
women's sexual behavior in face-to-face interviews. From various
vantage points, these sex researchers came to radically different conclusions about the meaning and causes of nymphomania. Through
popular magazines and newspapers, as well as medical and scientific

journals, the experts' messages reached millions of people anxious for sexual guidance and reassurance.

Nymphomania in the Laboratory

IN THE 1920S and 1930s, evidence that hormonal secretions affected sexual behavior created a furor in the scientific community. Researchers believed that enormous rewards awaited those who developed hormones, especially hormones that might be useful in the treatment of female disease and disorder. Mount Sinai Hospital gynecologist Robert Frank spoke of the "innumerable workers who are elbowing and jostling each other and jockeying for position in the neck-and-neck race to isolate and synthesize the much desired and long sought for hormone."[1] Keenly aware of the profit to be made, drug companies, even in the early days of hormonal research, funneled monies to university laboratories. If sex behavior turned out to be "all in the glands," the potential market for hormones would be enormous.[2]

Hormonal research came at a fortuitous moment.[3] Heightened concerns about birth control, venereal disease, and sexual compatibility in marriage had rendered questions about the libido no longer taboo. Those social reformers who worried about the shaky foundations of marriage welcomed scientific explanations of the nature of sexual desire. If scientists knew how desire worked and what caused it, presumably they might find the means to control it: either rejuvenate the lost libido of a frigid woman, or decrease the nymphomaniac's excessive desire. Robert Greenblatt of the University of Georgia Medical School optimistically proclaimed that "The psychotic tendencies of the nymphomaniac, the neuroses and unhappiness of the frigid female, and the problem of incompatible couples are amenable to hormone therapy."[4]

Echoing widespread concern about sexual issues, powerful institutions, such as the Rockefeller Foundation's Committee for Research in Problems of Sex, began to pour money into research. This spirited scientific race involved specialists from many fields, including a new field, which studied the hormonal secretions of the endocrine glands. Scientists analyzed tons of cows' ovaries and thousands of liters of human and animal urine attempting to isolate a "female" sex hormone. Finally, they found "gold in the urine of pregnant mares" (which contained high concentrations of relatively accessible hormones).[5]

The isolation and identification of the "female" sex hormone, estrogen, in 1929 suggested that the long-sought connection between the brain and women's reproductive organs had been found. In this theory, the hormones secreted by the ovaries—as with the womb or the ovaries themselves in an earlier age—provided the key to female behavior. Anatomically and psychologically, glandular secretions caused women to be women and men to be men. Ultimately, it would not prove that simple.[6]

For centuries, fascination with the differences between men and women had shaped both scientific and popular notions. Attempts to locate that presumed difference focused not only on genitals, but also on brains, skeletons, and by the 1920s on hormones. The scientists who set off in the twenties and thirties on their hormonal search did not jettison their cultural beliefs and concerns upon entering their laboratories. Indeed, biochemists and gynecologists expected to find distinct "male" and "female" sex hormones. These new chemical markers might prove once and for all that biology determined masculinity and femininity. Male and female social roles simply reflected their biological makeup.

Instead, hormone researchers discovered a paradox: women and men have both "male" and "female" hormones. According to one prominent endocrinologist, estrogen might have been called the "male" sex hormone, if researchers had first isolated it in what eventually proved to be the highest-secreting estrogenic animal—the stallion. Surprised and disconcerted, some scientists ventured novel explanations: female hormones came from the food men ate, not from male gonads. But many researchers recognized the complexities implicit in these new scientific findings.[7]

Eventually, most scientists abandoned the mutually exclusive categories and replaced them with relative ones: females produce *more* estrogen, males produce *more* testosterone. Even so, both scientific and popular writing retained the sense that "female" and "male" hormones stimulated intrinsically feminine or masculine behavior, that "wearing the pants" or "acting like a sissy" might be traced to biochemistry.[8]

This groundbreaking hormonal research galvanized the medical and scientific community. While giving lip service to psychological factors, some researchers triumphantly proclaimed that the sex drive was merely a phenomenon dependent on well-defined chemical substances. Robert Greenblatt, who was the leading scientist in a widely quoted study published in the *American Journal of Obstetrics and Gynecology*, declared the libido a "test tube chemical equation," which could be manipulated by increasing or decreasing hormones.[9]

In the course of research aimed at helping women with symptoms of menstrual pain or menopausal hot flashes, scientists raised other questions about sexual behavior. In a pioneering study of premenstrual tension, Philadelphia gynecologist Dr. S. Leon Israel, reporting in the *Journal of the American Medical Association* in 1938, found that 40 percent of normal women suffered disquieting symptoms before onset of menstruation. In particular, "nymphomania, when present, is an arresting symptom and commands the deepest sympathy." One of his patients, identified as M.T.C., a thirty-four-year-old, twice divorced white woman, during her premenstrual period went from "a quiet, industrious, mild mannered woman" to an "irritable, tensely restless, irascibly shrewish creature with headaches, insomnia, and nymphomania." Dr. Israel theorized that a deficiency of progesterone or an excess of estrogen might cause the condition. He treated her with progesterone and during this period she remained entirely symptom-free.[10]

Generally, these scientific studies—whether with human or animal subjects—did not define their use of the term "nymphomania".[11] Researchers assumed that the medical community knew what nymphomania was. But hormonal measurements of "excessive" sexuality posed problems similar to those confronted by earlier medical authorities. Being "oversexed" did not correspond to a specific, measurable quantity of hormones any more than it did to enlarged clitorises or overexcited nerve fibers.

While other "diseases" or "disorders" also had vague or uncertain meanings, nymphomania's definition—so entangled with the fantasies and fears surrounding supersexed women—was doubly suspect. In some of these case studies, we can see how cultural notions shaped even the science of assessing hormones in test tubes as a pronounced moral tone occasionally slipped through the objective scientific language. Consider the case of W.F., twenty-three years old and unmarried, who entered an endocrine clinic in the early 1940s suffering from painful menstruation, nervousness, fainting spells, and exaggerated sexual impulses. The implantation of a progesterone pellet soon reduced her symptoms, including "so marked a reduction in sexual desire that she no longer had any desire to 'run around.'" In censorious terms, the physicians concluded that she now "saw the evil of her ways," becoming fonder of her home and more willing to do her share of the family chores.[12]

Hormone research was in its infancy and scientists disagreed about the effects of treating women's sexual desire with hormones.[13] Indeed, testosterone was thought to affect the libido in two seemingly opposite ways: "male" sex hormones, some said, neutralized the action of "female" sex hormones and decreased libido, especially in cases of excessive sexual desire. Just as firm in their belief, other researchers suggested that these same hormones caused an increased sensitivity in the clitoris in some women and actually increased sexual desire. Interestingly, a twenty-five-year-old woman described as having a "mild" libido, defined as intercourse with her husband once or twice a week, began to have sexual relations once or twice a night following the implantation of testosterone pellets. In this case, the physicians referred to her "good libido," although other studies categorized such sexual activity as nymphomania.[14] Here, as in so many other examples, nymphomania was in the eye of the beholder.

Citing clinical experiments in which small doses of testosterone stimulated libido in the normal male and large doses depressed desire, neurologists at Washington, D.C.'s George Washington Hospital decided to study the effect of large doses of testosterone on "morbidly over-sexed females." Five white women complaining of intense sexual craving, accompanied by anxiety, depression, and restlessness, took part in the study. The women's sexual desire was "over-intense," although "normally directed," meaning heterosexual: the researchers had purposely excluded lesbians or women with what they termed "perverse sexual strivings."[15]

Following testosterone treatment, the "feeling of passion was gone" and the "sex tension completely disappeared" in four of the five women. The patients were now described as "placid" and "complacent." One woman, C.N., commented that she was grateful to be rid of the marked sexual excitement that had created marital problems. Another, P.L., was pleased that the treatment cured the feeling that "she was going mad." C.N.'s husband, who prior to the treatment was "unable to meet the added demands" of his thirty-two-year-old wife in the week before her menstrual period, enthusiastically approved the changes. P.L.'s "frequently tired" husband expressed his gratitude that his forty-two-year-old wife no longer became premenstrually "insatiable." Husbands, wives, and scientists all agreed that these "gratifying results" contributed significantly to the future stability and happiness of the patients' marriages.[16]

One unmarried woman in the study, however, bitterly attacked the doctors and the treatment. Like Catherine, the working-class girl we met in chapter 1, this twenty-five-year-old "brilliant," "moody" woman claimed that the doctors had "de-sexed" her. The physicians described her as a "psychopathic nymphomaniac." In recounting her history, they revealed her attempted suicide following expulsion from a southern university for immorality. She vehemently protested that she had never had relations with the man whose "tattling" led to her ejection from college. However, according to the researchers' case notes, she did collect "men as others would collect stamps or autographs. . . . On one occasion, during the football season, she journeyed to a distant city and cohabited with at least ten of the football squad on the night before the game." (Gratuitously, the authors added that the team lost the next day.) Released from the hospital, "she resumed her former psychopathic behavior, dressing fantastically, and seeking men whenever she could escape from the watchful eye of her brother."[17]

Once again, nymphomania's meaning is difficult to pin down. While other studies often used the two terms, "nymphomania" and "morbidly over-sexed," interchangeably, this study attempted, although without clear demarcation, to differentiate between the two. While the number of partners and the indiscriminant nature of the "psychopathic nymphomaniac's" sexual behavior might have been the reason researchers labeled her as such, at least one other patient in the study, L.N., also indulged in frequent "illicit relations," but was not labeled a nymphomaniac. In her case, "each indulgence was followed by remorse, but her craving was so intense that she just 'had to indulge.'"[18] Perhaps L.N.'s guilt was the reason the researchers did not interpret her sexual desires as nymphomania.

Research findings sometimes surprised scientists. A study published in the eminent journal *Endocrinology* recounted an experiment using testosterone to treat painful menstruation. Responding to the concerns of some women unable or unwilling to be injected or implanted with testosterone, Dr. A. B. Abarbanel of Sinai Hospital in Baltimore dissolved the hormone in sesame oil and instructed the ten patients, ranging in age from seventeen to thirty years old, to rub it in their armpits at specified times of the menstrual cycle. The gynecologist theorized that testosterone inhibited excessive uterine contractions, which presumably caused pain during menstruation.[19]

Commenting on the test patients, Abarbanel singled out a twenty-three-year-old, white, divorced woman. Her most outstanding symptom was a remarkable increase in libido in the week before menstruation, amounting to "practically that of a nymphomaniac." Over eighteen months, he measured her response to testosterone in the following categories: premenstrual breast tension, emotional instability, nymphomaniac tendencies, and dysmenorrhea (painful menstruation). Just what he meant by nymphomania is not clear, but Dr. Abarbanel presumably had some criteria in mind. He determined that testosterone decreased all the symptoms of nymphomania from "very marked" to "none" or "within normal limits."[20]

After the first flush of success, researchers began to admit that the libido was much more complicated than originally believed. Psychological as well as hormonal factors must be at work. Challenging those who hoped to isolate the libido in a test tube, Dr. William

Perloff, an endocrinologist at Philadelphia's General Hospital, reported the case of a twenty-four-year-old Japanese woman referred to the clinic because of amenorrhea (no menstruation). Although born without ovaries, the young woman still experienced what he considered a pathologically heightened sexual attraction toward men. She did not require physical contact to evoke these reactions; a male's mere proximity created an erotic charge. But her underdeveloped breasts, vagina, and uterus caused her shame and embarrassment and prevented her from pursuing these feelings. Instead, she satisfactorily masturbated to orgasm. According to Dr. Perloff, this case proved that "the so-called sex hormones" did not determine the sex drive. [21]

In the late 1940s and early 1950s, in the face of studies showing that—paradoxically—testosterone both increased women's libido and also diminished excessive libido, biochemists still could not find a simple test-tube explanation for sexual behavior. This did not stop researchers and chemical companies, however, from trying to find a sexual magic bullet to shoot down the disorder of too much or too little sexual desire. [22]

While mass-marketed hormones would have to wait until a later day, chemical companies touted other remedies, such as sedatives to treat the effects of endocrine imbalances, which, they theorized, led to nymphomania. In a 1951 pamphlet entitled *The Over-Sexed Woman*, the Dios Chemical Company, a St. Louis pharmaceutical company, declared that their product, Neurosine, a bromide sedative, relieved and controlled this troubling condition. The unnamed physician who wrote the pamphlet claimed that he and fellow physicians "not infrequently treated nymphomaniacs" in their offices. [23]

Although the author claimed medical credentials, *The Over-Sexed Woman* was a marketing brochure, not a scientific article. The Dios Chemical Company hoped to persuade physicians to prescribe Neurosine to calm nymphomaniacs' "excessive restlessness" and "pathological excitability." The pamphlet enumerated the various kind of nymphomaniacs that Neurosine would help: bashful, dreamy, masturbating adolescents; women in "double bondage to alcohol and sex"; potential lesbians; and women whose elderly husbands did not satisfy them. Quoting the popular advice book, *The Doctor and His Patients*, the author also diagnosed sedatives for aging women "caught in a terrifying, unnavigable stream of sex . . . until the endocrines have done their worst and retired into atrophy." In a bold marketing strategy, this Dios Chemical Company brochure established a potential market for their product among women of all kinds and all ages.[24]

Revealingly, the author advised Neurosine for the "incipient" nymphomaniac whose social behavior labeled her diseased. Who might this be? The doctor claimed he saw latent nymphomaniacs in every community. Unlike the milder cases of satyriasis that go unnoticed, he stated, "in our social system an unmarried woman is supposed to suppress any indication of sexual desire." Neurosine's proposed effects, "mental calm, aloofness, and imperturbability," would soothe these closet nymphomaniacs.

This laundry list of potential nymphomaniacs reads much like that found in Dr. Bienville's eighteenth-century study. In fact, the author of *The Over-Sexed Woman* paid homage to Bienville, declaring that the French physician had "pioneered the path for the non-habit-forming control of the nymphomaniac." Almost two centuries later—and despite the enormous social changes in women's lives in the twentieth century—the powerful image of the nymphomaniac continued to endure. Hormonal research was still in its early stages, but scientists were certain that given time and funding, they could find in their laboratories the answer to what caused too much sexual desire.

Nymphomania in the Psyche

AT THE SAME TIME that biochemists searched for the magic elixir of sexuality in a test tube, other experts continued to look for answers in the psyche. By the 1940s and 1950s, psychological as well as biological theories of hypersexuality had taken firm root in the medical and mental health communities. Medical professionals now began to spread their ideas to a much wider audience, who learned the real truth about what caused excessive sexual desires: deep psychological needs. Not the need for sex itself, but a confusing array of unconscious or conscious motivations caused nymphomania. According to psychiatrist Harold Ellis, "Sex is no real pleasure to the Messalina type. It's only an attempt to find relief from deeper unhappiness. You might call it a flight into sex."[25]

Experts proposed many possible psychological causes for the "flight into sex:" anxiety, a hunger for power, hostility, incestuous desires, latent homosexuality, narcissism, need for affection, rebellion, self-hatred, a sexually repressed childhood, among others. It was not immediately obvious to professionals why a particular individual chose sex rather than food, drink, sport, or good works to escape her unhappiness. Consequently, their task was to try to uncover the inner conflict which underlay an individual's excessive sexual desires and behavior. [26]

But psychological theories faced the same ambiguities as biologically oriented explanations: How much was too much sex? This culturally loaded question was not easy to answer. No one professed to know what the *right* amount of sex was. The key to nymphomania, many sex experts claimed, lay in the compulsiveness of the sexual activity or in the indiscriminate nature of the choice of partners. That particular approach to understanding the nymphomaniac became even more influential in later years and will be discussed in chapter 5.

In the 1940s and 1950s, under the influence of Freudian theories, a woman's rejection of her femininity was singled out as central. But, as we will see, this not easily measurable hypothesis nurtured its own uncertainties.

Psychological explanations encouraged people to think about sex in new ways, but as with hormone research, these scientific theories also incorporated older stereotypes. In previous centuries, medical authorities had believed that women's ovaries or wombs determined their supposedly passive and maternal nature. Now the psyche, considered to have its own innate norms, similarly shaped women's sexual nature. Allegedly, women's sexual desires were more diffuse and more difficult to awaken than men's and ultimately could be fulfilled only through motherhood. Women who did not fit this model aroused suspicion.

Even more so than in the 1920s, and despite splits among Freud's followers, in the 1940s and 1950s Freudian-influenced ideas exercised enormous influence over American notions of sex. As a generation of Freud's disciples fled Nazism and settled in England and the United States, they disseminated the master's theories ever more widely. By proposing a comprehensive explanation of sexuality, and couching it in scientific language, Freudianism offered answers to the vexing questions of what makes people do the things they do.[27]

Family-oriented magazines, such as *Coronet*, *Reader's Digest*, and *Ladies' Home Journal*, played a part in bringing these theories into millions of homes by publishing psychoanalytically oriented articles that examined contemporary marital sexual problems. In 1943, a *Reader's Digest* article entitled "A Woman's Responsibility in Sex Relations" warned that the divorce rate—one in every five or six marriages—was directly related to the "failure to make a satisfactory sexual adjustment early in married life." Citing the "paralyzing prudery and senseless taboos" with which many women entered marriage, the author discussed the works of various sex experts, including the Freudian psychoanalyst Wilhelm Stekel, who might help guide the public on matters of sex.[28]

While providing for a more open discussion of sex in America's heartland, these magazines also popularized grab bag notions of theories such as the "masculinity complex" and "penis envy." Simplistic explanations cited this or that theory, drew on this or that authority with little attempt at systematic analysis of very complex ideas.[29] Appealing to readers who wanted tangible answers to sexual problems, journalists and medical writers took these esoteric Freudian concepts out of context and presented them as if they were dogma, and implied that the theories provided simple solutions to sexual problems. Their "cookbook" approach to Freudianism simplified the ingredients of psychoanalysis to mindless generalizations, such as "tomboys grow up to be man-haters." Moreover, articles such as *Coronet's* "'Masculine' Women Are Cheating at Love" concluded that the expensive and time-consuming process of psychoanalytic treatment was not really necessary.[30] Popular magazines pointed their audience to other experts, including marriage counselors, psychologists, general practitioners, and the female sexuality experts, gynecologists.

Not surprisingly, specialists in women's diseases welcomed the opportunity and now claimed problem psyches as well as problem bodies as part of their domain. The authors of *The Gynecological Patient*, for example, declared that where once the priest, pastor, or general practitioner had been women's "friend, guardian and teacher . . . today, in the medical profession, obstetricians and gynecologists are perhaps best able to fill this position."[31] Not only the traditional gynecological concerns of women's reproductive diseases required their medical expertise, but women's emotional and sexual lives as well. Since many more women would visit a gynecologist than a psychiatrist or a psychoanalyst, gynecologists' examining rooms now became the site of psychological as well as physical probing.

Even gynecological textbooks began to incorporate Freudian and pseudo-Freudian notions, especially around issues of sexuality deemed deviant or abnormal.[32] Widely quoted in both the medical and the popular press, the gynecologist William Kroger and the endocrinologist Charles Freed, for example, joined forces in a 1951 textbook in which they examined nymphomania because "individuals suffering from it will often consult a gynecologist or endocrinologist for relief."[33]

As an example of nymphomania, they discussed the case of Mrs. A.R., a woman of forty-six, twice married, who came to see Dr. Kroger because of vaginal itching, heavy menstrual bleeding, and "strong hypersexual drives." The last symptom appears to be Dr. Kroger's diagnosis rather than the patient's concern. As the following case indicates, Mrs. A.R. did not visit the doctor because she feared she was oversexed.

According to her account, during the period leading up to her arrival in the medical office, she and her husband of fourteen years had greatly increased their sexual activity, engaging in as many as thirty-five sexual acts a week. She explained this by telling the gynecologist, "I feel that I am approaching the change in life and I may lose my attractiveness. Therefore, I would like to get all the sex I possibly can." What she most feared was that her husband would no longer be interested "when I lose my physical charms."[34]

Dr. Kroger labeled Mrs. A.R.'s behavior "weeks of nymphomania." Paying only lip service to her concerns, he did not comment on her fears about the potential sexual impact of impending menopause. Instead, he explained her sexual activity strictly in Freudian terms: the patient suffered from penis envy and a desire to castrate her husband. Never having accepted her femininity, she was sexually aggressive and hostile to her husband.

An additional revelation by Mrs. A.R.—that she had experienced orgasm throughout these weeks of sexual activity—contradicted Kroger and Freed's own textbook in which they claimed: "Nymphomaniacs are generally frigid and seldom experience 'vaginal orgasm.'"[35] Like other cookbook Freudians, the authors had selected out the ingredients they needed from the large body of Freudian theory. They did not change their diagnosis based on this contradictory evidence, but simply dismissed her orgasmic experience as "odd." Typical of most medical cases, this case provided no additional information about Mrs. A.R. except that her sexual drives had diminished following psychotherapy.

Even if the average gynecologist or general practitioner did not read these medical books, he and his patients would have encountered Freud in the popular press.[36] In fact, in 1950, *Time* magazine specifically discussed Drs. Kroger and Freed's use of Freudian concepts. "Unconscious resentments and hates such as a wish for revenge on men," *Time* quoted Kroger and Freed, accounted for "aggressive old maids, agitative female 'champions' in constant competition with men, narcissistic women and violent espousers of virginity." The article went on to discuss the Hungarian-born psychoanalyst Sandor Rado, director of the New York Psychoanalytic Institute, who categorized frigid women into gold diggers, prostitutes, and nymphomaniacs. Reflecting fifties attitudes toward women's proper place, Rado said that these women should be avoided because they tended to neglect their husbands and to follow their own interests by traveling alone and pursuing careers.[37]

Familiarity with these ideas by a wider reading public created a kind of medical-cultural feedback. Doctors encountered the concepts both in medical texts and in the popular press and ministered to their female patients based on vague, Freudian-influenced assumptions about women. While competing and contradictory messages also vied for women's attention, sexual discussions in mass-market magazines often included Freudian-inspired references to frigidity and to the feminine role. In visiting their gynecologist, women might have had these notions reinforced.

In the 1940s and 1950s, a period of enormous upheaval in gender roles, psychological notions of innate feminine nature would be harnessed to support contradictory messages. During World War II, millions of women went to work building warships, driving trucks, operating machines, flying airplanes, and doing jobs supposedly only a man could do. Originally, government-sponsored campaigns featured patriotic war work as the self-sacrificing, womanly thing to do. Posters portrayed "Rosie the Riveter" as strong, but decidedly attractive and feminine. Newspapers and magazines suggested that despite long hours and a frantic pace, women took pride and a sense of accomplishment from their work in the wartime industries.

Eventually, the tables were turned. Social policy began to favor reestablishing traditional gender roles; women in "men's" jobs were expected to leave the workforce to be replaced by the returning veterans. Some women undoubtedly left happily, but others either left grudgingly or were forced into lower-paid, more traditional jobs. No longer riveters and welders, women returned to more "feminine" employment as waitresses and secretaries.[38]

During the postwar years, in support of this domestic realignment, physicians, preachers, and the popular press reemphasized an old message: Being a helpmate to her husband and mother to her children was central to what made a woman a woman. Surprisingly, this did not mean that the popular press denigrated women's achievement in the public arena. On the contrary, mass-market magazines celebrated both the domestic ideal and women's accomplishments in the work world with articles not only on suburban homemakers and the PTA but also on women who successfully combined work and family.[39] Nevertheless, these magazines' bread and butter—promoting family stability and domestic togetherness—encouraged conventional notions of femininity. Primary responsibility for breadwinning and heading the household was still a man's job.

That some women were "rejecting" their femininity became a source of concern in both medical texts and the popular press. According to Dr. J. P. Greenhill's *Office Gynecology*, a medical textbook repeatedly revised and reissued during the period, the most important question a doctor should answer about a female patient was "does [she] accept herself as a woman?" Another contemporary textbook, *Psychosomatic Gynecology*, jointly authored by a gynecologist and a psychiatrist, claimed that women who were "deeply resentful of their feminine role" created both physical and psychological problems.[40]

The nymphomaniac afforded medical and popular discussions a surprising example of rejected femininity. Her apparent lustiness was not what it appeared, but a frantic attempt to hide an immature psyche. Now the sexy gal with the come-hither look was not the male fantasy come true, but a deeply troubled woman unable or unwilling to accept her female role. Threatening the stability of marriage, she rejected the essential feminine qualities of passivity, acceptance, sacrifice, and love. Medical writers worried that the normal husband could not fulfill the nymphomaniac's desperate search for sexual satisfaction. Divorce and even prostitution followed.

The image of the nymphomaniac overlapped with that of the lesbian who was being "rediscovered" as a sexual deviant in the postwar period.[41] According to psychiatrist Frank Caprio, author of what was considered the definitive book on lesbianism, *Female Homosexuality* (1954), "excessive heterosexuality (promiscuity) or what is known as the 'Messalina complex' may represent a disguised manifestation of latent homosexuality."[42] One telltale sexual expression of this hidden potential was the "wife who prefers to lie on top, and assume the active role."[43] Because Freudian-inspired psychoanalysts, such as Caprio, believed that latent homosexuality existed in everyone, they voiced considerable concern about its potential to wreck marriages.

Dr. Victor Eisenstein, chief psychiatrist at New York's Lenox Hill Hospital, echoed these fears in his *Neurotic Interactions in Marriage* (1956). Reviewing the sexual problems of married couples, he commented that an unresolved masculinity complex often led to nymphomaniacal behavior. These women existed in a "perpetual state of sexual excitement" because they were frigid. As an example of a "masculine" and "dominating" woman, Dr. Eisenstein described the case of a wife who had her husband masturbate her clitoris to the point of climax before she would allow him to insert his penis. By doing so, the author believed, she symbolically castrated her husband and declared her independence from the male organ. Ironically, future sex therapists would recommend just this technique to promote women's orgasm. But given Dr. Eisenstein's conception of passive female sexuality, his patient's sexual demands were seen as aggressive, a rejection of innate femininity, a sign of nymphomania.[44]

For years, Freudians had connected nymphomania and frigidity; now this image penetrated popular culture, even invading men's magazines. In 1954, for example, *Esquire* featured an article entitled "Nymphos Have No Fun." The round-heeled, sex-hungry dame of hard-boiled fiction, *Esquire* declared, did not exist outside of male jokes and locker room gossip. Turning to the experts, the authors quoted Freudian analyst Dr. Helene Deutsch: "The primitive woman who yields happily and without conflict to her sexual desires is as unknown to me as the primitive man. I've met her in fiction, nowhere else." In mock-nostalgic tones, *Esquire* declared that "science seems to have destroyed the hearty, love-happy nymph of song and story."[45]

Perhaps the "hearty, love-happy nymph" was ultimately too scary? Not surprisingly, men's magazines sought to reassure and support their male readers' egos. The notion that highly sexed women really suffered from underlying frigidity was paradoxically reassuring to men. The nymphomaniac-as-undersexed female assuaged the anxieties of men who feared that sex-hungry women would overwhelm them. Now a man's unwillingness or inability to meet a woman's sexual demands for more foreplay, intercourse, clitoral stimulation, or kissing did not have to reflect negatively on his manhood. He wasn't undersexed; she was!

The *Esquire* article repeated most of the confusing list of nymphomania's causes: narcissism, masochism, thwarted maternal instincts, repressed childhoods, incestuous attractions for fathers, latent homosexuality. But it was frigidity that provided the ultimate push-over-the-edge into sexual abandon. Not lascivious desires or hot blood, but lack of sexual satisfaction most often bred nymphomania. Recounting the much-told story of the Roman emperor Claudius's wife, Messalina, the authors described this archetypal nymphomaniac as a sexually voracious blond beauty who commanded the Praetorian Guard to do her sexual bidding. According to *Esquire*, Messalina's ferocious sexual appetite—like that of other legendary nymphomaniacs such as Cleopatra and Catherine the Great—concealed a restless, tormented woman. It wasn't sex but lack of sexual satisfaction that drove them to prodigious sexual feats.[46]

The outwardly nymphomaniacal but inwardly undersexed woman became a familiar type in other, less high-toned men's publications, such as the bi-monthly girlie magazine entitled *MR*.[47] In "My Bride Was a Nymphomaniac," (1956), an anonymous author told a story, typical of many men's magazines, which presented both a titillating tale of sexual excess and an underlying moral about the dangers of highly sexed women. The author even included a pseudo-medical diagnosis in which a woman's sexual exploits proved that "something was wrong with her mind."

Declaring that he wrote the article to warn others against the dangers of making his mistake, "Anonymous" revealed his "incredibly strange marriage to one of the most beautiful women in the world." He should have known that something was wrong with her, because Diane kissed him with a frightening passion on their first date, clinging to him "like a drowning person." His male ego was too flattered for him to resist, even when she took the sexual initiative. Her bold approach, he later realized, should have alerted him to the danger she posed.

Although his friends warned him that Diane's "bohemian" ways would not fit into his conventional, social world, Anonymous married her anyway, convinced that she would change. But his friends were right; Diane could not play the stereotypical feminine role as corporate wife to the rising young executive. Instead, she took up sculpting and brought an all-male artist crowd, "spouting left-wing philosophy," to their suburban house at all hours of the day and night. In the body of Diane, the twin nemeses of the 1950s—radical politics and aggressive female sexuality—infiltrated his domestic paradise.

Following an automobile accident in which Diane and her lover were killed, the husband found Diane's diary, which revealed her many infidelities. Anonymous concluded that Diane was a nymphomaniac. Steeped in popular Freudianism, the writer declared that like all nymphomaniacs, Diane subconsciously hated men. Presumably, her "insatiability" masked a desire to wear him and her other lovers out, to castrate him symbolically. Like the sex experts quoted in *Esquire*, Anonymous claimed that Diane, while apparently oversexed, was actually undersexed, masking her frigidity with nymphomaniacal excess. Warning all male readers who might fantasize about marriage to a woman who was crazy about sex, he concluded: "I do not want another nymphomaniac as a bride. One was more than enough."

Like the traditional fallen woman, Diane had to pay for her sins by dying at the end of the story. Sometimes, however, the woman was redeemed by seeing the error of her ways and was ultimately saved by the love of a powerful man. A *Coronet* magazine article entitled "Promiscuous Women Can Be Cured" (1955), for example, presented the case of Joan K., who grew up with little interest in girlish pursuits. Desiring to please her father who favored her two older brothers, she tagged along with them, learned to play baseball and football, and became almost as proficient as her brothers at these "male" sports. She chose a co-ed college and continued with what the article called her masculine behavior: drinking heavily and calling up her male classmates for dates instead of waiting to be asked.

Joan saw her male classmates as basically promiscuous and became promiscuous herself. But she felt no pleasure in the sexual experiences and sought help from a college counselor. The counselor helped Joan to understand that "in order to enjoy sex, she must cease to hate being a woman." Eventually, Joan "conquered her masculine strivings" when she fell in love with a strong and dominant man, the assistant football coach at the college. Freed from the necessity to prove to her father that she was equal to her brothers, Joan was able to give up her promiscuous ways and accept herself as a woman. The case concluded: Joan "is now herself the mother of two girls, and her sexual life is entirely satisfactory." [48]

The moral of these stories? Not only women's marital happiness, but their sexual satisfaction as well, depended on sublimating their competitiveness and accepting their feminine role. Women rejected the traditional roles of wife and mother at their peril. The "bohemian" Diane and the "masculine-striving" Joan symbolized the dangers of sexual nonconformity. *Coronet* stressed that Joan was fortunate because "the new knowledge that science has made available to her"— the knowledge that nymphomania was a curable, psychological disease—had brought her to her senses. Of course, it was the love of a strong, masculine man that made her truly happy.

The science of sex also promised to save women other than Joan from equally disastrous fates—divorce, promiscuity, or prostitution. From the late nineteenth century on, science and medicine had proposed a variety of answers to such social problems. Just as the cure for nymphomania might be found in the hormone researcher's laboratory, or in the conflicts buried deep in the female psyche, other scientists hoped to unlock a different set of sexual secrets.

"The Great Kinsey Hullabaloo"

TOWARD THIS END, the mid-twentieth century dean of sexual science, Alfred Kinsey, undertook years of research to demystify sex by investigating what actually took place in the bedrooms of America. An Indiana University zoology professor, Kinsey began his monumental research into sex in 1938 after realizing how little scientific material was available to him to teach an undergraduate course in human sexuality.

Kinsey approached the Rockefeller Foundation's Committee for Research in Problems of Sex for funding in 1941. By 1947, his Institute for Sex Research was receiving half the committee's budget. The zoologist's scientific expertise about a tiny insect known as a gall wasp—he had collected over four million specimens—shaped his approach to research in human sexuality. By interviewing over 12,000 white men and women about their sexual behavior, he put his faith in amassing and analyzing an unprecedented collection of sexual statistics. These interviews formed the basis for the groundbreaking, two-volume study of sex known collectively as the *Kinsey Reports*.[49]

With the publication of what one magazine dubbed "The Great Kinsey Hullabaloo"—*Sexual Behavior in the Human Male* in 1948 and

Sexual Behavior in the Human Female in 1953—scientific sex research launched its most explosive twentieth-century bombshells.[50] The first volume shocked readers by its revelations that men engaged in surprisingly high levels of premarital and extramarital intercourse. Five years later, in the midst of the ongoing and at times very heated controversy over *Sexual Behavior in the Human Male*—especially over the claim that 37 percent of adult males had experienced at least one homosexually related orgasm—the Kinsey Institute released its second volume, on female sexuality.

In a postwar period fraught with anxiety about reestablishing traditional gender roles, the second *Kinsey Report* caused even more furor than the first. In its time the hottest story in publishing history, *Sexual Behavior in the Human Female* hit the August 1953 covers of *Time, Life, Newsweek, Colliers,* and *Women's Home Companion* simultaneously. Thirty additional mass-circulation magazines featured the book on what was touted as "K-Day." Like a war maneuver, banner headlines and op-ed pieces—even a "Dr. Pinsey" character in the popular comic strip "Abbie and Slats"—invaded homes and newsstands. According to *Time* magazine, the *Kinsey Reports* did more for the open discussion of sex than any other event in human history. Nevertheless, the *Time* article was less sanguine about the "widespread breakdown in formal religion" which helped to foster the "revolution in sexual behavior" that Kinsey described.[51]

In determinedly unsensational scientific language, replete with charts, graphs, and extensive footnotes, the *Kinsey Report*'s revelations that much more sex was going on than society admitted both shocked and encouraged readers. Among the more startling conclusions, *Sexual Behavior in the Human Female* revealed that of the 5,940 white, non-incarcerated women included in the sample,[52] 26 percent engaged at least once in extramarital affairs; 50 percent participated one or more times in premarital intercourse; 14 percent regularly responded with multiple orgasms; 97 percent experienced erotic arousal before marriage; and higher percentages of women were having orgasms in the 1940s than in 1900.[53] Further setting the moralists' teeth on edge, the Kinsey Report declared that "the chances that a female can adjust sexually after marriage appear to be materially improved if she has experienced orgasm at an earlier age."[54] Christian evangelist Billy Graham thundered in response: "It is impossible to estimate the damage this book will do to the already deteriorating morals of America." [55]

In reality, Kinsey and his associates had social goals not diametrically opposed to the Reverend Graham's. They, too, hoped to strengthen the institution of marriage and to control promiscuity. In its opening pages, Sexual Behavior in the Human Female highlighted the social value of the scientific approach to the problems of sex. Nearly all societies everywhere in the world, it maintained, understood marriage to provide the cement of social organization. The importance of harmonious sexual relationships to marriage was evident: "where the sexual relationships are not equally satisfactory to both of the partners in the marriage, disagreement and angry rebellion may invade not only the marital bed, but all other aspects of the marriage."[56]

This Kinsey Report challenged two longstanding medical and popular assumptions: that the female's sexual response was slower, and that male and female orgasms were basically different. Scientifically accumulated data, the survey claimed, now proved these notions incorrect. The scientists believed that demystifying these aspects of human sexuality would contribute significantly to marital harmony. Based on this finding, marriage-manual sex techniques would have to change. Scientific objectivity notwithstanding, Kinsey and colleagues did have a social agenda: making the world, especially the marital bed, a better place for sex.[57]

In contrast to Victorian-era sexologists such as Richard von Krafft-Ebing and Havelock Ellis, the *Kinsey Reports'* authors found no place in the scientific vocabulary for terms like "normal" and "abnormal," "natural" and "unnatural." Challenging essentially all previous sexological research, the Kinsey team flatly declared that scientists who measured sexual behavior should not use these moralizing categories. Instead, human sexual behavior must be placed within its mammalian context: "the human animal behaves like the mammal that it is." Once the public understood this concept, notions of sexual perversity and deviance would fade away. How could female masturbation be considered abnormal and unnatural when 62 percent of all women in their sample—as well as rats, chinchillas, rabbits, porcupines, and many other female mammals—did it? And biologists and psychologists who assumed "perversions" of "normal instincts" in homosexual activities ignored the fact that sexual contacts between mammals of the same sex—from antelopes to shrews—occurred in practically every species studied.[58]

As scientists examining the sexuality of the human animal, the Kinsey team aspired to be unbiased and objective. To accomplish this, they created the concept of "total sexual outlet"—a measure of the incidence and frequency of orgasms from various types of sexual activity. Kinsey and his associates recognized that this focus might overemphasize the importance of orgasm, but justified its use on the grounds that in a large-scale survey, precise results required measuring an identifiable sexual occurrence such as orgasm. By quantifying the number of orgasms experienced in six outlets—heterosexual intercourse, masturbation, nocturnal dreams, petting, homosexual activity, and animal contacts—they hoped to enlighten the public about the real sexual behavior of real people in America. To the Kinsey team, not just married couple's coital activity was deemed legitimate sex. In fact, categorizing various different ways in which people achieved sexual satisfaction effectively dethroned heterosexual intercourse from its privileged position as *the* sex act. Studying such a broad range of human sexual behavior also shifted the focus away from the sexual pathologies that were at the heart of the clinical cases examined by psychologists and psychiatrists.[59]

By measuring "outlets," the *Kinsey Reports* challenged the notion that "too much" or the "wrong kind" of sex existed. Instead, the *Reports* declared, sexual behavior consisted of a continuum, and "no individual has a sexual frequency which differs in anything but the slightest degree from those next on the curve."[60] Accordingly, Messalina was really not that different from the girl next door.

To clarify their concern about non-scientific labels, the sex researchers warned:

> Such designations as infantile, frigid, sexually under-developed, under-active, excessively active, over-developed, over-sexed, hypersexual, or sexually over-active, and the attempts to recognize such states as nymphomania and satyriasis as discrete entities, can, in any objective analysis, refer to nothing more than *a position on a curve which is continuous*.[61] (emphasis added)

To the authors, empirical research confirmed the conclusion that some of the most successful and best adjusted persons in their study engaged in as much sexual activity "as those in any case labeled nymphomania or satyriasis in the literature, or recognized as such in the clinic."[62] A label of over- or undersexed merely reflected the labeler's own position on the curve. Kinsey himself pithily summarized this point of view. In a line that has become legendary, he replied to the question: "what is a nymphomaniac?" by answering, "someone who has more sex than you do."[63]

Sexual Behavior in the Human Female was particularly scathing toward those psychoanalysts and clinicians who insisted that to be sexually mature, a woman must transfer sexual feeling from her clitoris to her vagina. They blamed these foolish theories for "some hundreds of the women in our own study and many thousands of the patients of certain clinicians [who] have consequently been much disturbed by their failure to accomplish this biological impossibility." In direct refutation, the *Kinsey Report* declared that a vaginal orgasm was a physical and physiologic impossibility. Gynecological tests had conclusively proved that the interior of the vagina lacked nerve endings and was insensitive to touch. Nevertheless, the Kinsey team did admit that penetration might bring satisfaction for psychological reasons or because the clitoris was peripherally stimulated. [64]

Not surprisingly, the supporters of vaginal orgasm theory counterattacked. The Kinsey interviewees, they claimed, were unable to have a vaginal orgasm because they were frigid or nymphomaniacs, or both. Although vaginal orgasm's supporters and detractors debated the issues in professional journals during the 1950s, this controversy did not capture the public's attention. Not until the next major sex study—Masters and Johnson's *Human Sexual Response* in 1966—would the vaginal orgasm theory be substantially undermined.[65]

Both Kinsey's contemporaries and future social scientists also raised questions about the representativeness of the sample and disputed the reliability of individual responses to interviewers, especially because interviewees were being asked about sex. Despite these criticisms, the *Kinsey Reports* made an enormous contribution and remain to this day the largest empirical study of American sexual behavior. Perhaps their most important achievement was to awaken the public to the variety of sexual behavior engaged in by everyday people. For the first time, an enthralled public had proof that—in Kinsey's words—the "publicly pretended code of morals," including no premarital sex, no masturbation, no adultery, was regularly being breached.[66]

Nevertheless, Kinsey created a different set of problems by ignoring the emotional and social meaning of sex and focusing solely on the biological. By using the incidence and frequency of orgasm—counting the number of outlets—as the measure of sex, he ignored the fact that not all orgasms were alike. Quantification—how many times, with whom, and at what age?—demystified the sex act, but did not answer, why do it? or how did it feel? Kinsey's biologizing of sexuality, although allegedly value-free, established its own normalizing concepts: if mammals did it, it was natural and therefore good. [67]

Counting outlets supposed that a universal orgasm existed—across time, place, and species. In order to set human sexuality in a mammalian context, Kinsey portrayed sex as if age, upbringing, or partner made no difference to the experience; and as if sexual behavior meant the same thing in 1950 as it had in 1890. This approach assumed that without the inhibiting fetters of religion, morality, and culture, an untroubled, natural sexuality would emerge.

In the eyes of these beholders, nymphomania did not exist; "too many" orgasms was a moral, not a scientific judgment. But in killing off nymphomania, the Kinsey team created a different construct. Not the objective, scientific one they claimed, but a way of looking at sex that measured only behavior and not how people felt about it. In the coming decades, sexological researchers and their popular interpreters would overemphasize this biological point of view. Eventually, a new corrective—much like the corrective Kinsey provided to the earlier pathologizing perspective—would need to be developed.

ALL OF THESE sex experts—the scientists researching sex hormones, the Freudian-inspired physicians and popular writers, and

Kinsey and his colleagues—saw themselves as workers in the field of sexual enlightenment. Reflecting society's anxiety about changing gender roles, they searched for ways to better understand female sexuality and thus to strengthen marriage. Criticizing their Victorian grandparents' sexual blinders, each proposed that their particular perspective—endocrinological research, psychological theory, or quantitative methods—would solve the sexual issues of the day. Truth, they believed, could be found in the body's chemistry, in the depths of the psyche, or in human beings' similarity to mammals.

These mid-twentieth-century communities of experts validated three different views of nymphomania: biological, psychological, and nonexistent. From earlier notions of inflamed genitals to hormonal and psychological theories to Kinsey's attempt to lay the whole concept to rest, what constituted being "oversexed" was a moving target. Even so, to a public anxious for sexual advice, the authority of scientists, physicians, psychologists, and sex researchers to define hypersexuality carried enormous weight. As we will see in the next chapter, the power of that authority was also felt in another arena, when the notion of nymphomania was introduced into the courtroom.

4

nymphomania in the courts

FTER WORK ONE NIGHT in February 1948, two young Hancock, Michigan, bakery workers, a fifteen-year-old girl and her co-worker, Roger Bastian, went for a ride in the bakery's truck. According to the girl, Bastian took her to an uninhabited part of town and forced her to have sexual intercourse with him. Bastian denied his guilt and maintained instead that the young woman made advances to him. Actually, he claimed, her conduct offended him, he rejected her, and she became enraged.[1]

In this classic case of "he said, she said," the credibility of the rape complainant was at issue. Was her version of the events believable or was his? Moreover, according to Michigan's laws, a fifteen year old was not old enough to give consent to sexual intercourse. Even if Bastian could prove that his accuser actually wanted to have sex, that fact would not exonerate him from the charge of statutory rape: he must prove that sexual intercourse never happened.

For his defense, Bastian's lawyer attempted to introduce evidence proving that the "prosecutrix" was a nymphomaniac who only imagined the rape. (The very term "prosecutrix," unique to rape trials, stems from early English law and suggests that a vindictive complainant, rather than the state, was pressing charges for the sexual act.)[2] The defense claimed that her mental illness—nymphomania—led her to believe that she had been sexually assaulted, when actually no sexual activity had occurred. The Michigan judge ruled the evidence of nymphomania inadmissible and Bastian was found guilty.

But that was not the end of the case. In 1951, the Supreme Court of Michigan heard Bastian's appeal and ruled that the defendant was indeed "entitled to offer proofs, even though of a revolting nature, that [the] prosecutrix was a nymphomaniac." As a precedent for their ruling, the court cited an earlier Michigan statutory rape case, *People* v. *Cowles* (1929), in which the term "nymphomaniac" was declared to be "a standard one in medical parlance."[3] In 1951, the Michigan appellate court concluded that the question raised in the earlier case was still at issue: "whether the mind of the girl was so warped by sexual contemplation and desires as to lead her to accept the imaginary as real or to fabricate a claimed sexual experience."[4]

Legal Theory and the Nymphomaniac

THIS NOTION—that lust could so distort the mind of a fifteen-year-old girl that she would fantasize she had been raped—was not unique to these two Michigan cases. In fact, in the middle decades of the twentieth century, this pseudo-scientific notion was widely supported in the law. Articles in highly regarded legal journals legitimated the image of women's sexuality that underlay the rulings in the *Bastian* and *Cowles* cases as if scientifically proven. For example, referring to the "growing belief that many prosecuting witnesses [in sex offense cases] are emotionally unbalanced," the authoritative *American Law Reports* published a lengthy annotation in 1968 analyzing the admission of expert testimony in cases of mental disorder, such as nymphomania.[5] In the *Stanford Law Review* (1966), law professor Roger B. Dworkin stated unequivocally: "When current psychological evidence indicates the unreliability of women's reports of the incident, nothing should be left to the conceivably unreasonable opinion of the alleged victim."[6] And a 1967 Note in the *Columbia Law Review*, in which the author claimed that "stories of rape are frequently lies or fantasies," was even more forthright: "Surely, the simplest, and perhaps the most important, reason not to permit conviction for rape on the uncorroborated word of the prosecutrix is that that word is very often false."[7]

Lawyers who turned to medical-legal textbooks in the fifties and sixties also found similar and equally unsubstantiated claims. According to the *Attorneys' Textbook of Medicine*, women were prone to a mental condition that combines a mixture of lies and imagination which "not infrequently . . . is the basis of alleged sexual assaults."[8] Even crackpot theories—for example, the "riddance mechanism," which claimed that women unconsciously invited rape in order to rid themselves of the fear of being raped—were featured in legal journals as if scientifically valid.[9]

All of these midcentury legal theorists looked to the authority of one man, author of the most famous single modern work in the field of legal evidence, John Henry Wigmore, dean of Northwestern University Law School from 1901 to 1929. The ten-volume edition of his magnum opus, *Evidence in Trials at Common Law*, was published in 1940, revised in 1970, and is still used today.[10] Generations of law school students studied *Evidence*, hundreds of appellate court decisions cited it, and scores of legal scholars referred to it with reverence. Enormously influential, Wigmore's treatise defined the rules of evidence used in the United States legal system.[11]

In an often-cited section on rape, Wigmore immortalized the lying, fantasizing prosecutrix, while clothing the image in the appearance of objectivity. According to Wigmore, "[women's] psychic complexes are multifarious. . . . One form taken by these complexes is that of contriving false charges of sexual offenses by men."[12] Dressed up in medical terms like "nymphomania," supported by lengthy quotations from legal and medical experts, Wigmore's use of age-old suspicions of women who "cried rape" appeared "scientific" and thus legitimate. *Evidence* even contained a separate section entitled "Abnormal mentality of women complainants: nymphomania." Despite later revisions of other parts of the text, and the regular updating of supplements, at present the sections about nymphomania remain unchanged.[13]

Dean Wigmore was an impassioned advocate of the innocent man harmed by the false claims of a woman driven by perverted sexual desire. According to Wigmore, an "unchaste mentality" characterized rape complainants.[14] This was a twentieth-century corollary to the traditional belief—found in most legal treatises until quite recently—that if a rape victim had a reputation in her community for immorality, she was more likely to have consented to sexual activity again. Thus, if her body was not chaste, her rape charge was probably false.

Wigmore expanded that notion to include women's psyches as well. Firmly convinced of women's duplicitous nature, the eminent legal scholar challenged the courts "to awaken to the sinister possibilities of injustice that lurk in believing such a witness without careful psychiatric scrutiny." Because he assumed that the scales of justice unfairly tipped toward the prosecutrix, he insisted: *"No judge should ever let a sex offense charge go to the jury unless the female complainant's social history and mental makeup have been examined and testified to by a qualified physician"* (his emphasis).[15] Wigmore believed that the general lack of witnesses to rape made it a unique crime, the only one that required a compulsory psychiatric examination of the complaining witness.

Although this mandate never became part of the law, Wigmore's assumptions about women fraudulently accusing men of rape had a profound influence on legal theory.

Ironically, Wigmore saw himself as a modernizer—the objective man of science who challenged outmoded judicial procedures. Convinced that modern psychiatry held the key to rape complainants' false allegations, he cited experts on the troubled female psyche to support his theories. The psychiatrist Karl Menninger, for example, founder of the Menninger Clinic, wrote to Wigmore in 1933 that he believed psychiatric examinations should be required of rape complainants because "fantasies of being raped are exceedingly common in women, indeed one may almost say that they are probably universal."[16]

Dr. W. F. Lorenz, director of the Psychiatric Institute at the University of Wisconsin, agreed. Based on his work with the mentally ill, he thought that psychiatric examination was "imperative in every case where sexual assault is charged." And this was necessary for all women, not just those suspected of mental illness, because "frequently sexual assault is charged or claimed with nothing more substantive supporting this belief than an unrealized wish or unconscious, deeply suppressed sexual longing or thwarting."[17] Many decades of medical theories and millennia of cultural assumptions culminate in this extraordinary image of women.

The notion that women's sexual desires drove them to fantasize that they had been raped joined with the traditional stereotype of the lying, vindictive woman who falsely accused an innocent man. As far back as the seventeenth century, the Lord Chief Justice of England, Matthew Hale, had declared: "Rape is an accusation easily to be made and hard to be proved, and harder to be defended by the party accused, though ever so innocent."[18] As recently as the 1980s, many states still required judges to instruct the jury in words paraphrasing this pronouncement. No other crime called for a comparable warning to the jury.[19]

Shaped by folklore, myth, and biblical stories—such as that of Potiphar's wife, who accused her husband's slave Joseph of rape after he spurned her advances—rape laws had incorporated an image of women thought to be motivated by greed, revenge, guilt, or blackmail. Wigmore and others added an equally dangerous notion of the nymphomaniac who actually believed that she had been sexually attacked when no sexual activity had occurred. This idea was rooted in nineteenth-century claims that "hysterics," "nymphomaniacs," and "erotomaniacs" in mental hospitals often wrongly accused medical attendants of sexual attack.[20] Now, cultural assumptions had joined with medical opinion to create a unique image of female sexuality: women's irrational minds and weak wills so readily succumbed to sexual desires that they falsely claimed sexual assault.

Although this image of the nymphomaniac appeared in the nineteenth century, the influence of Freudianism on American legal theory greatly strengthened its impact in the twentieth century.[21] Just as nineteenth-century medical men had turned to biology to explain women's supposed propensity for false rape accusations, new theories about sexual longings buried deep in the female psyche added considerable weight to this stereotype.[22] The Viennese psychoanalyst Helene Deutsch, in her *Psychology of Women*, asserted that the basically masochistic character of the female sexual experience suggested that women were ambivalent about forced sex, fantasizing about and even subconsciously desiring rape. According to Deutsch, "rape fantasies have such irresistible verisimilitude that even the most experienced judges are misled in trials of innocent men accused of rape by hysterical women."[23]

Armed with these theories, a clever defense attorney—such as the one in the *Bastian* case—could employ a "nymphomania defense," attacking a rape victim's supposed unconscious fantasies of sexual assault to cast suspicion on her testimony. In a twist on the traditional attempt to prove the rape complainant a willing participant, defense attorneys might grill the accuser about her "insatiable desires" and "uncontrollable sexual weaknesses," not to present her as unchaste, but to prove that she had fantasized the rape. This approach was aided by the fact that, until the 1970s, the collection of rape evidence was still in its infancy and no rape counselors or rape crisis units helped women to report the assault immediately. Consequently, many women might not have had substantial physical evidence to prove the rape.

There is no question that some mentally ill women (and men) suffer from hallucinations and delusions, which include sexual imagery. However, generalizing from that population to all female rape complainants challenges the basic idea of scientific objectivity. The Wigmoreans vaulted across the uncharted territory from "wish" to "deed"—from a woman's fantasizing about or even wishing for forced sex to her actual participation in rape or to her belief that she had been raped when no sexual act had occurred. But they produced no evidence, nor does any exist, to prove that a woman's "rape fantasies" mean she actually wants to be raped.[24]

Nor did they prove that the female psyche is peculiarly prone to conjuring false images of sexual attack. The point is not that every woman who has accused a man of rape is telling the truth. What is at issue here is how loaded the cultural—and thus legal—imagery is against the "prosecutrix." Trapped by an older image of the hysterical, lying woman, and influenced by neo-Freudian concepts of women's basic masochism, twentieth-century judges, attorneys, and state legislators incorporated these concepts, in pseudo-scientific terms such as "nymphomania," into the legal system.

Returning to the *Bastian* case, we see what this meant for one young woman whose convicted rapist was granted a new trial based on this perception of women's sexuality. According to the Michigan appellate court, the trial judge had erred in not allowing the defense "to cross-examine the prosecutrix with reference to certain alleged conduct on her part tending to show that she was a sexual-psychopathic person," and thus a liar or a fantasizer.[25] In the excluded testimony, the prosecutrix admitted that in the months before the trial, but *after* her experience in the bakery truck, she had had sexual relations with eleven other young men. She insisted, however, that Ralph Bastian had been the first and that he had forced her to have sex.

Was she telling the truth or was she a nymphomaniac whose word could not be trusted? Based only on his observation of her in the courtroom, the defense's expert witness had declared that the prosecutrix was a "sexual-psychopathic person," the kind of individual whose credibility was "very poor." The appellate court ruled that this physician might have had even more reason to conclude that "the prosecutrix was actually a nymphomaniac" if he had heard the excluded testimony at the trial that the girl had later engaged in multiple sexual relations. Ultimately, these factors might have led the jury to acquit the defendant. In this case, the medical-legal theory, which interpreted her promiscuous sexuality after the rape as evidence of an abnormal mind, convinced the appellate court that she might not be telling the truth. For these reasons, they overturned the guilty verdict and granted a new trial.

Nymphomania, Fantasy, and Incest

IMAGES OF THE fantasizing prosecutrix played a role not only in rape cases but in cases of incest as well. Most people at this time found so unthinkable the idea that a father or trusted relative would sexually molest a daughter or niece that many denied it happened. Others blamed the victim. Since most incest cases handled by the criminal justice system dealt with poor and working-class families, authorities generally assumed that crowded living conditions and the taken-for-granted immorality of the poor caused the breaking of this unspoken taboo. Like rape, incest supposedly did not happen to respectable girls: only rarely were middle-class fathers or brothers prosecuted for incestuous acts.

Fervent belief in middle-class children's basic innocence and asexuality shaped the way incest was understood. Professionals and ordinary people alike clung to the belief that sexual desires and behavior before puberty signaled abnormality. If relatives sexually abused daughters or nieces, the girls had either brought it on themselves or invented the whole story. Mid-twentieth-century official reports reflected this notion, focusing on the "unusually charming and attractive" molested child who might be the "actual seducer, rather than the one innocently seduced."[26] Contrary opinions existed, but the *Comprehensive Textbook of Psychiatry - II* (1975) summed up prevailing notions: "The daughters collude in the incestuous liaison and play an active and even initiating role in establishing the pattern."[27]

Researchers signaled their belief in the victim's moral corruption by describing cases such as that of Pat L., who "at the age of four began a sexual relationship with a 54-year-old man [her stepfather] which continued until she was 11."[28] The idea that four year olds initiate sexual relationships with fifty-four year olds reflected earlier beliefs. In the nineteenth century, for example, many believed that very young children who took an interest in their genitals were "precociously depraved," presumably an evolutionary throwback to a more primitive time.

Freud, of course, had exploded the belief that children were asexual. Only ancient prejudice, he maintained, could deny the fact that sexual life began soon after birth. Freud further shocked his contemporaries by proclaiming that children focused their earliest sexual desires on their parents. The psychic conflict caused by society's demand to repress these desires, he believed, led to the hysterical claims of childhood sexual molestation which his adult female patients brought to him. Freud had originally accepted these stories of childhood seduction and rape to be real events. Later he changed his mind about the truth of such tales, a volte-face that would have major effects not only on psychoanalysis but on the law as well.[29]

Freudian theory combined with nineteenth-century notions of "precocious depravity" to create a volatile mid-twentieth-century mix. Many psychiatrists and other medical authorities understood incest either as a fantasy or as the work of "sexualized" girls, such as Pat L. The influence of these sex experts, as we saw in the previous chapter, greatly increased after World War II. Having been hired by the thousands to detect sexual deviation and other abnormalities within the armed forces, psychiatrists and psychologists sought to solidify their professional status in the postwar period. Testifying in court both reflected and helped to legitimate their claim to expertise in sexual issues. Progressive legal scholars, echoing Wigmore, supported that claim and called for an enlightened court to require the widespread use of experts in sex offense cases.[30]

Not all legal authorities were convinced. Even though most states gave judges the right to admit psychiatric testimony, many chose not to.[31] But in this still-contested terrain, psychiatric evidence potentially posed an effective argument.

Nymphomania-induced distortions of reality and the admissibility of expert psychiatric witnesses dominated one mid-1960s California incest case, *People* v. *Russel*. Fourteen-year-old Roxanne Russel testified that, in April 1965, her father had "called her into his bedroom and there performed an act of sexual intercourse with her; that during the ten months following this date [he] performed such acts with her about once a week."[32] Seeking to prove that she was lying, the defense requested a psychiatric examination of Roxanne to show that "her mental or emotional condition affected her veracity"[33]—to show, in effect, that she was a nymphomaniac who had fantasized the incest. Although the judge approved the request to examine Roxanne, he ultimately refused to admit the psychiatrist's report into evidence on the grounds that the jury, not experts, must determine her credibility.

Convicted of incest, the father, Thomas Russel, appealed to the Supreme Court of California, claiming that the jury needed to hear this expert evidence because as laymen they might have been unable to detect Roxanne's nymphomanialike condition. According to Russel's lawyer, Roxanne's perverted imagination drove her to fabricate her lurid tale of repeated sexual molestation. The contested psychiatric examination supported this assumption by concluding: "[While] this patient fails to reveal any evidence of psychosis . . . no indication of hallucination or delusional pattern . . . [she] appears to have a serious emotional problem marked by impulsive and unpredictable behavior, as well as a tendency to lose contact with and distort reality."[34]

A California psychiatrist, David R. Rubin, summed up his twenty-minute examination of Roxanne with a written diagnosis which stated that she deliberately "lies when she feels it is convenient for her."[35] To substantiate his claim that she was a liar—and thus invalidate the entire tale of sexual intimacies—the appellant pointed to the falsehoods in her testimony. While on the stand, Roxanne at first said that her father had engaged in sexual intercourse with her approximately four times, but not more than ten times. On redirect examination, she testified that she had lied because she was "embarrassed in admitting how many times it actually occurred." According to Russel's lawyer, and in the words of Dr. Rubin, this changed testimony was evidence of Roxanne's inability "to distinguish between what occurred in reality and the production of her own phantasies."[36]

The Supreme Court of California ruled that this psychiatric testimony should have been admitted: especially in a sex offense case where "the legal discretion of the judge should be exercised liberally in favor of the defendant." Referring to Wigmore, the court claimed that psychiatric examinations were necessary in sex cases like this one because the complaining witness's state of mind played such a big role. Consequently, the appeals court reversed the jury's guilty verdict.[37]

In this and other incest cases—as in the rape cases of the period—a particular image of female sexuality shaped the opinions of the court.[38] Not until the late 1970s and early 1980s would the attitudes toward incest begin to change. Female psychology supposedly rendered women and girls peculiarly prone to repressed sexual desires; these metamorphosed into sexual fantasies. Within this set of cultural beliefs, only "a-stranger-in-a-dark-alley" attack—one that was accompanied by signs of struggle, followed by immediate reporting—might be seen as "real."[39] Sexual intercourse with an acquaintance or relative obviously did not fit this model. Consequently, suspicion surrounded not the molesters but the Roxannes of the world and their nymphomaniacal fantasies.

Psychiatric expert testimony and the use of pseudo-medical terms such as "nymphomania" cast these culturally bound notions in a scientific light. Using Freudian theories, legal modernizers called for the admission of psychiatric testimony about the emotional or mental conflicts allegedly plaguing rape complainants. Supposedly, ordinary jury members might not be aware of the depth of these female proclivities and thus required the guidance of experts. But cultural forces, not science, were at work here.

Nymphomania and the Supreme Court

EVEN THE HIGHEST court of the land found credible these pseudo-scientific images of nymphomaniacal women. In 1966, the U.S. Supreme Court heard *Giles* v. *Maryland*,[40] in which Joyce Roberts accused the two Giles brothers, James and John, and Joseph Johnson of rape. Roberts testified that about midnight, July 20, 1961, she, her boyfriend, and two other young men went to a secluded spot on the Patuxent River to go swimming. Upon leaving, they discovered that their car was out of gas; two of the friends left to find a gas station. At this point, "three young Negroes"—the Giles brothers and Johnson—appeared, allegedly threatened them, and attacked the car with rocks. Ms. Roberts escaped into the woods. She later testified that she was captured and raped by the three men. The defendants claimed that Roberts was a nymphomaniac and had consented. The jury in Montgomery County, Maryland, found the Giles brothers (Johnson's trial had been severed from that of the other defendants) guilty of raping sixteen-year-old Joyce Roberts and sentenced them to death. Their various appeals eventually reached the Supreme Court.

The tragic history of mob lynching and state executions of hundreds of black men unjustly accused of raping white women haunts this case. Racial issues, such as the disproportionate use of the death penalty against convicted black rapists, the institutionalized racism of Montgomery County, the racial composition of the jury, and the inadequate legal defense provided poor blacks accused of capital crimes have rightly dominated the subsequent discussion of *Giles* v. *Maryland*.[41] But little attention has been paid to another issue this case raised: how did the Supreme Court, under the liberal and progressive leadership of Chief Justice Earl Warren, understand and interpret the term "nymphomania"?[42]

Before the Supreme Court reviewed this case, the defense filed several appeals in lower courts, arguing, among other issues, that the state had withheld evidence of Roberts's nymphomania, which the court referred to as a "type of mental illness" that affects the witness's credibility.[43] The Giles brothers' lawyer, Joseph Forer, presenting the case at a post-conviction hearing, declared: "And by definition, rape being intercourse against the will of the woman, it is virtually impossible to rape a nymphomaniac." To which the presiding judge retorted, "No one has the right to rape a nymphomaniac."[44] Forer quickly agreed that nymphomaniacs, like prostitutes, were not fair game for rapists. But nymphomania did mean, he asserted, that Roberts's credibility was extremely doubtful. The judge concurred, remanded the case for a new trial, and the state appealed.

After additional legal maneuvering, the Supreme Court agreed to hear the case in 1966. *Giles* v. *Maryland* was concerned with the classic rape question: Did she consent? To prove that Roberts had willingly participated, the Giles brothers' attorneys appealed to the Supreme Court to determine whether the trial court had suppressed evidence concerning the victim's mental condition and her reputation for promiscuity. If known, this evidence might have supported "a defense that Roberts suffered from an uncontrollable weakness [nymphomania] that the Giles brothers might reasonably have mistaken for consent."[45]

In this case, unlike statutory rape cases, the defense argued that she had consented, not that she had fantasized the act. Expert testimony of her lascivious desires should have been admitted, according to the defense, because such evidence might have convinced the jury that Roberts agreed to have sex. In what Justice Abe Fortas called "this immensely troubling case," the Court split its verdict five to four. Justice William Brennan, joined by the Chief Justice and Justice William O. Douglas, announced the judgment of the Court: evidence of Roberts's nymphomania had indeed been improperly suppressed. The evidence, according to Brennan, went as follows: Several months after the rape, but before the trial, Roberts had sexual relations with two boys at a party, took an overdose of pills, was hospitalized in a psychiatric ward, and told a friend that she had been raped by the two men. Joyce Roberts's father filed a formal charge of rape, which she refused to support, although she admitted to the examining police officer that "she had had sexual relations with numerous boys and men, some of whom she did not know."[46]

In a concurring opinion, Justice Byron White, citing with approval *People* v. *Bastian*, agreed that evidence of nymphomania was generally admissible. However, he found nothing in this particular trial record to prove that the prosecutrix was so afflicted. Presumably, Justice White did not interpret Joyce Roberts's alleged sexual conduct or her psychiatric hospitalization as an indication that she was a nymphomaniac. In addition, he maintained, even if she was a nymphomaniac, that did not automatically make her an incompetent witness.

Justice White agreed with a lower court judge's conclusion that Roberts might be a nymphomaniac and still be telling the truth about not consenting to sex. Even so, he and Justice Fortas joined the majority opinion because they believed that the lower court should review the suppressed evidence more fully. The four dissenting judges, on the other hand, declared that "it would be difficult to imagine charges more convincingly proved than were those against these three youths for raping this teenage girl."[47] The Supreme Court's majority opinion remanded the case to the Maryland Court of Appeals for further proceedings.

In preparation for a new trial, the state's attorney learned that Joyce Roberts was unwilling to return to testify at a new trial. Five years after the alleged rape, she was eight months pregnant and fiercely protective of her new life as a Florida wife and mother of two. The state of Florida refused to extradite her. In 1967, after spending two years on death row and four years in the Maryland Penitentiary, John and James Giles were cleared of all charges.[48]

In addition to profound issues of racial injustice, *Giles v. Maryland* raised several additional questions: Was Roberts a "nymphomaniac"? What was sexual excess on the part of a teenage girl, and did it mean mental or emotional illness? And finally, what effect did any of this have on her credibility, on whether or not she had consented? Of course, the justices did not resolve these questions. They did, however, add the Supreme Court's imprimatur to the notion that nymphomania was real, a diagnosable disease or disorder that had consequences in the law.

State Legislative Codes Adopt Nymphomania

THE SLIPPERY AND ELUSIVE notion of the sex-crazed, fantasizing prosecutrix appeared real to state legislators as well. Reflecting mid-twentieth-century medical categories of sexual deviation, at least one state legislature specifically included nymphomania in its official law codes. According to the state of Georgia statutes:

> Generally, expert testimony as to the credibility of a witness is admissible if the subject matter involves organic or mental disease. This includes testimony concerning insanity and other forms of mental derangement, such as hysteria, delusions, hallucinations, nymphomania, sexual psychopathy, and retrograde amnesia.[49]

Even without their own individual codes, the appellate courts of various states, including Iowa, Nebraska, and Wisconsin, cited the

Georgia state statute to justify their use of expert witnesses to assess whether the complainant's sexual drives hindered her ability to tell the truth.[50] This formulation persists even today: in Georgia's most recent revision of its state law code, the clause remains intact.[51]

The Cable-Car Nymphomaniac

STRANGELY ENOUGH, in legal areas other than rape cases, a few women themselves—or the lawyers who represented them—have claimed to be nymphomaniacs. In a 1970 personal injury case, a twenty-nine-year-old San Francisco woman sued the Municipal Railway for $500,000 in damages sustained when the cable car on which she was riding careened backward down the Hyde Street hill and crashed. According to her lawsuit, the crash left her with physical injuries and a "demonic sex urge."[52] In this case, law, medicine, and popular culture joined in highlighting a relatively new aspect of nymphomania. Reading the newspaper accounts, the public became aware that at least one set of psychiatric experts—testifying in her behalf—believed that her excessive sexual desires really masked her need for cuddling and affection. She wanted sex not for sex's sake, they claimed, but for emotional sustenance.

Variously described by the newspapers as a "buxom blonde" and "modestly attractive," the "Cable-Car-Named-Desire" nymphomaniac became an instant cause célèbre. In two and a half days on the witness stand, the former dance teacher testified that during the five years since the accident she had had over one hundred lovers. Six of them testified at the trial to their "easy access to her." When asked by her attorney why she needed so many men, she feistily replied: "That's like asking a mouse why it eats cheese."[53]

Originally, the plaintiff's lawyer had planned to present her as "trouble free and upward bound in career" before the crash destroyed her psychic equilibrium. He had hired a private investigator to find the men "who had dated her before the accident and NOT gone to bed with her" in order to "show that the girl [at that time] was quiet and nice."[54] However, the plaintiff herself revealed on the witness stand that she had had "two affairs of the heart" while at the University of Michigan in the 1960s and also kept a diary in which she confessed to being "horny." An enthralled courtroom heard the woman explain this diary entry by saying: "if you tell a man you need affection he wouldn't understand you, if you tell him you are horny, he'll make love to you."[55]

Dueling psychiatric notions about this combination of sexual behavior and emotional need were at the heart of the case. The four psychiatrists who testified for the plaintiff hoped to demonstrate that the crash had turned her into a nymphomaniac. They maintained that the route was an indirect one—her sexual desire became obsessive because her scrape with death shattered her emotional security. The consequent damage to her psyche drove her into the arms of scores of lovers. An expert witness, psychiatrist Dr. Andrew Watson, testifying on her behalf, related her condition to a scientific study which claimed that depressed people needed a lot of cuddling that, in turn, led to excessive sexual intercourse.[56]

The city of San Francisco, on the other hand, called only one witness. Dr. Knox Finley, a psychiatrist who routinely examined claimants against the city, presented another theory about nymphomania. Along with other experts at the time, Dr. Finley insisted that nymphomania could only result from brain damage: "It's my opinion that any excessive sexual drive could not possibly be attributed to the cable car accident because there is no indication whatsoever that the brain was damaged." At most, he believed, the accident might have caused a "temporary emotional upset and neurosis, if you want to call it that, a benign one."[57]

In addition, Finley claimed that the young woman's "emotional problems have always been with her to some degree."[58] The defense appeared to be presenting its case from two angles: the plaintiff was not a nymphomaniac because there was no brain damage; and even if she were one, the cable car accident had not caused the condition because she had always been neurotic and sexually overactive.[59]

The trial ended after ten days in the public spotlight. The eight-woman, four-man jury entered the jury room having heard the judge's instructions: they must find that the city's negligence led to some injury to the plaintiff, although not necessarily the specific condition of nymphomania. In a 9–3 decision, they did so. Without specifying the particular injuries, they awarded her $50,000, which while only one-tenth the original claim, was still a very considerable sum in 1970.[60]

Both sides declared victory. The young woman's attorney maintained that the jury had recognized that psychic injuries required compensation. The city claimed that the dramatic cut in the award signaled the jury's belief that the accident played a minimal role in her subsequent problems.

For the public, days of titillating newspaper headlines and detailed sexual stories left an indelible image of the "buxom blonde cable-car nymphomaniac." Dissecting excessive sexual behavior for widespread public consumption, the court case displayed the uncertain nature of nymphomania. Even though psychiatric theories heightened the sense that nymphomania was a knowable entity, the legal debate promised more than it could deliver. Nymphomania's definition remained elusive. Following this brief moment of fame, the woman who had been the focus of all this attention disappeared from the news.

Rape Law Reform and the "Nymphomania Defense"

COURTROOM TACTICS AND law journal articles helped to shape the definition of nymphomania in the postwar period. Sensational trials, such as the San Francisco cable car case, reinforced notions of female sexual excess presented in popular magazines. Rape cases magnified one particular aspect of nymphomania: the alleged connection between a woman's sexuality and her ability to tell the truth.

Starting in the 1960s, widespread social changes would challenge these stereotypes. Fair and equal treatment before the law became a battle cry of an emboldened women's movement. The sexual double standard so blatantly displayed in rape cases came under especially heated attack.

In the early 1970s, an unlikely combination of feminists and "get-tough-on-crime" conservatives joined forces to change rape laws throughout the country. Feminists attacked the bias against women embedded in rape laws; conservatives demanded changes in the arrest and conviction rates of rapists, reported by the FBI to be the lowest rate of all violent crimes. Mounting a fierce campaign in state legislatures, law journals, and the mass media, this coalition confronted state rape statutes essentially unchanged since their enactment two hundred years earlier.[61]

After an intense state-by-state, sometimes legislator-by-legislator campaign, forty-five states passed new rape legislation by the early 1980s. In a crucial set of reforms, legislatures redefined rape as a violent, not a sexual crime, eliminated the corroboration requirement, and passed "rape shield" laws which aimed to protect the victim on the witness stand from a humiliating dissection of her past sexual life. In 1986, Congress too ratified rape reform legislation similar to that in the states. In effect, the laws tried to make a woman's sexual history irrelevant and inadmissible.[62]

But reformers overestimated the potential impact of these legislative victories. Recent reviews of rape reform legislation conclude that while real change occurred in certain aspects of the law and in the treatment of the victims, the results remain equivocal. Law reform does not automatically lead to a change in the cultural stereotypes prevalent in the criminal justice system. Judges, district attorneys, and police officers still retain a tremendous amount of discretion in dealing with women who accuse men of rape.[63]

Many gaping holes remain in the shield that supposedly protects rape victims from questions about their sexual history.[64] Consider the following possibly far-fetched but still potential loophole, which I will call the "nymphomania defense." Law professors Charles Alan Wright and Kenneth Graham, authors of an influential, multivolume treatise on the federal rules of evidence, *Federal Practice and Procedure*, have proposed the following scenario. Suppose a psychiatrist, testifying as an expert witness, wants to offer an opinion that the complainant actually consented to the alleged rape. "His opinion of her present consent is based upon her prior sexual behavior; e.g., psychiatric testimony that the victim is a 'nymphomaniac.'" The admissibility of this evidence would depend upon the trial court judge's interpretation of the state's rules of evidence; but if admitted, it would mean that the prosecutor would presumably have to do what rape reform legislation was supposed to prevent. In order to rebut the assertion of the expert witness, the prosecutor would have to expose the victim to an examination of her past sexual behavior.[65]

Moreover, according to Wright and Graham, "since 'nymphomania' is usually claimed to embrace prevarication as well as promiscuity, such an interpretation would [also] open the door to use of prior sexual conduct on the issue of credibility."[66] Again, the intent of the rape reform legislation—to divorce a woman's sexual conduct from her trustworthiness—would be nullified. Regardless of the lack of scientific rigor apparent in the diagnosis of nymphomania, her sexual behavior might then be scrutinized on the witness stand. While courts differed on the admissibility of such expert witness testimony, civil libertarians contended that the accused's Sixth Amendment rights required that all relevant evidence be admitted.[67]

A 1986 case, *Missouri v. Jones*, illustrates the potential for this approach. In a dissenting opinion, Judge J. Blackmar, later the chief justice of the Missouri Supreme Court, posed a hypothetical question: "Suppose a defendant asserts that the accuser was a nymphomaniac who threw herself at him and proffered charges only because of subsequent disagreement, or even because he refused her approach. Should he not be able to corroborate his claim that she regularly made advances to men?"[68] Blackmar's opinion concluded that a person accused of rape had a constitutional right to introduce such evidence.

Judge Blackmar did not define nymphomania, nor did he suggest what evidence would be required to prove the accuser was a nymphomaniac. Neither did those legal scholars who agreed with him.[69] Moreover, Blackmar's vague statement about an accuser who "regularly made advances to men" remains hopelessly elusive. How regularly? How many men? Finally, the judge made no attempt to substantiate a relationship between these "advances" and either the complainant's ability to tell the truth or her consent to a *particular* sexual act.[70] Remarkably, he even cited Genesis and the biblical story of Potiphar's wife. In Judge Blackmar's judicial opinion, the centuries-old image of lying, seductive women and falsely accused men lives on.[71]

A bizarre example of this stereotype's tenacity can be found in a 1991 case, *Chew v. Texas*.[72] At the trial, the prosecution presented evidence that Felipe Chew and others forced a twenty-year-old victim into a car late one night while she was on her way home from a family party. She was taken to a ranch, where she later testified that as many as fifteen men had raped her.

Chew's defense alleged that she was a nymphomaniac and had consented to the sex. To substantiate that claim in court, the defense attorney asked the accuser whether she had experienced "an uncontrollable" desire on the night of the attack.[73] When she responded "no," he called a "qualified psychiatrist with expertise in sexual disorders," Dr. Lawrence Taylor, to determine whether the rape complainant had an "insatiable" sexual desire. In typical courtroom fashion, the defense attorney presented Taylor with a hypothetical question based on the events of the night in question. Specifically, he asked whether a person who consented to have sex with multiple partners while in close proximity to other people displayed the characteristics of nymphomania. Dr. Taylor affirmed that diagnosis and then elaborated on the illness of nymphomania, describing it as a condition "occasionally found in females, consisting of an unmanageable sexual desire which results in a dramatic frequency of sexual contact with a partner as well as *indiscriminate sexual contact with groups*" (my emphasis).[74] Not surprisingly, this stunning construction conveniently fit the evidence presented by the defense.

Other hypothetical questions were posed to the expert witness outside the hearing of the jury. The judge had already excluded the defense's attempt to present testimony from a number of men who described numerous sexual encounters with the complainant *subsequent* to the rape. However, in the judge's chamber, the defense asked Taylor to comment on what this kind of "sexual misconduct" might mean. The psychiatrist responded that the facts were "in keeping with a diagnosis of nymphomania." Furthermore, "that when females afflicted with this illness are caught or confronted, they have a tendency 'to cover up.'" He concluded: "a female so afflicted could possibly be raped but that it was not probable." This evidence did not reach the jury because of rape shield laws, but following Chew's conviction, it formed the basis of his appeal.[75]

Chew appealed on the grounds that the Texas rules of evidence which excluded the testimony alleging her subsequent sexual encounters—conduct supposedly consistent with that of a person suffering from nymphomania—violated his Sixth Amendment right to confront his accuser. In somewhat tortured legalese, the Texas Court of Appeals agreed: "Certainly, the alleged affliction of the complainant which the appellant sought to show by the suppressed evidence had the tendency of creating a propensity, on someone so afflicted, of not only consenting to group sexual contacts, but of inducing them." Furthermore, Chew had the right to cross-examine her to prove that she had a motive for her false allegation of rape, that is, that she had wanted "to hide her sexual affliction from the public as well as from her jealous husband."[76] According to the appeal, if the jury had heard this evidence, they might have believed Chew's contention that the complainant consented to the sexual activity for which he had been convicted of rape. Citing the Supreme Court's recognition "that the Sixth Amendment guarantees significant cross-examination rights, which include exposure of a witness' motivation in testifying," the Texas Court of Appeals reversed the decision and granted Chew a new trial.[77]

In a blistering dissent, one appellate court judge labeled the crime a "gang rape." The evidence of nymphomania, which the defense wished to present, he said, involved sexual behavior *subsequent* to the rape and therefore could not be used to show something about the complainant's character and truthfulness at the time of the crime. However, "if appellant had offered evidence of the complainant's *reputation* for nymphomania *in March 1988* [at the same time that the sexual assault took place] this case would present a different question" (emphasis in the original).[78] Thus, all the participants—the defense, the state, the majority, and even the outraged dissenting appeals court judge—assumed that nymphomania existed; that it was a clearly definable disease with symptoms and characteristics that could be discussed authoritatively as evidence in a trial. Sixteen years after passage of the Texas rape shield laws, *Chew* v. *Texas* makes clear that the truthfulness of a rape victim's testimony could still be challenged, in Texas at least, by evidence of the complainant's sexual behavior admitted under the guise of a diagnosis of nymphomania.[79]

Imagery of the Oversexed, Fantasizing Woman Lingers On

NO STATISTICS EXIST on how often cases that use a nymphomania defense similar to *Chew* v. *Texas* are introduced into courts of law. We do not yet have a systematic and extensive publication of lower court proceedings. Since only appellate and higher courts regularly publish their rulings, we do not know how many trials introduce nymphomania or some equivalent to get around rape shield laws.[80] Cases that introduce the nymphomania defense and lead to acquittal never get to the appeals court for obvious reasons: the prosecution cannot appeal a jury's verdict to acquit.[81] Nor do we know how many cases never come to trial because the district attorney or the rape complainant believes that the possible use of such a defense makes the case unwinnable.

But ultimately the number of cases is not the issue: what is remarkable is that this antiquated image of the oversexed, fantasizing woman still exists at all.[82] Two decades after widespread rape reform legislation and significant changes in sexual attitudes and behavior in society, the potential for the use of nymphomania in the legal arena—even if remote—remains extremely troubling.

What explains this persistence? In part, the conservative nature of the law itself leads to nymphomania's endurance: based on precedent and case review, past legal decisions continue to carry great weight. While the measured pace of legal change benefits society, it also allows outmoded concepts like nymphomania to linger on.

Furthermore, in an adversarial legal system, attorneys are motivated to try whatever approach might help them to win their case. Like other far-fetched arguments, the "nymphomania defense" provides an opportunistic strategy in a variety of legal arenas. Of course, such defenses do not always work, but their occasional success means that similar strategies will be tried in the future.

Interestingly, as we will see in the next chapter, the medical and psychological definitions underpinning nymphomania's legal use metamorphosed in the last quarter of the twentieth century. In fact, nymphomania disappeared from the American Psychiatric Association's manual of disorders. And yet the almost magical power of the stereotypes about female sexuality persists in the culture—and consequently in the legal system—affecting jurors, police officers, judges, legislators, and attorneys.

5

the sexual revolution

The New Sex Experts

IN THE 1960S, scientific research seemed to confirm a startling conclusion: women had an unlimited capacity to enjoy sex. Based on ten years of research, William Masters and Virginia Johnson concluded in 1966 in their best-selling book, *Human Sexual Response*, that the human female was much more highly sexed than previously supposed. "Many females, especially when clitorally stimulated, can regularly have 5–6 orgasms within minutes." Generalizing from the experience of the women volunteers whose orgasms they had measured and recorded, Masters and Johnson stated that the more orgasms a woman had, the more she could have, and the more intense the orgasms became.[1]

This model of "nymphomaniacal" or limitless female sexual desire as normal signaled a dramatic transformation from earlier claims that a woman needed a Prince Charming to awaken her Sleeping Beauty–like sexuality. Masters and Johnson's research challenged the prevailing medical viewpoint that such multiorgasmic women were "freaks." According to the authors, "the female is *naturally* multiorgasmic." Although Kinsey had earlier also identified 14 percent of the women he interviewed as multiorgasmic, this finding had been largely ignored. Now, in what Masters and Johnson called the "orgasm preoccupied" sixties, women's multiorgasmic ability took center stage, calling into question time-honored stereotypes about oversexed women. After all, if ordinary women could and did have lots of orgasms, what was the measure of sexual excess?[2]

When questioned in a *Playboy* interview about the nature of nymphomania, Masters and Johnson commented: "Many of the misconceptions about nymphomania stem from the lack of understanding that the female can be multiorgasmic." An unenlightened man, confronted with a woman who wanted more than one orgasm, might hide his panic by labeling such a demanding sex partner a nymphomaniac. Once again, a new perspective—this time that women were multiorgasmic—shifted the way that nymphomania was viewed.[3]

One commentator, psychiatrist Mary Jane Sherfey, believed that Masters and Johnson's work proved that so-called oversexed women were only doing what came naturally. In *The Nature and Evolution of Female Sexuality*, first published in a professional journal and then widely reprinted, Sherfey proposed that women's sexual drive was similar to that of various primates in heat. Calling attention to the women volunteers who had experienced upward of fifty orgasms in less than an hour in Masters and Johnson's laboratory, Sherfey theorized that all women had the capacity for such endless orgasms. At the dawn of modern civilization, she argued, it had been necessary to "ruthlessly subjugate" women's inordinate sexual demands. Settled, property-owning societies, which needed to establish parentage, required forceful suppression of female sexuality.[4]

But Masters and Johnson's research had proven that wanting or having many orgasms was not a sign of disease or disorder, as psychiatrists, physicians, and moralists had claimed. Instead, Sherfey stated, their work had shown that this sexual capacity was a "universal and physically normal condition" and grew out of "women's inability ever to reach complete sexual satiation." A woman might be sexually satisfied with three to five orgasms. Theoretically, however, she could go on having orgasms indefinitely until exhaustion interrupted her physical ability.[5]

In addition to the startling conclusion about female sexual capacity, Masters and Johnson also presented research findings which challenged lingering Victorian notions that women were less sexually desirous, less responsive, and less orgasmic than men. Dismantling these old-fashioned assumptions had been Masters and Johnson's intention from the beginning of their research. Like most twentieth-century sex scientists, they believed that traditional notions of women's lesser sexual interest had created many unhappy marriages. In attempting to confront that bias, they had signaled a new emphasis on women's sexual satisfaction by the unprecedented inclusion of a female co-leader of the research team. Consequently, their findings would prove to be extraordinarily liberating in reclaiming women as sexual beings.

Central to their research was their claim that all human beings go through a cycle of sexual responses that is virtually identical. By this they meant that both women and men respond to sexual stimuli in four identical stages: excitement, plateau, orgasm, and resolution. Based on their measurements of over 10,000 male and female orgasms, this four-stage cycle challenged much received wisdom about sexuality.[6] In the best white-coat, scientific tradition, they presented this conclusion as an objective and value-free measurement of how all human bodies responded when sexually stimulated. Nevertheless, later research would suggest that the similarities they proposed in the human sexual response cycle were more ideological than real.

Many problems existed with Masters and Johnson's methodology. They used only women volunteers who identified themselves as readily and easily orgasmic. Thus, the volunteers already embodied the hypothesis that Masters and Johnson were testing. Further skewing the representativeness of the sample, the paid volunteers were almost exclusively white and middle class. Sweeping generalizations about female sexual response based on this sample were obviously questionable.

Even more telling, the sex researchers' assumption that—all other things being equal—women would have orgasms as easily as men did was also flawed. Of course, all other things are never equal. Similarities in women's and men's pounding hearts, contracting muscles, and secreting genitals in the laboratory's never-never-land ignored the fact that in ordinary bedrooms, cultural expectations and power differences shape the sexual relationship. And the heart of the research—physiological experiments in which Masters and Johnson and their research team observed couples having intercourse—totally disregarded the effects of love, affection, hostility, boredom, fear, and many other factors that affect sexual response.

Like many scientists of sex, Masters and Johnson believed that stripping away the psychological factors and removing the genital experiences from their social context would uncover the "essence" of sex. Their assumption of a *there* there, outside of time, place, and the myriad conditions which shape sexuality, presupposes that if all sexual repression were stripped away, a basic sexual nature would burst free. This sex-equals-biology approach did have revolutionary aspects, especially for women whose sexual expression was most in need of being "freed" from leftover Victorian notions. Sexual desire, however, is not a simple, biological force in need of liberation. Age, upbringing, economic circumstances, ideology, religion, the historical moment, availability of a partner—in addition to one's body—all shape sexuality.

The body-as-machine metaphor also contained so many problematic elements (for example, sex as a series of pushing the right buttons and rubbing the right parts) that critics, including many feminists, soon challenged it. But that is getting ahead of the story. Despite its flaws, as well as its important contributions, the key to the widespread influence of Masters and Johnson's research was timing.

Feminism and the Sexual Revolution

H*UMAN* S*EXUAL* R*ESPONSE* burst upon a world primed to receive it. Several years earlier, *Time* magazine had published a cover story entitled "The Second Sexual Revolution." The magazine worried that all America had become one big Orgone Box, a reference to Wilhelm Reich's half-forgotten device which, he had claimed, would capture and reinvigorate an individual's sexual energy. Now, *Time* bemoaned, it was no longer necessary to sit inside the box to benefit from its sexual stimulation because the whole country had become one big sex machine. "From innumerable screens and stages, posters and pages, it flashes the larger-than-life-sized images of sex." The "big machine" touted books that once were considered pornographic, gloried in the erotic lyrics of pop music, and promoted "the message that sex will save you and libido will make you free."[7]

Much earlier in the century, a few sexual rebels, most notably Emma Goldman and Margaret Sanger, had championed women's right to have numerous sexual partners, to experiment sexually, and to initiate sexual relations on their own terms. Now, these ideas moved into the mainstream. Alongside demands for civil rights, gay rights, and the end to the war in Vietnam, the 1960s and 1970s witnessed large numbers of women demanding their *right* to sexual satisfaction. For the first time, a mass movement—not just an avant-garde—attempted to bring equality into sexual relationships.[8]

Economic, demographic, and social forces—not the least of which was a growing number of young women living on their own in large and small cities and college towns—fed this transformation. Seeking adventure for a few years before settling down to marriage and motherhood, these secretaries and editorial assistants, college students and management trainees, flight attendants and aspiring actresses discovered and helped to create a much-talked-about, sexually active singles scene. Emboldened by the greater availability of reliable birth control, these young women (and men) were also cheered on by a new optimistic psychology. Some enthusiasts adopted the theories of humanistic psychology's founders Abraham Maslow and Rollo May and turned their call for self-actualization and personal growth into a justification to "do your own thing."[9]

Of the many, many books in the 1960s and 1970s which reflected and defined a broad spectrum of women's responses to the sexual revolution, a few stand out. The sexual restlessness of the housewives whom Betty Friedan interviewed for *The Feminine Mystique* (1963) existed alongside the sexual adventures of Helen Gurley Brown's newly created "glamour girl of our times," described in her 1962 best-seller, *Sex and the Single Girl*. Both books shocked many readers: Friedan's because it portrayed such desperately unfulfilled white, middle-class women who were supposed to be living the American suburban dream; Brown's because it boldly proclaimed: "Nice girls do have affairs, and they do not necessarily die of them."[10]

Other important books, such as the 1972 how-to guide, *The Joy of Sex*, replaced old-fashioned marriage manuals in which husbands introduced wives to the sex act. Appealing to a broad age group, Alex Comfort's cookbook structure assumed that women, as well as men, would enthusiastically choose from the various menus of sexual acts described. The Boston feminist health manual, *Our Bodies, Ourselves* (1971), with its emphasis on sexual autonomy, celebrated all aspects of women's sexual self and inspired women to take charge of their own sexuality. Nancy Friday added to the literature with a compilation of women's sexual fantasies, *My Secret Garden* (1973), in which women reveled in sex on their own terms. Sexually exciting fantasies of seducing men on trains and dancing naked on tabletops, not to mention being tied up and ravished by strangers, all challenged old notions of the "good" woman's passive, submissive sexuality. Even books written with the stated intention of upholding the traditional roles of men and women in marriage, such as Marabel Morgan's *The Total Woman* (1973), included explicit instructions on sexual technique. [11]

Starting on the East and West coasts and in Chicago, and moving eventually to cities and towns across America, a rebirth of the feminist movement also fueled the demands for a woman's right to sexual expression. Meeting in hundreds of consciousness-raising groups, women of all ages—married and single, divorced and widowed, lesbian and heterosexual—discussed, analyzed, and compared notes about their sexual experiences, fantasies, and desires. Sometimes raucous, sometimes painful, these discussions gave women permission to trust their own experiences. They described orgasmic moments, shared stories about losing their virginity, rated their lovers, told their most explicit sexual fantasies, and actually looked—some for the first time—at their own clitorises and inside other women's vaginas. No longer would experts be able to define sexuality for women, to tell them what and how they should feel about sex. Together, women were redefining their own sexuality. Millions of women who never joined consciousness-raising groups or even thought of themselves as feminists learned about these new ideas from widespread, although not always favorable, media coverage.

Central to this redefinition was a far-reaching and much-debated attack on the sexual double standard. From radical groups like Redstockings to liberal organizations like the National Organization for Women, the women's movement called for a transformation of the traditional roles of women and men. One of the rallying cries of women's liberation—"the personal is political"—captured the essence of the critique. Although male domination of women affected all spheres of life, from the work world to the political arena, perhaps its most insidious invasion was into the quintessential personal and intimate relationship between men and women, the sexual act. By politicizing sex, the women's movement called attention to the fact that what went on in the bedroom was not really private. In fact, the relationship in the bedroom replicated women's subordinate position and economic dependence in the outside world. Changing that role required much more than marriage manuals and sex technique workshops. Individual Band-Aid solutions would not work. Women's liberation called for overturning the gendered world of female submissiveness and male dominance. Lesbians took the logic of this argument one step further: sexual relations with men equaled sleeping with the enemy.

Masters and Johnson's findings accelerated the debate. In their laboratory, they had created an extraordinary research tool, an adjustable plastic penis controlled by the female volunteers who measured physiological changes in their vaginas and recorded them on film.[12] For the first time, researchers could "see" inside women's genitals and translate the tantalizing mystery of those organs into data on internal secretions. The physiological responses Masters and Johnson charted remained intriguingly similar regardless of how orgasm occurred. Whether women masturbated, engaged in intercourse, or experienced coitus with the artificial penis, the response was the same. In terms of what went on in the body, this finding—that both masturbation and intercourse caused similar changes—finally buried Freud's claim of a split between an "immature" clitoral and a "mature" vaginal orgasm. Half a century after Freud had proposed that distinction, Masters and Johnson proved that, physiologically, there was no difference.

Despite earlier critiques by Kinsey and others, why had "the myth of the vaginal orgasm" held sway for so long? Anne Koedt, feminist author of a widely reprinted essay with that title, argued that the myth endured because it served men's needs. "Men have orgasms essentially by friction with the vagina, not the clitoris. . . . Women have been defined sexually in terms of what pleases men."[13] Consequently, in the "standard" sexual position, only one partner regularly experienced an orgasm. A recognition that women's sexual satisfaction lay in the clitoris—the only organ in either the male or female body solely devoted to pleasure—challenged coitus as the primary sexual act.

Other feminists, such as the author of *Memoirs of an Ex-Prom Queen*, Alix Kates Shulman, decried the fact that generations of women had been declared "frigid" because they were not orgasmic during "normal" sexual intercourse. Now Masters and Johnson had provided the anatomical research for why that was so. Shulman interpreted their work and advised women: "Think clitoris."[14]

Feminists recognized other radical implications of Masters and Johnson's research. The sex scientists' advocacy of women's right to sexual satisfaction, for example, assumed that these pleasures would take place in the marital bed. Yet their research demonstrated the efficiency—even the superiority—of certain sexual acts, such as masturbation, in achieving the orgasmic goal. It would not be long before commentators recognized—some with horror, some with delight— the potential irrelevance of men in this scenario of women satisfying their own, or each other's, sexual needs. According to Koedt, "Lesbian sexuality . . . could make an excellent case, based on anatomical data, for the extinction of the male organ."[15]

No Such Thing as Nymphomania?

THE WOMEN'S MOVEMENT'S frontal assault on men's privileged role, and the equally insistent demand for women's sexual rights, reverberated throughout society. Not surprisingly, all the discussion and the media coverage about changing attitudes toward female sexuality further muddied the conceptual waters surrounding nymphomania. If "normal" and "healthy" women felt entitled to pursue sexual pleasure, where was the line between "too much" and the "right" amount of sex to be drawn? Once again, the criteria for nymphomania shifted.

Perhaps nymphomania did not even exist. Reviewing the state of nymphomania studies in the early seventies, Indiana University Medical School psychologist Eugene E. Levitt called attention to the ambiguity and relativity of such terms as "hypersexual," "uncontrollable," and "oversexed." While most definitions of nymphomania used some variant of those terms, they were not easy to quantify. "No knowledgeable sexologist," according to Levitt, "has been imprudent enough to try to attach numbers to these words."[16]

Levitt's analysis, published in the Kinsey Institute's journal, *Sexual Behavior*, criticized the cultural assumptions implicit in the diagnosis. Granted, contemporary sexologists' biases were not quite as strident as those of earlier writers, such as the physicians who in the 1937 *Encyclopedia of Sexual Knowledge* referred to nymphomaniacs as women who "exceed the bounds of decent behavior." Nevertheless, because there was no empirical research on nymphomania, Levitt pointed out that at best, all of the theories and definitions were based on clinical case studies. This biased sample consisted of people who were disturbed about their sexual behavior, so troubled that they sought professional help. Inferring from these patients that most sexually promiscuous people were psychologically disturbed was simply too big a leap.[17]

Try as they might, Levitt said, clinicians had great difficulty in keeping their value judgments out of their discussions of the criteria for nymphomania. Many physicians and psychologists assumed that for women, "a sexual relationship that does not include a deep, emotional involvement is distorted," a sign of mental disorder. Levitt asked what evidence existed for this assertion. Not all women, he argued, wanted or needed a grand passion to lead a satisfying sexual life. Also, why was a woman's indiscriminate choice of inappropriate lovers characterized as a disease? Exaggerating this point for emphasis, Levitt declared, "A woman who has slept with 'all the desperadoes of Texas' has not, *ipso facto*, earned a special, categorical designation." In this twist on the words of Max Huhner, a famous sexologist from an earlier era, Levitt suggested that these women did not constitute a subcategory whose special characteristics set them off as diseased. They simply had more sex than others did, which some might consider was a moral issue, but was definitely not a medical one.[18]

In addition, Levitt questioned the prevailing view among psychoanalysts that nymphomaniacs were frigid. According to traditional psychoanalytic theories, a nymphomaniac's hypersexual behavior was thought to be based on an endless search for the unattainable orgasm. But, as with other theories about nymphomania, Levitt criticized this generalized thesis for lack of supporting evidence. Finally, the *opportunity* to engage in sexual behavior "appears to have been chronically overlooked in previous attempts to define nymphomania." Simply being young, attractive, and living in an urban area, rather than homely, middle-aged, and living in a rural community significantly increased a woman's chances of having more sex partners. So-called nymphomania might reflect opportunity rather than sexual appetite. Given these caveats, Levitt concluded: "Nymphomania is an outmoded, chauvinistic word that should be abandoned by science and medicine, and ought not to be used by any thinking person."[19]

Other voices in the sixties and seventies championed the abandonment of the term "nymphomania." According to Donald Hastings, a psychiatrist at the University of Minnesota Medical School and author of a book for physicians, *Impotence and Frigidity* (1963), "a person is 'oversexed' or 'undersexed' only in comparison to a specific sexual partner." In fact, one husband's too highly sexed wife was another man's perfect partner. Thus, "terms such as 'nymphomania'" should be eliminated. Stanford University Medical School psychiatrist William Fry placed the blame squarely on male chauvinism which kept alive the myth of nymphomania: "Sexually aggressive males feel guilty about their depredation and need to manufacture stories about a great number of nymphomaniacs lusting for their attention."[20]

Eustace Chesser, psychiatrist and author of more than twenty books on sexuality, love, and marriage, agreed. "The nymphomaniac is a wide-spread male fantasy," he wrote. "The man whose sex drives are denied free satisfaction dreams of meeting a woman who is completely uninhibited." But she is only a figment of his imagination, a reflection of his fears and anxieties about his own sexual prowess.[21]

According to Chesser, because the public was ignorant of the great variation in sexual desire, they wrongly labeled certain women—such as "Mrs. L.," his twenty-four-year-old "strongly-sexed" patient—as nymphomaniacs. In reviewing her case, Chesser described Mrs. L. as expecting intercourse at least once every night and appearing to have a limitless appetite for orgasm. Although her thirty-two-year-old husband had been "delighted to find her so responsive" on their honeymoon, he eventually became exhausted by her nightly demands for a second and third erection. Infuriated at his request that she take tranquilizers, the disgruntled wife "started a se-

ries of brief affairs with almost any man who came her way," ultimately divorced Mr. L., and was subsequently happily married to a
younger man.[22]

Presumably, in the eyes of this new husband, Mrs. L. was not
"oversexed," but just right. Chesser believed that while society might
condemn Mrs. L. as a nymphomaniac, actually it might have been the
fault of her first husband for not satisfying his wife. Mr. L. had admitted that his young wife seemed more satisfied after masturbation than
after intercourse. Chesser concluded that Mr. L.'s inadequate technique, as well as his lesser sexual desire, had led to the failure of this
marriage.

The doctor's analysis of Mrs. L.'s putative nymphomania was
firmly rooted in the camp of those who believed that women labeled
nymphomaniacs simply experienced stronger sexual drives than
their partners did. Like many other authorities, his discussion of
nymphomania reflected the uncertainty and anxiety over the right
way to perform the sex act. Greater knowledge of physiology and
more open discussion of sex in the sixties and seventies had not alle-
viated that concern. In fact, the sex act was weighted with even more
meaning now that women were expected to have orgasms—even
multiple orgasms—regularly.

More than likely, if Mrs. L. had walked into a doctor's office a century earlier, she would have been diagnosed as a nymphomaniac. By
the 1970s, her marital and extramarital sexual demands meant something quite different. Chesser, at least, determined that Mrs. L.'s sexual
urges weren't excessive or abnormal. Evidently, modern researchers'
assumptions about the multiorgasmic, multipartnered type as a potential Everywoman had complicated the notions of "excessive" female
sexual desire or behavior. So much that had been labeled female hypersexuality in the nineteenth century—masturbation, oral sex, post-
menopausal sex, pre- and extramarital sex—was now not only

regularly practiced but even glamorized by popular culture. Nymphomania could no longer be defined by "too much sex" (counting the number of partners) or by "too much desire" (measuring the intensity of the sex drive). New measures were needed.

New Pathology: Sex Without Love or Affection

EMPHASIS NOW SHIFTED from the frequency of the sexual act to its meaning. If the traditional reproductive, marital context no longer limited men and women's sexual behavior, what would be the criterion for excess? For many in the mental health field, sex without love or affection became the new pathology. As attitudes toward premarital sex became more liberal, new psychological criteria for healthy sex replaced the old standards of saving oneself for the wedding night. Now the question was, did you love your sex partner or at least feel some emotional attachment? This new definition captured the fears about depersonalized, hedonistic sex that co-existed alongside liberalized sexual attitudes. Swinging singles, gay liberation, partner-swapping clubs, increases in both unmarried mothers and abortions, and the effects of the sexual revolution on women's sexual autonomy, all helped to shape the sexual concerns of the day in this particular direction.[23]

In light of these changing attitudes, Alfred Auerback, University of California at San Francisco professor of psychiatry and past vice president of the American Psychiatric Association, argued that "The nymphomaniac is a compulsively promiscuous female who engages in a great many sexual contacts with many different partners . . . *without feelings of love or sharing*" (emphasis added). Lots of sex was no longer the key to nymphomania. In fact, while the modern definition included many-partnered sexual behavior, the most important aspect was that nymphomaniacs "are attempting to solve problems involving personal identity rather than seeking sexual gratification per se." According to Auerback, nymphomaniacs came from disturbed homes where the parents vacillated between being overly loving and rejecting and distant. Fearful that any deep emotional commitment would result in further pain and rejection, these sexually troubled women sought transient relationships with men they treated only as objects. [24]

Although men also suffered from these sexual problems and articles about satyriasis or "Don Juan syndrome" occasionally appeared in popular and professional journals, society continued to admire men's sexual conquests as a sign of masculinity. As James Leslie McCary, a noted psychologist and author of one the first college textbooks on human sexuality, pointed out: "The public does not show as much concern over men who are 'oversexed' as it does over similarly 'afflicted' women." Likewise, the psychoanalyst Eugene Pumpian-Mindlin, using the pop culture superhero James Bond as an example, pointed out that Bond's sexual exploits brought him fame and glory. On the other hand, his female co-stars, who at first glance appeared to be leading glamorous, sexually liberated lives, often met with untimely deaths. The moral ground might have shifted somewhat, but female movie characters, as well as real-life women, would still be held to a stricter standard of sexual behavior and punished for breaking social norms. [25]

Like scientific investigators in general, Auerback attempted to categorize his subjects into specific types so that he might better understand their motivation. However, his broad and general classifications, such as the "career girl" who used sex to compete in a man's world, the "bored housewife" who sought sexual satisfaction in her humdrum life, or the "rebellious teenager" who tried to find acceptance, appear to be a grab bag of female types. Nevertheless, his support for the changing definition of nymphomania lent credence to the newer notion that low self-esteem and profound feelings of unworthiness, and not sexual desire, drove a nymphomaniac to search for love and acceptance throughout her life.[26]

Similarly, UCLA psychiatrist Stanley Willis understood nymphomania to be a form of "pathological self-enhancement." The nymphomaniac purposely avoided deep emotional attachments because she feared the dependency or the possible rejection inherent in commitment. Willis repudiated some colleagues' claims that nymphomania represented nothing more than the "greater personal and sexual freedom possible in a modern and less puritanical society." Like Auerback, he pointed a finger at unloving parents, and the promiscuous woman's fear of repeating the pain of early emotional trauma.[27]

To illustrate, he described a case of a "thrice-married mother of four children, who had a good education and came from an affluent, highly privileged, talented family." She had spent a childhood torn between grief and rage at her parents, who either ignored her or recruited her as an ally in their hostile battles with each other. Over the years, she had established a pattern: after provoking rejection, she would engage in a burst of promiscuous behavior. Now in her third marriage, she engaged in numerous transient affairs with her husband's colleagues, usually following a fight with her husband. If he was out of town, she "drove the city streets at night picking up available sexual partners as she found them."[28]

Willis did not reveal the outcome of his work with this patient, and appeared to be more interested in what the case revealed about larger, social forces. Willis believed that while childhood neglect had shaped his patient, just as importantly, she lived in an age in which the erosion of traditional mores had led to widespread cultural anxiety. To Willis, promiscuity represented nothing less than "impending social or cultural disintegration." He indicted the culture itself for worshipping "glamorous and exciting prototypes of promiscuous behavior, such as James Bond," rather than providing a model of mature, stable sexual unions. And like other critics, he blamed the increasing commercialization of sex for leading people away from the old-fashioned values of family and monogamy. [29]

The clinical psychologist Albert Ellis also influenced the discussion of nymphomania with his publication in 1964 of *Nymphomania: A Study of the Oversexed Woman* (co-authored with Edward Sagarin). Author of over two hundred articles and twenty books in both professional and popular venues, Albert Ellis was an ardent defender of liberal sexual values. To him, the vast majority of women depicted as "nymphomaniacs" in novels and movies were "nothing but highly-sexed females who are quite promiscuous and whose behavior would hardly be noticed if they were males." [30]

The failure of both medical professionals and the general public to distinguish between this garden-variety promiscuity and a psychological disorder called "nymphomania" led to the widespread misunderstanding of the term, Ellis believed. To clear up the confusion, he chose to define nymphomania by differentiating "compulsive" from "selective" promiscuity. The key to nymphomania was the self-defeating, driven nature of the sexual behavior. Unconcerned about the women who simply had lots of sex partners, he focused on those whose indiscriminate choice and "feelings of self loathing" marked them as nymphomaniacs. Ellis's brand of therapy stressed that these women needed to learn to value themselves even if society looked contemptuously at their sexual exploits. [31]

Ellis's attempt to distinguish "highly-sexed" women from "compulsive" ones, however, contained its own problems. The question of where to draw the line remained. Sweeping generalizations such as "many compulsive hypersexed women become semi-professionals" (prostitutes) was a throwaway line based on no empirical research. Without any evidence to support it, Ellis also contended that nymphomaniacs made poor prostitutes, because they were willing to give sex away rather than charge for it. [32]

Ellis did challenge the notion generally supported by psychoanalysts that nymphomaniacs were frigid and did not have orgasms. He recounted the case of Eloise R., a "good-looking, college educated" twenty-two-year-old divorcée with nymphomaniacal tendencies. Because "the only technique Eloise would permit was sexual intercourse with the male surmounting her," she did not have an orgasm with her first husband, who thought she was frigid. [33] In a desperate attempt to achieve that goal, the young divorcée sought the company of many "uncouth" men. Now she planned to marry again and wanted Ellis to cure her.

Ellis's therapy included instructing Eloise in basic sex education, such as oral sex and positions other than the missionary one. The results: "Once she began to achieve orgasms with her fiancée, Eloise lost most of her inclinations to have sexual relations elsewhere." Ellis believed that "her nymphomania was at an end. Eloise had no incentive for compulsive promiscuity." He did not comment on the relative ease with which sex education had cured Eloise of what he presumed to be a serious disorder. [34]

In the 1960s and 1970s, nymphomania was both dismissed as a useful term and redefined in a number of ways: as a desperate search for love and affection, a compulsive escape from anxiety, and the pathological result of low self-esteem. Nymphomania's new definitions captured the sense of emptiness and alienation that critics of sexual permissiveness found to be pervasive in contemporary society. But other observers raised the suspicion that sex without strings had become a sign of mental disorder only when *women* began to sow their wild oats. [35] Traditionally, men's sexual escapades, visits to prostitutes, and love-'em-and-leave-'em attitude might have been condemned by some, but generally this behavior had not been seen as a sign of mental illness. Now that some women were actually seeking sex for the sake of pleasure and not as a prelude to happily-ever-after, the rules had changed.

Given the conceptual murkiness of nymphomania's definition, a few professionals attempted to quantify it. One 1967 survey of California physicians reported their diagnoses of patients' sexual complaints. Nymphomania, or excessive female sexual desire, constituted a miniscule 0.12 percent of the 13,687 ailments. The survey did not make clear whether the sixteen and one-half nymphomaniacs were physician- or self-diagnosed, but since these were patients, this survey shed no light on how often nymphomania might turn up in the general population. University of Houston psychologist James Leslie McCary, based on a twenty-five-year psychotherapy practice in which he had seen only one nymphomaniac (whom we will meet later in the chapter) and no men suffering from "satyromania," hazarded a guess about the number of sexually afflicted women and men: "Considerably less than one-tenth of one percent of all women are so afflicted [with nymphomania] and the number of men [satyromaniacs] is even smaller."[36]

Cases of Nymphomania Reach a Broader Public

FASCINATION WITH THE SUBJECT remained high in spite of new arguments that only a few women—or none at all—seemed to qualify as nymphomaniacs. In the 1960s and 1970s, more liberalized obscenity laws and the recognition that sex sells led to a flurry of full-length books for "the professional and the layman" which presented various "cases" of nymphomania.[37] Absent from these contemporary cases was the mainstay of older medical literature: the institutionalized woman who tore off her clothes, masturbated in public, and sexually attacked any available man. By the 1950s, "endogenous" nymphomania—excessive sexual behavior caused by something "in the body," such as brain lesions or hormonal imbalance—received far less attention as new drugs now tranquilized mental hospital patients.[38] In fact, many medical practitioners confessed to never having encountered this kind of nymphomania, although they often referred to it in passing as "real" or "true" nymphomania before moving quickly on to more familiar descriptions of nymphomania's psychological motivations.[39]

Yet the term "nymphomania"—confusing and ambiguous as ever—remained. Its appeal was apparent in the increasing boldness of the publishers of cheap paperback books to market works, such as *InsatiableWomen, UnfaithfulWives* (1972), which combined sexually titillating color photos with a sprinkling of quotes from medical experts. Purporting to be "carefully researched," replete with M.D. and Ph.D. authors and bibliographical references, this genre of books recounted information not very different from the material found in medical texts, offering both a world of sexual misinformation and a modicum of "sex education" about oral sex, clitoral orgasms, and sexually satisfied women.[40]

Some of the popular medical books, in fact, claimed to have the cure for nymphomania. Mirroring the medical and psychological community's confusion, these books maintained that improving the husband's sexual technique would remedy the disorder. This uncertainty about what nymphomania really was—whether simply the unsatisfied wife of a clumsy husband or an indication of deep psychological problems—had been present from the earliest attempts to define nymphomania and remained a concern in the modern popular and medical literature. According to physician Edward Podolsky and writer Carlson Wade in *Nymphomania* (1961): "Many husbands are responsible for keeping their wives in a state of constant sexual agitation. . . . Such wives tend to become nymphomaniac females, after a time." Citing various authorities, Podolsky and Wade claimed that "even the most compulsive of nymphomaniac females will find a certain amount of relief from the sex craving if she experiences a clitoric orgasm." In case after case, from the sexually repressed "Marion" to "Phyllis," who experienced her only orgasm with another woman, it was orgasmic success in marriage that would ultimately provide relief for these "oversexed" women. Despite the book's vampirelike photos of women in the throes of sexual ecstasy, *Nymphomania* was really a kind of marriage manual. With the correct technique, supposedly any marriage—even one to a nymphomaniac—could be saved.[41]

Popular works on nymphomania also adopted simplistic Freudian explanations: nymphomaniacs were not really oversexed; in fact, their sexual insatiability covered up their frigidity. *Casebook: Nymphomania* (1964) detailed four such cases, including "Angelique Adams," the sexually manipulative but unsatisfied child who grew up to be a power-hungry and sex-starved movie star, and gender-bending "Lois Love," who assumed the masculine role in seducing "girlish" young gay males, a unique (not to mention inventive) twist on the typical nymphomania story. All four of the cases graphically portrayed the nymphomaniacs' unfulfilled quest to find orgasmic release.[42]

In obviously self-serving ways, mass-market books portrayed themselves as beacons in a storm of sexual misinformation. By their frequent use of experts, they tried to legitimate their claim that they presented a frank, objective discussion of sex to a public in search of enlightenment. In the introduction to *Casebook: Nymphomania*, for example, Albert Ellis attempted to reassure the reader that although the cases presented were fictionalized, they were nevertheless "authentic" and "representative" because they were based on "actual psychiatric histories," which the writer, Victoria Morhaim, had "culled from a large number of clinical records to which she had had access."[43]

Notwithstanding such protestations of legitimacy and science, in turning the experts' theories about nymphomania into common parlance and sexually explicit "cases," this pseudo-medical literary subgenre could not escape the same contradictions, the same confusion of medicine and morality, which plagued professionals' attempt to understand nymphomania.

The DSM and Nymphomania

MEANWHILE, PSYCHIATRIC OFFICIALDOM contrived to struggle with the meaning of nymphomania. Remarkably, at a time when many doctors questioned its very existence, nymphomania continued to appear into the 1980s in the official classification of mental disorders compiled by the American Psychiatric Association (APA). The APA's *Diagnostic and Statistical Manual of Mental Disorders* (colloquially referred to as the *DSM*) was a relatively obscure administrative codebook, rather than a diagnostic tool, when it first appeared in 1952. Nymphomania was then classified as a "sexual deviation" and shared this designation with homosexuality, erotomania, misogyny, and others, although satyriasis was not included. *DSM-I*, as it would later be called, simply labeled and did not further define the deviations except to state that such a diagnosis did not cover more extensive syndromes, such as schizophrenic reactions.[44]

The successive generation of *DSM*s that replaced this first slim volume had an increasingly important impact. During the 1970s, as insurance companies expanded their coverage for psychotherapeutic treatment, they demanded specific medical diagnoses in order to reimburse patients and therapists. They turned to the *DSM* to legitimate those diagnoses. In response, and with the stated purpose of making the treatment of mental illness more scientific, the APA transformed the third edition of the *DSM* in 1980. *DSM-III* burgeoned to over 500 pages and almost 300 specific disorders, along with a substantial increase in the number of everyday behaviors included as symptoms of these psychological disorders.[45] More and more sex problems, which previously might have been seen as part of the ups and downs of life, became diseases to be treated.[46]

Befitting the expanded *DSM*, nymphomania and the entire category originally called "sexual deviation" became a new classification, "psychosexual disorders." For the first time, the *DSM* provided definitions of disorders, instead of simply listing them. In the subcategory "other sexual disorders," *DSM-III* identified nymphomania and Don Juanism as "distress about a pattern of repeated sexual conquests with a succession of individuals who exist *only as things to be used*" (emphasis added).[47] In so doing, the APA put its professional imprimatur on what had recently become the disorder's defining characteristic: sex without love or affection. At least one prominent psychiatrist, Stephen B. Levine, criticized the *DSM* definition for shifting emphasis away from what had traditionally been hypersexuality's major symptom: the "disruptive increase in [sexual] desire."[48]

DSM-III's new definition of nymphomania was not very helpful. On the one hand, the *DSM* located the sexual dysfunction of nymphomania, like psychosexual disorders in general, in the individual body or psyche and ignored social and political influences, including the effects of the sixties and seventies gender battles on women's and men's sex lives. On the other hand, unlike most of the psychosexual disorders identified in *DSM-III*, the category of "other sexual disorders" included no specific diagnostic criteria and no instructions to the mental health practitioner as to how to recognize it.

Later editions of the *DSM* would shift the focus once again and briefly connect nymphomania to a new concept: sexual addiction. The 1987 revised manual, *DSM-III-R*, dropped the specific terms "Don Juanism" and "nymphomania," and included for the first time "distress about a pattern of repeated sexual conquests or other forms of nonparaphilic [nondeviant] *sexual addiction*, involving a succession of people who exist only as things to be used" (emphasis added).[49] The term "sexual addiction" did not remain for long, however, and *DSM-IV* (1994) eliminated any reference to it in a definition of sexual disorders that otherwise resembled the one found in *DSM-III-R*.[50] Yet although the APA dropped the concept of sexual addiction, and many mainstream psychologists and sex therapists give no credence to the concept, popular acceptance of the idea of sex as an addiction was another matter, as we will see in the next chapter.

New Approaches to Incest Victims

MEDICAL AND LEGAL LITERATURE often blamed incest on the nymphomanialike tendencies of the victim, the child-temptress who seduced her male relative. In the 1970s and early 1980s, what scientists call a "paradigm shift"—a dramatically new way of understanding a phenomenon—occurred. Some professionals began to insist that nymphomanialike behavior did not cause incest, and portrayed the child not as a temptress, but as a victim. As the political winds shifted, people were more willing to believe that adult males (and sometimes females)—not predatory, nymphomaniacal Lolitas—were responsible for incest.[51] Yet, obvious as this new view may seem, the transition to this way of thinking was never in fact complete.

During these same years, feminist activists, as well as victim self-help groups, forced a rethinking of traditional notions of incest. Joining forces in speakouts, women brought the dreadful secret of incest out into the open.[52] Hundreds of women testified to the fact that child sexual abuse was not limited to families living on the other side of the tracks. Incest was alive and well in American homes at all economic levels, from lawyers to laborers.[53]

Kiss Daddy Goodnight (1978) demanded the title of a groundbreaking book on incest, in which graphic first-person accounts revealed how fathers and uncles and older brothers took advantage of their positions of power. These women's stories challenged the twisted social mores that had made women and girls feel dirty and guilty—even responsible—for having been sexually abused.[54]

New scholarly research also began to expose the lethal link between male privilege and blaming women for their own victimization. Feminist critics, in particular, exposed the ways in which widely held ideas about dangerous and licentious female sexuality had shaped assumptions about incest. Male perpetrators had excused their actions by rationalizing that their female victims were really Jezebels, and had even convinced some of their victims that "you're-a-bad-girl-for-making-me-do-this."[55]

As part of a larger critique of traditional gender roles, commentators in the seventies and eighties raised the question of why the incest victim had stirred so little compassion in the scientific literature. In particular, why had most researchers downplayed or ignored the long-term effects of incest?[56] Blinded by their assumption that females were the real seducers, or at least willing participants, many mental health professionals had denied or simply could not see the effects of incest on the child. They interpreted seductive behavior on the part of a child or adult female patient as "proof" that she had been the initiator of previous sexual relations. Increasingly, new research declared that sexual "acting out"—not only in the therapist's office, but in promiscuous sexual behavior in general—was the *result* of sexual abuse, not its root cause.[57]

Medical and popular literature began to reflect this new understanding: the trauma created by a trusted relative's betrayal could lead to compulsive, promiscuous sexual behavior, behavior that had earlier been labeled nymphomaniacal.[58] Yet, as the following case demonstrates, vestiges of the older notions still lingered. In an ongoing monthly column in *Medical Aspects of Human Sexuality*, which featured various professionals presenting their "most unusual sexual cases," psychologist James Leslie McCary described a case of nymphomania in 1979. Referred to him by a neurosurgeon who could find no physical explanation for the young woman's persistent headaches, Mrs. M. was described by McCary as a nineteen-year-old white woman of lower-middle-class background, married, and the mother of an eight-month-old child. Mrs. M. talked readily of her insatiable appetite: she and her twenty-year-old husband had sexual relations every night for several hours "or for as long as he could sustain the pace." The husband reported that he was bewildered by the fact that "she remained as sexually hungry after hours of coitus and dozens of orgasms as she had been at the beginning of the act." Mrs. M.'s headaches disappeared only after the rare occasions when she was sexually satisfied, although the account did not make clear what was meant by that term or how this "sexual satisfaction" differed from her nightly orgasmic experiences.[59]

McCary traced the roots of Mrs. M.'s incessant sexual needs to her childhood. Starting at the age of nine, and continuing two or three times a week for the next seven years, she had had sexual intercourse with her stepfather. When she was about fourteen years old, intense guilt had led her to confess the sexual involvement to her mother. Her mother had turned on her, blaming the daughter for the sexual behavior, calling her a worthless human being. The sex continued for the next two years, until the stepfather finally left the household. According to Mrs. M.'s account, she then became sexually involved with almost every boy in her high school. Following her marriage, she occasionally had extramarital relationships, none of which gave her relief from her overpowering sexual need.[60]

In therapy, according to McCary, Mrs. M. at first acted very seductively. The doctor convinced her that her behavior toward him "was merely an attempt to prove her value and worth as a human being." His sympathetic understanding of Mrs. M.'s sexual overtures reflected psychology's new insights into the effects of incest. Nevertheless, even he interpreted the nineteen-year-old's excessive sexual behavior as a futile search for acceptance and love caused by her mother's rejection, not as the effect of the stepfather's persistent sexual abuse. While McCary's diagnosis might partly explain her sexual behavior, it also served to deflect attention—and responsibility— away from the stepfather's actions.[61]

Over the next decade, incest survivors—along with substance abusers, sex addicts, and their co-dependents—concentrated on the individual task of personal healing. Although dramatic and wrenching, the individual revelations of sexual abuse to be found on every television talk show were personal, not political. While crucially important to many victims, as long as the "recovery" from incest was part of a therapeutic mode in which an individual must be "healed," a critique of the gender relations in which it was embedded could not take place. The question of power—so central to the original feminist analysis of incest—was lost in the more individual focus on treatment and recovery and in the growing backlash against feminism itself. [62]

Today, experts and the public more readily acknowledge the reality of child sexual abuse, although no agreement exists about its causes. Criminal justice and mental health professionals no longer automatically assume that the sexually abused daughter seduced her father, nor that her participation in the sexual act means that she enjoyed it. Police and child protection services take allegations of child sexual abuse very seriously, often removing the child from the home. But the increased attention paid to these allegations has had an unexpected consequence. In child custody cases, family court judges may look with a jaundiced eye at these claims, assuming that they are a hostile strategy in the war over who gets the children. The full impact of these recent changes has not yet been measured.[63]

In the wider culture, the sexualization of girl's bodies continues apace.[64] Many ads portray prepubescent girls as objects of desire, encouraging eight year olds to wear training bras, sexy nighties, and vampy, high-heeled size two shoes. Tabloid magazines and local television broadcasts in the late 1990s seized upon one child—the murdered six-year-old, JonBenet Ramsey—continually displaying her indelible image. The pictures of JonBenet's lipsticked and powdered beauty pageant face remind us that thousands of pint-sized "nymphets" regularly strut their stuff, performing bump-and-grind renditions of "Hey, Big Spender" and the like, in their efforts to win a prize in one of hundreds of weekly beauty contests.[65]

Of course, more than children's sexuality is on display. While medical and psychological literature beginning in the 1960s debated whether nymphomania even existed, popular images of sexually aggressive women have become ever more familiar. As explicit sexual images saturate the culture, and previously defined extremes of sexual conduct move into the mainstream, what defines an oversexed woman? In the next chapter, we examine the ways in which tabloid magazines, TV talk shows, and popular culture in general help to shape what we think about nymphomania.

6

happy nymphos
and sexual addicts

A T THE TURN of the twenty-first century, sexy women smile and beckon everywhere: on the front pages of supermarket tabloids and on the sides of buses; lusting after their neighbors' husbands on TV talk shows and singing about their sexual prowess before soldout concert audiences. In an era when $25 at the Hands-On Car Wash in Fort Lauderdale buys bare-breasted females in thong bottoms to wash your car, what happens to the idea of oversexed women? In a culture saturated with sex, who is a nymphomaniac?

No longer a medical diagnosis, the idea of nymphomania still lingers in the popular culture, although its meaning is vague and uncertain. Lots of sexual desire, even many sexual partners, does not automatically label a woman "sick" as it might have in the past. The woman who says, "I was a bit of a nympho last weekend," voices both delicious pleasure and a little anxiety about her behavior, but presumably she does not think that her mental health is in jeopardy.

In 1993, *The New York Times* captured the post-sexual revolution attitude toward nymphomania in its tongue-in-cheek comment about the Victoria's Secret catalogue models, who were "good girls, well brought-up, slightly nymphomaniacal, but only behind closed doors and only when in love." Presumably a little bit of nymphomania adds a naughty, but still acceptable frisson to ad campaigns as well as to Saturday night escapades. And in 1999, journalist Dinitia Smith referred with amazed amusement to the CIA's attempt to cast moral aspersion on Eartha Kitt's anti-Vietnam activities in 1972 by labeling her a "sadistic sex nymphomaniac."[1]

This seemingly lighthearted attitude toward nymphomania reflects the previous decades' changes in sexual mores. From behind the closed doors of doctors' offices and men's locker rooms, a "happy nympho" emerged in the 1960s and 1970s. An enthusiastic sexual adventuress, the happy nympho reflected modern sexual theories about women's multiorgasmic potential. As new popular portrayals of women's sexual appetite replaced older notions of female passivity, sexually aggressive heroines, such as Isadora Wing, protagonist of Erica Jong's 1973 bestseller, *Fear of Flying*, strode boldly into popular consciousness. No longer limited to men's fantasies of acquiescent, ever-willing women, the happy nympho took charge of her own sexuality.

Of course, lusty, lascivious women had appeared before in history, but never so pervasively or so publicly. Women whose sexual behavior might previously have labeled them nymphomaniacs now appeared on television talk shows, such as the *Jenny Jones* show, "Sexual Promiscuity Without Apology."[2] And women's magazines teased readers and heightened sales with cover stories featuring "Confessions of a Serious Nymphomaniac."[3] The little old lady from Dubuque was now routinely exposed to a sexual explicitness formerly found only in red light districts or behind-the-counter men's magazines. From advertising to the corner newsstand, from supermarket tabloids to on-line zines, the modern media explosion created an unprecedented public focus on sexual images.

The fact that happy nymphos had gone public signaled the arrival of new sexual rules, a shift in the line of what was considered appropriate sexual behavior, especially for women. But the same old sense of unease lurked within the widespread exposure and discussion of sex: How much sex was too much? How much was not enough? And who decided?

Reflecting those anxieties, a sexual counterrevolution gained momentum in the 1980s. A newly emerging conservative movement attacked what it perceived as a Sodom-like collapse of morals, manifested in the form of premarital sex, gay rights, abortion, pornography, and sex education. At the same time, a dawning recognition of the horror of the AIDS epidemic provided additional ammunition for a panicked public. Out of these shifting cultural sands, the nymphomaniac emerged in yet another guise: the "sex addict." In this Alcoholics Anonymous–inspired model, sex—like alcohol and drugs—could lead to addictive behavior.

Tracing the rise of both the happy nympho and the sex addict in the vast, amorphous, diverse, and transient popular culture, we find that no single example from a magazine or a movie carries much weight. The idea of nymphomania itself is constantly "shape shifting," making it doubly difficult to pin down. Nevertheless, if we look for selected portrayals of nymphomania in representative or revealing areas of popular culture—in women's magazines, mainstream and pornographic films, and television talk shows—something significant about the changing attitudes toward female sexuality in recent decades emerges.

Women's Magazines

FOR OVER A CENTURY, women's magazines have offered advice about romance and domestic life. In the 1960s, according to *Ms.*

magazine, Helen Gurley Brown revolutionized the women's magazine formula and revamped *Cosmopolitan* when she became the first editor to admit that women were sexual.[4] Following her lead, most women's magazines—from chic, urban sophisticates like *Glamour* and *Harper's Bazaar* to wholesome, middle-American magazines like *Redbook*, and including general magazines aimed at African Americans, such as *Ebony* and *Essence*—became increasingly emboldened about discussing sex. Depending on their philosophy and readership, women's magazines in particular addressed the issue of how to be a good "bad girl," displaying just enough sexiness without stepping over the line. The approach paid off: features, stories, and advice columns on sex sold lots of magazines to women eager for advice and direction on how to navigate the new and dangerous post-sexual revolution waters.

One of the main tasks that women's magazines set for themselves was to reassure the reader that, even in the age of sexual liberation, some of the old values still held. Sex surveys provided the evidence. *Redbook*'s 1974 survey of 100,000 married women—a number unprecedented in sex research—delivered the "good news about sex." The survey concluded that most of the respondents "liked their husbands, their marriages, and their sex lives." The survey became something of a standard in subsequent women's magazine discussions of sex, reassuring women that in the age of sexual liberation, "good sex" was not incompatible with marriage.[5]

Not surprisingly, the magazines reflected the wider culture's ambivalence about women's newfound sexual freedom. A 1979 *Mademoiselle* feature, for example, described "flings" as a "source of fun and a matter of simple survival [for singles]." But the writer undercut this message by recounting her own fling with a gorgeous Irishman, which wound up as the worst of both worlds: "It had the callousness of a casual affair and the painful conflicts of a serious love."[6] A 1980

Harper's Bazaar article presented mixed messages about female sexuality, not by turning to personal experience, but to the experts. On one side, according to Helen Singer Kaplan, director of the Human Sexuality Program at New York Hospital, women were as capable as men were of enjoying transient sexual relationships. In the opposite corner, Anthony Labrum, professor at the University of Rochester Medical School, warned that "Women need loving, caring and more romanticized relationships, not sexual intercourse within five minutes."[7]

Magazines underscored such warnings by calling attention to the fact that the sexual revolution had not ended the double standard. In a 1986 *Harper's Bazaar* article, "Sexcess and Excess: Are You a Nymphomaniac?", anthropologist David Givens suggested that the very different labels given to female and male sexual excess— "nymphomania" and "Don Juanism"—reveal their bias. Nymphomania conjures up madness, while Don Juanism hints of nobility and Spanish courts. Liberation notwithstanding, he stated, "Men are [still] less stigmatized by this behavior."[8] A few years earlier in the same magazine, best-selling author Nancy Friday commented: "for all its apparent openness, our society doesn't yet loudly applaud a fully sexual woman."[9] While presented as realistic assessments, these frank discussions also served to remind female readers that stepping over the sexual line—even though the line had shifted—still resulted in more serious repercussions for women than for men.

Women's magazines vacillated in their discussions of sex, often presenting mixed messages about the end of the sexual revolution while at the same time featuring titillating stories about one-night stands. In 1985, the September issue of *Glamour* magazine, for example, introduced the results of a longitudinal sex survey to answer the question: "Whatever happened to the sexual revolution that was supposed to change society forever?" The conclusion? "It bottomed out," according to sociology professor Robert Sherwin, who had conducted a twenty-one year survey of virginity at Miami University in Ohio. Remarkably, the percentage of co-ed virgins on his campus had gone from 75 percent in 1963 to 38 percent in 1978. But that was old news. What was important to Sherwin and to *Glamour* was that in recent years, the trend had begun to reverse itself. By 1984, 43 percent reported they were virgins. Extending these findings to other college campuses, *Glamour* attributed the changes to a fear of venereal diseases, to a more conservative political climate on the campuses, and to an upsurge in affiliation with Christian religions that advocated no sex before marriage.[10]

On the other hand, the next issue of *Glamour* presented an article generally condemning one-night stands, yet several women described their brief encounters in positive terms. According to one woman who recounted a blissful night of pure lust: "I've come to the conclusion that if I'm in the mood and the situation feels right, I'll go to bed with a man and not concern myself with whether or not it's going to be a one-night stand . . . I no longer need to be reassured that I am still 'worthy' enough to be seen again."[11]

Magazines such as *Ebony* and *Essence*, which were aimed at an African American audience, also exhibited ambivalence about the sexual revolution. In particular, according to contributing editor Bonnie Allen of *Essence*: "The image makers had always portrayed us as hot-to-trot mammas, and we didn't want to 'act our color' and give them what they expected."[12] Consequently, black women have to walk an even tighter tightrope than white women do in response to the new sexual values. Nevertheless, Robert Staples, sociology professor at the University of California at San Francisco, commented in *Ebony* that the most sexually active single black women, those between the ages of twenty and thirty-five, had embraced the idea that sexual gratification was their right. Middle-class black women energetically sought out potential sexual as well as marriage partners at the typical upwardly mobile meeting spots, health clubs and the happy hours of local watering holes. In addition, the longtime staple of the black community—the churches—provided a meeting ground as well.[13]

Like their white counterparts, blacks also felt the backlash of conservatism in the 1980s. In a reference to a "media blitz" on sexually transmitted diseases, Bonnie Allen commented: "[The Moral Majority] couldn't control us by preaching traditional moral standards, so it's found a way to control us through fear of infection."[14] Despite the backlash, the novelist Bebe Moore Campbell, a frequent contributor to *Ebony*, recognized that the sexual revolution brought something new and important to black women: "the right to choose her partner and initiate lovemaking, as well as a new sense of sexual self-awareness that is intrinsically personal."[15]

In the post-sexual revolution, no magazine was more successful at manipulating the new rules about good girls and bad girls than the grandmamma of them all: *Cosmopolitan*. It continued Helen Gurley Brown's winning formula: Take a beautiful, semi-dressed model, place her on the cover looking enticingly at the potential reader, surround her with sexually provocative headlines, and *voilà!* three million readers a month buy the magazine.[16]

Cosmopolitan attracted a readership of mostly working-class, married young women with voyeuristic fantasies of the "Cosmo Girl" they would never be. Although *Cosmopolitan* capitalized on the sexual revolution's many changes, and loudly proclaimed that "nice girls did," ultimately the magazine upheld conventional values. Take, for example, a 1995 article, "Confessions of a Serious Nymphomaniac." Here, the *Cosmo* girl is quite proud to be a "nymphomaniac," especially since she's now found Mr. Right, "the treasure at the end of the nymphomaniac trail."[17]

Nymphomania

Accompanied by a soft-focus photo of a beautiful, semi-clad blond model and her male partner, the article tells the larger-than-life story of a "happy nympho" and her fifty-eight lovers. She recounts her sexual adventures with a surfer, a punk rocker, her professor at graduate school, a taxi driver, a yoga teacher, and the orderly in the hospital where she got a nose job. Thoroughly enjoying herself, this "serious nymphomaniac" eventually realizes that she wants not only sex but love and babies, too. Following marriage, two children, and divorce, she recognizes that she cannot return to her earlier carefree sexual life. Instead, she becomes—what might appear to be a contradiction in terms—a monogamous nymphomaniac, lusty and voracious for one man only. *Cosmo* presents her as a normal, healthy, sexy woman whose love-of-her-life "despairs of ever satiating me, [and] would probably say I'm as much a nymphomaniac as ever." Luckily for her, Mr. Right was "damn happy" about this state of affairs.[18]

In this late twentieth-century fairy tale, no handsome prince needs to awaken Sleeping Beauty's sexual desire. The princess herself makes the moves. The simple fact that this positive spin on female sexual desire appeared on newsstands around the country indicates a profound cultural shift. Over the last two or three decades, the feminine ideal of women's magazines has expanded so that sexual desires and behavior that might earlier have labeled a woman a nymphomaniac are now applauded. And yet, the old traditional story still holds: the happy-ever-after ending to the "serious nymphomaniac's" tale requires the exclusive love of one extraordinary, handsome, heterosexual male. The recounting of her many sexual adventures provides the reader with vicarious thrills without ever having to pay the price society might exact on a real-life woman who flaunted the fact that she had had fifty-eight lovers. Finally, the potential challenge to the status quo is resolved by the nymphomaniac's choice of monogamy and her admission that "no matter how intense my moments of rapture might be, I always knew I was searching for something more *lasting.*"[19]

Not only *Cosmopolitan*—the magazine that brought America sex and the single girl—but other magazines and their advice columns occasionally featured discussions about what constitutes too much sex. *Elle*'s popular "Ask E. Jean" grappled with the nymphomania question from a female reader, calling herself "Befuddled," who wrote in 1995 about a "disturbing trend" in her last four or five semi-serious relationships: "I have this insatiable sex drive." "Befuddled" is concerned that "for about the first month of having sex with someone . . . we have sex all the time, and he tells me I'm the best he's ever had. Then I guess I wear him out or something because suddenly he's not quite interested. . . . I'm accused of being a nymphomaniac, and he's out the door." Now she's decided to swear off sex until someone shows up who looks like he's going to stay for a while.[20]

E. Jean responds humorously to "Befuddled:" "Ninety-nine out of 100 male analysts would take your money and attempt to 'treat' your so-called nymphomania, so get down on your knees, sugar lips, and thank god you wrote to me." After that stick-in-the-eye to male mental health professionals for creating the problem, E. Jean cheers "Befuddled" on to enjoy the male sex to excess. Forget about the notion that she's wearing them out: that's what men are for!

Like Mae West, E. Jean celebrates the notion that "too much of a good thing is wonderful," but her advice also contains a caveat. If "Befuddled" is looking for a serious relationship, she should withhold sex. Why? Not because her sexual "insatiability" is immoral or un-healthy—the columnist's hip approach would not abide those old-fashioned notions. Instead, *Elle*'s expert turns to pop evolutionary theory as the reason to give "Befuddled" and her readers essentially Ann Landers–like advice: play hard to get. "Befuddled" should hold off having sex with a man because "millions of years of evolution [are] telling him (rightly or wrongly) that if you'll have sex with him right off the bat, you'll have sex with a bunch of other fellows, too—the very *last* trait a man wants in a mate." Supposedly, E. Jean is on the side of "Befuddled's" right to have lots of sex. But she also recognizes and reasserts that the double standard still requires the young woman to play a different game if she wants to keep her man.

It is not surprising that the advice seeker was befuddled. Permitted, even encouraged, to pursue sexual pleasure, she does not understand why the rules keep changing in the middle of the game. Her concern differs dramatically from that of the nineteenth-century "Mrs. B." who, as we saw in chapter 1, was so troubled by her lascivious dreams that she sought the advice of a doctor. In contrast, this 1990s woman does not fear sexual desire itself; she simply does not understand why it keeps frightening her boyfriends away.

Women are not alone in their concern that they are over-sexed; sometimes their boyfriends worry, too. In a regular column, "Sex Questions Guys Are Too Embarrassed to Ask You," *Mademoiselle* replied to the "stacks and stacks of letters" it received every month from guys who read the magazine and wrote to ask all kinds of questions about the women in their lives. In 1996, *Mademoiselle*'s columnist, Blanche Vernon, responded to twenty-nine-year-old Brad, who had written: "I think my girlfriend is a nymphomaniac,"—with a flippant: "And this is a bad thing?" Recalling the old Kinsey definition: "most guys define a nymphomaniac as any woman who wants to have sex more than they do," Vernon also commented that "true nymphomania"—compulsive, all-consuming sexual behavior—did exist. But she didn't think this was Brad's—or most men's—problem. Confronting the stereotype that men's sex drive should always be greater than women's, she thought it likely that Brad's girlfriend "had a healthy sexual appetite—perhaps more robust than yours—and you're worried about being able to satisfy her." Figuratively, Vernon then patted Brad on the head and told him not to worry: "If she cares about you, she's not going to run off with your best friend." Not so reassuringly, and with a sly poke at men's sexual fears, she continued, "[even if your best friend's] high school nickname was Trigger."[21]

Another popular advice columnist, Dr. Ruth, whose forthright sexual guidance and grandmotherly demeanor brought her many admirers, addressed the following question from a reader: "My girlfriend has never, ever said no to me in over two years. Would you call her a case of nymphomania?" Answering with an emphatic no, she adds yet another humorous twist to the discussion of nymphomania. "You may like to think of her that way—it makes you feel proud and lucky, like the man whose girl is pretty and good-natured and fun and never makes him jealous and also owns a golf course." Dr. Ruth thinks the word is meaningless, and "all too often a man calls a woman that because she likes a lot more sex than he does." Attempting to quell his concern, Dr. Ruth urges him to take pride in what is essentially a happy nympho, to be pleased with how much his girlfriend likes to have sex with him.[22]

Although such magazine advice columns are frequently flippant, still they tap into readers' concerns. In these several cases, the columns sought to assuage the writers' anxieties about how much sex is too much. For their women readers, in particular, these magazines give permission to expect and to demand satisfaction, to see themselves as highly sexual, to become "happy nymphos." At the same time, the columnists and the letterwriters register the fears and uncertainties created by these newly legitimated sexual desires and demands.

Nymphomaniacs in the Movies: The New Pornography

ON THE FAR REACHES of the popular culture, even pornography—that most male-oriented, hidebound presentation of female sexuality—began to change. Just as marriage manuals, sex surveys, popular advice columns, the women's movement, and sex scientists Masters and Johnson all attempted—in very different ways—to understand and describe women's sexual desire and pleasure, so too did pornography. Whereas images of ever-willing women had always been pornography's bread and butter, something new was added in the seventies and eighties: women who actively sought their own pleasure, instead of simply responding to male desire.[23]

In *Deep Throat* (1972), one of the first pornographic films to reach a mass audience, a woman's search for sexual pleasure became the central theme of the film. Granted, the female protagonist's satisfaction was finally achieved in an extraordinarily sophomoric male fantasy: the nurse played by Linda Lovelace finds that her clitoris is located in her throat and her supreme pleasure comes from performing oral sex on her many male patients. Even so, alongside the traditional focus on the male performers' pleasure, the heroine's fireworks-producing, "Star-Spangled Banner"–accompanied orgasm explodes on the screen as a sign that women's sexual satisfaction would no longer be given short shrift.[24]

Changed, too, were the audiences now watching these new pornographic films and videos. Shown at first-run, downtown movie theaters, not at sleazy, former burlesque houses, 1972's big three porn films, *Deep Throat*, *Behind the Green Door*, and *The Devil in Miss Jones* (in which Miss Jones's hell is an eternity of sexual frustration) played to record-breaking audiences. For the first time, couples—not just the proverbial dirty old men in raincoats—lined the streets to attend films considered "hard core," those that graphically displayed various sexual acts. And not only in hip San Francisco and Manhattan, but much more surprisingly, in Tucson and in Duluth. These growing audiences would feed into the even more sizable current market that watches "blue movie" cable TV channels, rents porn videos at the local video store, and surfs the net for pornography Web sites. Today, the magnitude of the multi-billion-dollar porn revolution easily becomes clear.[25]

The new markets and new female consumers—estimated at as high as 40 percent of those renting approximately 100 million X-rated videos annually[26]—required at least some experimentation in the tried-and-true porn formula. The happy nympho response, tentatively presented in *Deep Throat*, would be played out more emphatically in later films. Marilyn Chambers, whose fresh-faced image on millions of boxes of Ivory Snow coincided with her Cannes Film Festival debut in *Behind the Green Door*, epitomized the happy nympho in *Insatiable* (1981) and *Insatiable II* (1984).

In both films, she plays the spirited, self-confident, wealthy, high fashion model, Sandra Chase, who initiates sex with whomever she wants. In a "porn-utopia," not troubled by the real world's differences in power between the sexes, she cheerfully seduces and is seduced. She's not sexually passive unless she chooses to be. Sandra Chase is the sexual actor, instead of the sexual object as in most porn films, and her "insatiability" doesn't mean that she's not sexually satisfied. She embodies the opposite of the older, medicalized sense of the term "insatiable"—a "frigid nymphomaniac," a woman who has lots of sex because she is never sexually satisfied. In fact, this happy nympho personifies a whole new definition of insatiable: she remains ever desirous, even though sexually fulfilled.[27]

Happy nymphos also began to appear in films made by a few female porn stars who moved behind the lights to produce and direct their own films. One of the best known, Candida Royale, established Femme Productions in 1984 because she wanted to make a different kind of porn film—one that showed women celebrating their own lustiness. Films such as *Christine's Secret* (1984) or *The Gift* (1996) present the typical porn film's variety of sexual acts and positions, but do so from the woman's point of view. Consequently, they emphasize the sensual, while not ignoring the genital, aspects of sex.

The proliferation of lesbian porn films, not as a sexual come-on for men, but for the pleasure of their female viewers, also offers new images of female sexual agency. These more women-centered porn approaches shift the modern spotlight away from the male sexual organ—the ultimate icon of porn—toward an exploration of female sexual fantasy and desire. Another porn star, Annie Sprinkle, in her 1992 video, *Sluts and Goddesses Workshop*, eliminated men altogether and celebrated the female body's ability to pleasure itself. In the video, spectacular vibrator-induced orgasms graphically display women's multiple orgasms, a pornographic rendering of what Masters and Johnson's research had proclaimed as a unique female capability. [28]

Backlash: The Anti-Pornography Movement

AT THE SAME TIME that the porn industry was on its way to making more money than all three television networks combined, antipornography became the rallying cry for a new national purity crusade. Much like Carry Nation, who at the turn of the twentieth century had targeted drink as the evil which fueled men's lusts, latter-day conservatives used their verbal axes on pornography. [29]

For the newly emboldened political right, pornography provided the spearhead to foment a counterrevolution against all that had gone wrong in society: sex outside marriage, abortion, gay rights, and single mothers, to name just a few. Conservative crusaders such as Pat Robertson galvanized public opinion around the threat that pornography posed to the nation, especially to women and children. In 1986, the Attorney General's Commission on Pornography agreed. Based on the commission's theory that reading or watching pornography drove men to commit sexually violent acts—the exact opposite of the conclusion of the 1970 President's Commission on Pornography and Obscenity—their final report recommended greater restriction of sexually explicit material.[30]

Feminists, too, joined the anti-pornography struggle in "take back the night" marches through red light districts and in other direct tactics, such as publicizing photographs they took of men going into porn shops. The often-quoted remark, "Pornography is the theory, rape is the practice," captured the outrage of those who argued that X-rated films and videos encouraged violence against women. Susan Brownmiller, earlier author of *Against Our Will: Men, Women, and Rape*, maintained that the feminist objection to pornography was "based on our belief that pornography represents hatred of women, that pornography's intent is to humiliate, degrade, and dehumanize the female body for the purpose of erotic stimulation and pleasure."[31]

In the optimistic sixties, the analysis of pornography had been part of a larger feminist critique of sexism, an example of one of many ways in which men turned women into sex objects. By the far-less-hopeful eighties, following years of uncovering the deep-seated roots of misogyny, anti-pornography feminists now indicted pornography as one of the most important keys to men's domination of women.

An outspoken leader of the movement, Andrea Dworkin, captured much media attention in works such as *Woman Hating* (1974) and other writings in which she characterized male sexuality and its most visible expression, pornography, as "the stuff of murder, not love."[32] Together with University of Minnesota Professor of Law Catherine MacKinnon, Dworkin formulated ordinances in Indianapolis and Minneapolis which included a new legal definition of pornography as "the sexually explicit subordination of women, graphically depicted, whether in pictures or in words."[33] In this novel approach—later declared unconstitutional—the ordinance allowed those who could prove that pornography had harmed them to sue the purveyors for damages.

Anti-pornography feminism captured the public's imagination as *the* feminist position, resonating with the more conservative mood of the time, and capitalizing on the anger stirred by women's revelations of rape and incest. But there was another side to the debate. Other feminists claimed that the single-minded focus on pornography helped to perpetuate neo-Victorian assumptions about sexuality and played into the hands of conservatives who wanted to restrict not only pornography but sex education and reproductive rights as well.

In addition, Ellen Willis, at the time a writer for *The Village Voice*, understood that the anti-pornography movement was a danger to women's expression of sexuality, one that would restrict women in an attempt to protect them. Anti-pornography's "goody-goody concept of eroticism is not feminist but feminine," she wrote. "It is precisely sex as an aggressive, unladylike activity, an expression of violent and unpretty emotion, an exercise of erotic power and a specifically genital experience that has been taboo for women."[34]

Other "pro-sex" feminists joined Willis in her belief that women's liberation required sexual liberation, not a return to Victorian notions of women's sexual passivity and moral superiority to men. They maintained that one of the most problematic aspects of the anti-pornography campaign was that it shifted exclusive attention to women's victimization, rather than keeping feminism's sights on empowering women to challenge society's oppressive institutions and ideology. Not surprisingly, anti-pornography feminists contended that only by listening to the voices of individual victims could society's rampant misogyny be forced to change.

The bitter struggle over pornography split the women's movement but had little effect on the vast expansion of the pornography industry. During the late eighties and the nineties, pornography began to influence mainstream culture. Fueled by the enormous profits to be made, fashion magazines, MTV, the Internet, advertising, and cable TV teased the consumer with ever more sexually explicit material. Today, even though pornography remains on the fringes of popular culture, its particular slant on the changing images of female sexuality reaches ever wider audiences.

Nymphomania and the Movies: In the Mainstream

NOT SURPRISINGLY, Hollywood films sometimes borrowed images from pornography. A *Chicago Tribune* movie reviewer wrote that in *Basic Instinct* (1992), "the hints of sadomasochism, bisexuality, and nymphomania latent in [Marlene] Dietrich's character [in *The Blue Angel*] have now become blatant."[35] The reformulated femme fatale, Catherine Trammel, played by Sharon Stone, is a "cold, calculating and beautiful novelist with an insatiable sexual appetite."[36] Apparently, her independent, aggressive, bisexual desire and her many-partnered sex life define her nymphomania. Like the porn character Sandra Chase, Trammel chooses whom she wants to have sex with—from her live-in female lover, Roxy, to the male detective played by Michael Douglas, to the rock star whose grisly murder opens the film. An object of desire of the five detectives interrogating her about the murder, Trammel herself takes charge of this semi-porn "beaver shot" scene by slowly uncrossing her legs to reveal that she is wearing nothing underneath her very short dress.

Unlike an earlier movie-nymphomaniac, Dorothy Malone's Academy Award–winning performance as Marylee in *Written on the Wind* (1956), Catherine Trammel is not abandoned by the hero for the "good" woman at the end of the film. In fact, *Basic Instinct*'s conclusion is intentionally ambiguous, but certainly does not suggest either of two traditional endings: that she will pay for her sins or that any of her lovers will domesticate her.[37]

What does a viewer actually take away from this film? Perhaps the audience, feeling manipulated to identify with Catherine Trammel, rejects the work's strongest, savviest, and most unsavory character. After all, much like earlier film portrayals of sexually aggressive women, Trammel's sexuality is clearly linked to criminality and deviance. But unlike other contemporary sexual monsters, such as the Glenn Close character in *Fatal Attraction* (1987), Catherine Trammel does not pay for her sexual sins. In fact, both the Catherine Trammel character and Sharon Stone's Hollywood persona exemplify a woman who transgresses the rules: neither is simply the object of male desire. Like other "happy nymphos," they present themselves as sexually autonomous, powerful, and in charge of their lives.[38]

In another less well known mainstream film, *Rambling Rose* (1991), Laura Dern plays the very opposite of a femme fatale: a sympathetic, sex-obsessed-because-love-starved "nymphomaniac." Set in 1920s small-town Georgia, the story revolves around the upheaval nineteen-year-old Rose causes when she arrives to work in the Hillyard household. Innocent of the sexual tumult she is creating, Rose trails a string of young swains behind her, and demonstrates her enthusiastic desire for the Hillyard patriarch, Robert Duvall's "Daddy," by literally throwing herself into his arms.

Later, when Daddy and Mrs. Hillyard discuss Rose with a medical specialist, the two men determine that she is oversexed and agree that "for her own good" she needs to have a radical hysterectomy to "cure" her nymphomania. In this remarkable scene, Mrs. Hillyard jumps to her feet and soundly chastises the two startled men for their arrogance in assuming that they have the right to make this decision. Because this is a 1990s film, and not the actual South where hysterectomies for nymphomania were performed at least until the 1920s, Rose escapes this drastic treatment.[39]

These two film images of the oversexed female joined many others in the increasingly fragmented late twentieth-century popular culture, which presented the viewer with a variety of ways to understand nymphomania. A quick review includes the following celluloid images. In Hal Hartley's *Amateur* (1994), Isabelle Huppert plays a former nun who calls herself a nymphomaniac, even though she is a virgin. When asked by the amnesiac young man whom she has rescued, "How can you be a nymphomaniac and never [have] had sex?" she answers, "I'm choosy."[40]

Sharply clashing with the black comedy overtones of *Amateur*, the bisexual heroine of another independent film, *Chasing Amy* (1997), presents a different sexual stance. She passionately defends the behavior which got her the high school label "finger cuffs," so named because—like the eponymous Chinese puzzle—she had been locked together in a dual sexual act with two male friends. "I've tried it all!" she declares to her boyfriend. "That is until we—that's you and I—got together and suddenly, I was sated."This sympathetic portrayal of a sexually experimental young woman presents the boyfriend as a jerk for not being able to accept her prodigious sexual past.[41]

Looking earlier at one of the defining teen flicks of the 1980s, we find yet another representation of nymphomania. In *The Breakfast Club* (1985), five white, mainly privileged, high school students spend a Saturday detention learning about themselves and each other. As if around a campfire, they sit in a circle and listen as the "weird one,"Allison, played by Ally Sheedy, makes the shocking claim: "I've done just about everything there is. Except a couple of things that are illegal. I'm a nymphomaniac." Questioned by the brainy geek of the group, "Isn't nymphomania a sexual myth?" Allison replies, "It's a state of mind." When Molly Ringwald's popular prom-queen character,

Claire, reluctantly reveals to the group that she is a virgin, Allison backtracks. "I'm not a nympho," she admits. "I'm a compulsive liar." It is not clear whether the filmmakers were intentionally echoing the legal connection that we have seen drawn between female sexuality and pathological lying or simply portraying one more example of Allison's neuroses.[42] In any case, nymphomania is used here to indicate a psychologically troubled teenager.

In an early Spike Lee film, *She's Gotta Have It* (1986), the heroine, Nola Darling, was widely hailed as a sexually liberated black female. Given the unrelenting cultural stereotype of black women as "oversexed"—a legacy of slavery which provided the rationale for white masters to sexually exploit their female slaves—a positive, sexually self-affirming, cinematic portrayal of black women would have been truly radical. On the surface, Nola Darling appears to be just that, a woman determined not to belong to any of her three lovers, Jamie, Greer, or Mars. But when Greer accuses her of being sexually abnormal—"I'm not saying that you're a nympho, slut, or whore, but maybe a sex addict"—Nola wonders if he might be right. She seeks out a black woman psychiatrist, who reassures her that her so-called friend "confuses a healthy sex drive with sickness."[43]

Up to this point, it is unclear how Spike Lee will resolve the dilemma of a sexually healthy black woman who's "gotta have it." Significantly, he chooses to reinstate male control in a scene in which Jamie pushes Nola to the bed and forcibly takes her from behind. As a final humiliation, Jamie coerces her to answer, "Yours," to his question, "Whose pussy is this?" The conclusion of the film presents a mixed message. On the one hand, Nola rejects *all* her lovers, declaring that she alone controls her body and her life. On the other hand, the image of what happens to a black woman—any woman—who dares to assert her sexual rights lingers on as a powerful message.[44]

The wide range of film nymphomaniacs presented in the eighties and nineties suggests how amorphous the notion has become. Consider the following: the Spanish film *Labyrinth of Passion* (1982) depicts the unabashed nymphomaniac Sexilia, aka Sexi, as the heroine of an energetic sex farce filled with outlandish characters and their misadventures on the streets of Madrid. In *Everyone Says I Love You* (1996), Woody Allen uses nymphomania as part of an ongoing joke about how he always chooses the wrong woman. When his ex-wife chides him with yet another inappropriate choice: "What about Madeline? Madeline was a nymphomaniac!" Allen responds defensively, "O.K., so she had a little problem with fidelity." And in a hilarious Coen brothers comedy, *The Big Lebowski* (1998), old-man Lebowski's daughter claims that her father's new porn-star wife, Bunny, is a "compulsive fornicator" who "is taking my father for the proverbial ride." In language straight out of a medical manual, she continues by explaining that while sex "can be a natural, zesty enterprise . . . there are some people—it is called satyriasis in men, nymphomania in women—who engage in it compulsively and without joy."[45]

A wide variety of film versions of nymphomania circulated throughout popular culture in the years after the sexual revolution: an ultra-chic, explicitly bisexual, lethal femme fatale; a screwball sexual heroine just having fun; a sexually needy young woman looking for love; and a sexually assertive black woman who's "gotta" be put in her place. Some of these films also connected compulsiveness, pathological lying, and frigidity to nymphomania, reflecting the influence of medicine and law on popular culture. The movies portrayed old stereotypes while also introducing newer, ambiguous, and occasionally humorous images of oversexed women. According to the film critic, Molly Haskell, none of them offered what the early women's movement optimistically assumed female sexual liberation would bring—a fully realized, passionately sexual woman.[46]

The Fifteen Minutes of Fame
of a Real-Life "Nymphomaniac"

OFF THE BIG SCREEN, yet another kind of nineties nymphomaniac played a starring role in the popular imagination: the Broward County, Florida, deputy sheriff's wife, Kathy Willets, who claimed that nymphomania drove her to become a prostitute. By presenting herself as a "nymphomaniac," Kathy Willets transformed what might have been just another arrest of a call girl into a media sensation. The saga epitomizes so many of the ways nymphomania has been popularly portrayed—pathologically, salaciously, and humorously—that I will examine it in detail.

The Kathy Willets story provides all the ingredients close to the heart of modern popular culture: a lurid sex scandal, the accused presenting themselves as victims, and the potential to catch some "big shots" literally with their pants down. In July 1991, when she and her husband were arrested for prostitution and wiretapping her clients' calls, Kathy and Jeff Willets ignited a media frenzy, both in the United States and abroad.[47] The couple appeared on top television talk shows, including *Larry King Live*, *Maury Povich*, *The Phil Donahue Show*, and several times on *Geraldo*. At the last minute, they and their lawyer walked off *Oprah Winfrey* because several of Kathy's clients had been secretly slated to appear at the same time.[48] With more than a hint of hyperbole, Geraldo Rivera introduced them in 1992 as "key players in some of the most sensational sex scandals . . . headlined not only in their native Florida, but around the country, indeed all around the planet."[49]

The story began when a disgruntled customer tipped off the police that the Willetses' split-level home in a Fort Lauderdale suburb actually housed a mom-and-pop sex shop. Raiding both the premises and Jeff Willets's squad car, the police found videotapes of Kathy sexually servicing customers. Secretly watching and videotaping while hidden in a bedroom closet, Jeff had also kept "The List"—client names, dates, times, and explicit comments on the sexual preferences of at least fifty locally prominent doctors, lawyers, and businessmen. A furious legal battle ensued to shield the names from public scrutiny, and only one name immediately surfaced, that of the vice mayor of Fort Lauderdale, who ironically had earned his reputation crusading against topless bars. He resigned, citing "personal reasons."

Meanwhile, the Willetses' lawyer—a well-known, flamboyant defense attorney, Ellis Rubin—capitalized on a novel defense sure to capture media attention. Kathy and Jeff would plead not guilty because sex-for-sale was simply therapy for their medical condition: she was a nymphomaniac, he an impotent voyeur. In fact, Rubin claimed, Kathy never asked for money; men simply left "gifts" of up to $150. Rubin announced at one of many press conferences—on some days Florida newspapers alone assigned more than a dozen reporters to cover the story—that he planned to present testimony by "experts" who had advised the couple to allow Kathy to "act out" her nymphomaniacal fantasies.[50]

At the end of August 1991, Rubin introduced another new twist: Kathy's nymphomania was caused by the effects of withdrawing from taking Prozac for depression in early 1990. When she stopped taking the drug, Jeff told a national audience on *Larry King Live*, "her libido went into overdrive and it got to the point where having sex three, four times per day wasn't enough for her. I couldn't keep up."[51] Told that the Willetses planned to sue, a spokesperson for Prozac's manufacturer, the Eli Lilly Co., insisted that Prozac did not heighten sexual desire, and commented further: "A lot of people have blamed Prozac for a lot of things, but this is the most bizarre yet."[52]

In a tell-all society, the Willetses' revelations of a wife having sex daily with as many as eight partners while her husband watched wowed newspaper readers and television talk show audiences. Most titillating was Kathy's bombshell that she never got enough sex. With feigned astonishment, Larry King asked, "Do you have the urge right now?" which evoked a nonchalant, "Sure," from Mrs. Willets.[53] Her story provided a juicy opportunity for television interviewers, audiences, newspaper columnists, tabloid reporters, and various sex experts to talk publicly about sex, to question what was "normal" female sexual desire, and to express outrage at the Willetses' wanton disregard for morality. In a gee-whiz tone, Larry King observed to Kathy and Jeff Willets, "I guess we've heard about this [nymphomania] all our lives. It's rare that you get a chance to do an interview about it."[54]

Some TV discussions suggested just how fluid the label had become. A twenty-three-year-old husband, also named Jeff, with an alleged nymphomaniac wife appeared along with the Willetses on another *Geraldo* show, "My Wife Can't Get Enough Sex." When questioned by a member of the audience, the young husband admitted that his wife's "insatiable" demands actually amounted to wanting to have sex about four times a week. In protest against the new, sexually assertive woman, Jeff complained that he didn't like his wife to "come on to me." He wanted to be the initiator.[55]

In a nod to newer, more inclusive definitions of marriage and sexual relationships, a lesbian couple, Lisa and Lorrie, also appeared on the show. Lisa found common ground with both the Jeffs in that she claimed not to be able to keep up with the sexual demands of her partner, Lorrie. In a facile summation typical of talk show psychological patter, Geraldo concluded that—as in the case of Kathy and Jeff—"wife Lorrie's" sexual aggression had put off the "husband Lisa." While entertaining and somewhat titillating, all the talk suggested that participants and audiences alike shared some unease about what the sexual revolution had wrought.

For a time in early 1992, Kathy Willets switched from claiming to be a nymphomaniac to calling herself a "sex addict." Befitting this new way of defining her sexual behavior, Kathy now revealed that what had driven her to prostitution was her serious lack of self-esteem, a theme echoed throughout the sex addiction literature. In February 1992, she told the audience on *Geraldo* that it was not the sex or the money she was looking for. Instead, it was "the moral support, the emotional support, the friendships that I received from these gentlemen made me feel really good." Whether conscious or not, Kathy's temporary shift to sex addiction reflected rather astute cultural antennae and firmly established her role in a society more than a little taken with notions of victimhood and uncontrollable sexual illnesses.[56]

Kathy would redefine herself once again when she emerged into her most recent persona: topless dancer and porn star. In 1994, performing at a strip joint called Alcatraz, forty miles south of Detroit, Kathy drew crowds as a celebrity of sorts. Interviewed there, the Willetses no longer talked of sex addiction, perhaps recognizing that a happy nympho image, rather than a victim persona, would do more in the long run to enhance Kathy's audience appeal. "Kathy enjoys what she's doing," Jeff rhapsodized. "What better way for a nymphomaniac to get all the sex she needs?" Appearing on *Maury Povich* in 1996 to promote her starring role in a porn film, *A Naked Scandal:The Kathy Willets Story*, Kathy further reinforced this image by claiming that making "adult videos" now helped her to deal with her nymphomania.[57]

By this time, the Willetses had long since faded from the headlines and TV screens. Even when they were front-page news, Kathy and Jeff had been treated as something of a joke. The Florida state prosecutor, according to *USA Today*, referred to the case as "Ken and Barbie Do Dallas," alluding to a similarly named, notorious porn movie.[58]

Nevertheless, buried beneath the ribald humor, some very real late twentieth-century sexual anxieties surfaced. The talk show hosts, the television audience, and the thousands of people who wrote to Kathy all had questions: How much was "too much"? What was "normal" sexuality? When did sexual desire cross the line into disease? Was Kathy a nymphomaniac? A sexual addict? In a society in which sex was thought to be central to a person's identity, in which a successful sexual relationship was touted as the key to the good life, these questions carried enormous weight. The fact that they had no simple answer—or had multiple answers—heightened concern.

The Willetses' story provided media commentators the opportunity to raise these questions in a something-for-everyone forum: scandalous disclosures, moral tut-tutting, and a modicum of sex education all at once. It featured a heroine who embodied several popular notions of the oversexed woman: on the one hand, she was the happy nympho whose voracious sexual appetite led to lots of sex partners and to starring in porn movies and performing in topless bars; simultaneously, she was the victim of a medical condition and a self-described "sexual addict."

The New Nymphomaniacs: Sexual Addicts

KATHY WILLETS ONLY BRIEFLY toyed with and ultimately discarded the sex addict label. Oprah Winfrey, the reigning queen of TV talk shows, however, maintains that sexual addiction is the number one addiction in the country, affecting over 20 million people, with over 2,000 support groups meeting nationwide.[59] The National Association of Sexual Addiction Problems claims that women comprise one-tenth of the sufferers, while other authorities believe that women account for as many as one-third of those identifying as sex addicts. Reflecting the treatment gold mine that sexual addiction has become, the Web site of the National Council on Sexual Abuse and Compulsivity lists 125 counseling services, recovery centers, and addiction programs, including numerous M.D.s, Ph.D.s, and certified social workers who minister to the condition. [60]

The idea that sex could be an addiction developed in the late 1970s and 1980s at a time when addiction appeared to be everywhere: not only alcohol and drugs, but too much gambling, shopping, working, eating, or having sex.[61] Behavior that in the past might have been seen as a sin, a failure of the will, or simply too much of a good thing, became identified as a disease. The theory behind this new way of looking at old concerns presumed that just as people could become dependent on alcohol or drugs, they could also get "hooked" on shopping, gambling, or reading romance novels. Biological theories proposed that such behavior created endorphin "highs," or that genetic coding or biochemistry predetermined those most susceptible to addiction. Psychological explanations assumed that low self-esteem or anxiety drove individuals to compulsive, self-destructive behavior.[62]

As we saw in chapter 5, it was also at this time that the ugly secrets of incest and child sexual abuse began to receive widespread public attention. Without verifiable statistics, studies claimed that as many as one in four females and one in eight males had been sexually abused as children and that untold numbers of additional children had suffered emotional neglect or psychological abuse. Sexual addiction professionals maintained that this presumed epidemic of sexual or psychological abuse and neglect was the key to addictive behavior.[63] They proposed that childhood traumas led to feelings of emptiness, which adults tried to fill with food, liquor, drugs, sex, or material goods.

This new diagnosis of sexual addiction also reflected a pervasive unease about the permissiveness of the sexual revolution. As we saw earlier, a conservative shift in the late 1970s and 1980s had been accompanied by increasing concern that sex was out of control: porn widely available, teenage pregnancy on the rise, anything-goes sex clubs and gay bathhouses operating openly, and free-and-easy attitudes run amok. In the wake of the AIDS epidemic and extensive publicity about alleged sexual abuse in day-care centers, something of a sexual panic had set in. Under the rallying cry of reestablishing "family values," an increasingly powerful right-wing religious movement had strongly endorsed the perception that sex was both dangerous and out of control.[64]

Influenced by evangelical notions of repentance and salvation, pop psychological literature today portrays sexual addicts as having much in common with sinners of the past. Following the model of Alcoholics Anonymous, the various self-help groups, including Sex Addicts Anonymous, Sexaholics Anonymous, and Sex and Love Addicts Anonymous, have adopted a version of the twelve-step program that requires participants to place themselves in the hands of a higher power. Addiction gurus, such as Stephen Arterburn, author of *Addicted to "Love"* (1996), ask readers to rate their "recovery readiness" by determining how willing they are to replace "unhealthy dependencies with a surrender to a reliance upon God."[65] To become sexually sober, the most restrictive recovery groups advocate no sexual activity unless one is married and forbid masturbation, pornography, or sexual fantasies, as well as lesbian or gay sexual alliances. As in other addictions, there is no "cure" and an individual continues to be "in recovery" for life.[66]

The early literature on sexual behaviors as addictive disease, such as Patrick Carnes's pioneering *The Sexual Addiction* (1983), presented a single path to recovery for both female and male sex addicts. That approach soon changed as women therapists, including Charlotte Kasl, author of *Women, Sex, and Addiction* (1989), argued that society's different messages about sexuality shaped women and men's addictive behavior in distinct ways. According to Kasl, female sex addicts use sex to feel powerful, just as men do. However, as the title of a best-seller suggests, the *Women Who Love Too Much* are raised to please men, and are more likely to be sexually "co-dependent," offering sex in the hopes of finding romance, love, or a relationship.[67] Kasl understands sexual co-dependency to be "only a slight exaggeration of the culturally prescribed norm for women: the passive, sweet, servile female who believes that she must be sexual to receive love and care." In the author's terms, not only women who have lots of sex partners but also the great majority of women who act out their "basic training in dependency" suffer from co-dependency, a psychological disorder whose treatment requires therapists who understand how cultural messages contribute to addiction.[68]

Some dissenting voices within the sexual addiction community suggest that maintaining this distinction between female and male sex addicts is simply another form of gender stereotyping. According to the National Council on Sexual Addiction and Compulsivity, "The idea of being 'love addicted' may be preferred by sexually addicted women because it fits the romantic, nurturer model of woman, whereas the term 'sex addict' connotes an image of a 'nymphomaniac,' 'slut,' or 'whore.'"[69] From a feminist perspective, the neo-Victorian assumption that women are "love addicts" fits the still reigning perception of women's sexuality "as less powerful, less compelling, and less profound than that of men."[70]

The idea of sex addiction continues to strike a responsive, popular chord. All manner of self-identified sex addicts, love and relationship addicts, co-dependents, and children of sex addicts have become staples of tabloid newspapers and television talk shows, from *Jerry Springer* to the Christian Broadcasting Network's *700 Club*. Gaining increasing popularity in the nineties, the talk shows' need for ever more sensational examples of sexual deviance feeds and is fed by the growing addiction movement. TV producers know—and the ratings reflect the fact—that the testimony of sexual addicts is much more compelling than that of shopaholics. Attempting to fill the airwaves day after day, Sally Jessy Raphael, Pat Robertson, Jenny Jones, Oprah Winfrey, and other talk show hosts compete to present the repentant victim of a variety of titillating addictions. [71]

Compared to the early days of AA, when small groups of peers met in church basements and listened to group members testify to an inability to control their drinking, now television audiences of millions hear Connie, a recovering sex addict, confess: "I would medicate sexually when I felt lonely. Instead of eating, I filled myself up with sex."[72] Playing to the viewers' anxieties, many shows provide a sex quiz of sorts, a list of broad and general questions to which the audience can answer in the privacy of their own homes to determine if they too are sex addicts or living with one.[73] Talk show aficionados claim that the candidness of these confessions encourages others to recognize their addiction and seek help. Critics attack such displays as voyeuristic and manipulative, arguing that they feed a mindless desire to substitute simplistic, feel-good messages for people's struggle to find meaning in their lives.

Just as nineteenth-century gynecologists and their women patients understood excessive sexual desire as an organic disease, today, both therapists and the general public have learned to talk the talk of sex as an addiction. Reflecting a more conservative time, sexual behavior is believed to be normal and healthy only when it takes place within a monogamous, committed relationship; anything else is a symptom of a psychological disorder. Responding to fears of out of control sexuality, a widespread movement of self-help groups provides participants with a supportive community whose message that sexual addiction can be controlled offers great comfort.

But formulating sexual addiction as a disease has a downside. Seeing sexual desire as something inside the body or psyche—an explosive *internal* force in need of control, repression, and regulation—ignores all the other influences that shape sexuality. A narrow medical model obscures the need for social change, emphasizing individual solutions exclusively.[74]

Interestingly, the tables have been turned in the older nymphomania vs. satyriasis debate, which characterized any sexually active woman as a nymphomaniac but rarely diagnosed her male counterpart with satyriasis. Today, sex addiction is more likely to wear a male face, including professional basketball players, film stars, and even a president of the United States. On the one hand, this suggests that the women's movement's attack on the old boys-will-be-boys rationalization, together with the feminist exposure of the prevalence of rape and incest, has permeated the popular culture. On the other, when Oprah Winfrey asked Douglas Weiss, author of *The Final Freedom: Pioneering Sexual Addiction Recovery*, why there were more men than women sex addicts, he replied: "Men are still socialized as sex addicts. They ask each other 'did you get some, did you get it,' and grow up seeing sex as something you accomplish." In his eyes, nothing much has changed.[75]

At the beginning of the twenty-first century, nymphomania is no longer a significant category either as an organic disease or as a specific mental disorder. And yet it lives on in the popular culture, embodied in the happy nympho, on the one hand, and the victimized child who grows up to be a sex addict, on the other. Equally facile and two-dimensional, these new twists in familiar stereotypes of female sexuality suggest that the questions, How much is too much? How much is enough? And who decides? have still not been satisfactorily answered.

afterword

THERE IS NO simple conclusion to the history of nymphomania. Having traced the rise and not-quite-fall of this idea over two centuries, we see that behavior thought to be nymphomaniacal thirty, fifty, or a hundred years ago is commonplace today. Yet even though the sexual revolution appears to have changed the double standard about who gets to enjoy sex or how much sex is "normal," a deep ambivalence still exists in the society toward female sexuality. The old double standard has been replaced by a more nuanced and complicated set of beliefs. Women still find themselves in a double bind: expected to be sexual, but not too aggressive; tolerated as lesbian, as long as not too butch; assumed to be sexually experienced, but not more experienced than their male partner.

The meaning of sex itself has also changed over the past two centuries. We no longer think of sex mainly in terms of reproduction; rather, we understand sexuality to be central to our sense of self. We believe that satisfying sex is crucial to a happy marriage and to the good life. Our belief that we have the right not only to have sex but also to enjoy it, however, has upped the ante in the sex stakes. Increasingly over the course of the twentieth century, people worried: Were they doing it right? Often enough? Too often? Would it be better with someone else?

More information and greater public discussion of sex in recent years have not quelled those concerns. In fact, we seem to have created a kind of sexual Tower of Babel, with many contradictory voices endlessly talking about sex on all the available airwaves and everywhere else in the media.

In our modern, scientific era, we want to believe that there is some definitive way to demarcate what is normal and what is oversexed. We look for some inherent biological line over which we must not step. And yet the history of attempts to define nymphomania suggests that even the professionals' definitions change more often than they provide illumination. At times, they display all the rigor of "I-know-one-when-I-see-one." [1]

In the course of writing this book, it became clear to me that some historical ideas are like viruses: over time, they mutate and adapt to changed circumstances. And while they may flourish more in some environments and certain periods than in others, they never totally vanish. Nymphomania fits this category, over the years assuming different guises in response to the changing sexual milieu, but never disappearing. At the moment, the term is intrinsically not very important, even something of a tired joke. And yet, as we have seen, the very protean quality of its metamorphoses over time reveals a great deal about culture, medicine, psychology, law, and the evolving history of female sexuality.

At the risk of mixing metaphors, nymphomania can also be compared to an iceberg: its power comes from what is hidden. Beneath the deceptively simple surface of a word meaning "excessive sexuality" lie centuries of Western attitudes toward women—from fears about voracious, sexual personas such as Messalina to fantasies of ever-willing women circulating throughout popular culture. Today's society shamelessly promotes the idea of excess, commercially exploiting sex to sell every conceivable product and service. Yet our fears that sex is out of control are just as visible as ever.

On a final, revealing note, as I was completing this afterword, I spoke to a colleague who, like many others over the course of my work on this book, announced: "I know a nymphomaniac." Filled to the brim with several hundred pages of elaborations on the topic, I asked: "And what is it that makes her a nymphomaniac?" He looked slightly puzzled. "Well, you know, she wants to have sex all the time." If only it were that simple.

notes

Introduction

1. "Nymphomania" comes from a combination of two words originally from the Greek: *mania,* meaning madness or frenzy, and *nymph,* meaning a bride, or more generally a maiden. In mythology, nymphs were semi-divine beings inhabiting rivers, the sea, the woods, or the hills, whose beauty could drive men to madness. In Latin, *nymphae,* plural of *nympha,* means the inner lips of the vulva, adding another dimension to the meaning of the term.

2. There has been relatively little historical study of nymphomania per se, although in recent years a wide variety of studies about sexuality, too numerous to be cited, have been published. For nymphomania, see my articles, "Nymphomania and the Historical Construction of Female Sexuality," *Signs: Journal of Women in Culture and Society* 19 (1994): 337–67, and "Nymphomania and the Freudians," *Psychohistory Review: Studies of Motivation in History and Culture* 23 (1995): 125–42. The most recent full-scale examination is a popular, psychological work with a short chapter on the historical background which simply repeats some of the tall tales about Messalina, Cleopatra, and Catherine the Great. See Albert Ellis and Edward Sagarin, *Nymphomania: A Study of the Oversexed Woman* (New York: Gilbert Press, 1964). Three articles and a dissertation are of interest: G. S. Rousseau, "Nymphomania, Bienville and the Rise of Erotic Sensibility," in *Sexuality in Eighteenth-Century Britain,* ed. Paul Gabriel Bouce (Manchester, UK: Manchester University Press, 1982), pp. 95–119; Jean Marie Goulemot, "Fureurs Utérines," *Dix-Huitième Siècle* special issue: *Représentations de la vie sexuelle* 12 (1980): 97–111; Oscar Diethelm, "La surexcitation sexuelle," *L'évolution psychiatrique* 31 (1966): 233–45; Anne Gold-

berg, "A Social Analysis of Insanity in Nineteenth-Century Germany: Sexuality, Delinquency and Anti-Semitism in the Records of the Eberbach Asylum," Ph.D. diss., UCLA, 1992; as well as an essay by Marianne Maaskant-Kleibrink, "Nymphomania," in *Sexual Asymmetry: Studies in Ancient Society*, ed. Josine Blok and Peter Mason (Amsterdam: J. C. Gieben, 1980), pp. 275–89.

3.   See Jacques Ferrand, *A Treatise on Lovesickness*, trans. and ed. Donald A. Beecher and Massimo Ciavolella (Syracuse, NY: Syracuse University Press, 1990), pp. 174, 264, 505. Many sources discuss Greek theories; see, e.g., Lesley Dean-Jones, "The Politics of Pleasure: Female Sexual Appetite in the Hippocratic Corpus," *Helios* 19 (1992): 74–78; Helen King, "Once Upon a Test: Hysteria from Hippocrates," in *Hysteria Beyond Freud*, ed. Sander Gilman, et al. (Berkeley: University of California Press, 1993), pp. 3–91.

4.   John D'Emilio and Estelle B. Freedman, *Intimate Matters: A History of Sexuality in America* (New York: Harper & Row, 1988), pp. 41, 45–46; Carol F. Karlsen, *The Devil in the Shape of a Woman: Witchcraft in Colonial New England* (New York: Norton, 1987), pp. 159–60; Thomas Laqueur, *Making Sex: Body and Gender from the Greeks to Freud* (Cambridge, MA: Harvard University Press, 1990), pp. 3–4; Mary Ryan, *Womanhood in America*, 3rd ed. (New York: Franklin Watts, 1983), pp. 44, 90; Ornella Moscucci, *The Science of Woman: Gynaecology and Gender in England, 1800–1929* (Cambridge: Cambridge University Press, 1990), pp. 2–28; Laurel Ulrich, *Goodwives: Image and Reality in the Lives of Women in Northern New England, 1650–1750* (New York: Knopf, 1983), p. 104; and Jeffrey Weeks, *Sexuality* (London: Routledge, 1986), pp. 38–39.

5.   Karlsen, *The Devil*, pp. 256–57; Laqueur, *Making Sex*, pp. 194–96; Ruth H. Bloch, "Untangling the Roots of Modern Sex Roles: A Survey of Four Centuries of Change," *Signs: Journal of Women in Culture and Society* 4 (1978): 245; Mary Beth Norton, *Liberty's Daughters: The Revolutionary Experience of American Women, 1750–1800* (Boston: Little, Brown, 1980), p. 110; Londa Schiebinger, "Skeletons in the Closet: The First Illustrations of the Female Skeleton in Eighteenth-Century Anatomy," in *The Making of the Modern Body*, ed. Catherine Gallagher and Thomas Laqueur (Berkeley: University of California Press, 1987), pp. 42-46.

6.   Nancy Cott, "Passionless: An Interpretation of Victorian Sexual Ideology," *Signs: Journal of Women in Culture and Society* 4 (1978): 219–36; for an opposing view, see Karen Lystra, *Searching the Heart: Women, Men, and Romantic Love in Nineteenth-Century America* (New York: Oxford University Press, 1989), pp. 58–60; see also Carroll Smith-Rosenberg, *Disorderly Conduct: Visions of Gender in Victorian America* (New York: Knopf, 1985), p. 302.

7.   Laqueur, *Making Sex*, pp. 79–96.

8.   Dean-Jones, "The Politics of Pleasure," p. 73; Michel Foucault, *The His-*

tory of Sexuality, vol.I: *An Introduction* (New York: Random House, 1978); Michael Mason, *The Making of Victorian Sexuality* (Oxford: Oxford University Press, 1994), pp. 177–82, 194.

9. Carroll Smith-Rosenberg and Charles Rosenberg, "The Female Animal: Medical and Biological Views of Woman and Her Role in Nineteenth-Century America," *Journal of American History* 60 (1973): 332–56; Ruth Bloch, "American Feminine Ideals in Transition: The Rise of the Moral Mother, 1785–1815," *Feminist Studies* 4 (1978): 101–26; Anne Digby, "Women's Biological Straitjacket," in *Sexuality and Subordination: Interdisciplinary Studies of Gender in the Nineteenth Century*, ed. Susan Mendus and Jane Rendall (London: Routledge, 1989).

10. Patricia Cline Cohen, *Murder of Helen Jewett: The Life and Death of a Prostitute in Nineteenth-Century New York City* (New York: Knopf, 1998), p. 184; D'Emilio and Freedman, *Intimate Matters*, pp. 39–48; Norton, *Liberty's Daughters*, p. 228.

11. D'Emilio and Freedman, *Intimate Matters*, pp. 42–48; Ellen K. Rothman, *Hands and Hearts: A History of Courtship in America* (New York: Basic Books, 1984).

12. Groneman, "Nymphomania," 350–53; E. H. Hare, "Masturbatory Insanity: The History of an Idea," *Journal of Mental Science* 108 (1962): 1–25; Mason, *The Making of Victorian Sexuality*, p. 182. A. P. Duprest-Rony, "Satyriasis," in *Dictionnaire des Sciences Médicales*, vol. 50 (Paris: Pancoucke, 1820), discusses contemporary notions of satyriasis.

13. John Rutledge Martin, "Sex and Science: Victorian and Post-Scientific Ideas in Sexuality," Ph.D. diss., Duke University, 1978, p. 50; Mason, *The Making of Victorian Sexuality*, pp. 195–96.

14. What appears to us as a contradiction between their biological theories about "Woman" as controlled by her reproductive organs (thus all women would presumably be the same) and the distinctions the Victorians drew between middle and lower class, black and white women, was explained in light of evolutionary theory. The more "highly evolved" white middle-class woman was also more civilized, refined, and moral, and consequently had less sexual desire. See Victoria Bynum, *Unruly Women: The Politics of Social and Sexual Control in the Old South* (Chapel Hill: University of North Carolina, 1992), p. 89; Sander Gilman, "Black Bodies, White Bodies: Toward an Iconography of Female Sexuality in Late Nineteenth-Century Art, Medicine and Literature," *Critical Inquiry* 12 (1985): 204–42; Gerda Lerner, *Black Women in White America: A Documentary History* (New York: Pantheon Books, 1972), pp. 149–71; Cynthia Eagle Russett, *Sexual Science: The Victorian Construction of Womanhood* (Cambridge, MA: Harvard University Press, 1989), pp. 26–28, 51–54; Weeks, *Sexuality*, pp. 39–41; and Deborah Gray White, *Ar'n't I a Woman?: Female Slaves in the Plantation South* (New York: Norton, 1985), pp. 27–46.

15. Clinical observations of nymphomania, or *furor uterinus* as it was more likely to be called until the seventeenth century, had been discussed by medical theorists as early as the fifteenth century, and numerous medical school dissertations and scholarly texts examining the disease appeared in the sixteenth and seventeenth centuries. Cases of *furor uterinus* were reported in England, France, Germany, Italy, Portugal, and Spain. See Oscar Diethelm, *Medical Dissertations of Psychiatric Interest Before 1750* (Basel: Karger, 1971), pp. 62, 139.

16. I chose illustrative cases from a variety of medical sources and included only those cases in which the term "nymphomania" was part of the diagnosis. The medical journals I consulted include *Alienist and Neurologist*, *American Gynecological and Obstetrical Journal*, *American Journal of Insanity*, *American Journal of Medical Science*, *American Journal of Obstetrics and Diseases of Women and Children*, *American Journal of Urology and Sexology*, *American Practitioner*, *Boston Medical and Surgical Journal*, *British Gynaecological Journal*, *Journal of the American Medical Association*, *Journal of Nervous and Mental Disease*, *Journal of Psychological Medicine and Mental Pathology*, *Lancet*, *Medical and Surgical Reporter*, *New York Medical and Physical Journal*, *Transactions of the American Association of Obstetricians and Gynecologists*, and *Transactions of the American Medical Association*. I also consulted dozens of nineteenth- and early twentieth-century medical texts.

17. See Nancy Theriot, "Women's Voices in Nineteenth-Century Medical Discourse: A Step Toward Deconstructing Science," *Signs: Journal of Women in Culture and Society* 19 (1993): 1–31. See also Charles Rosenberg, "Disease in History: Frames and Framers," *Milbank Quarterly* 67, supp. 1 (1989): 1–15.

18. Wardell B. Pomeroy, *Dr. Kinsey and the Institute for Sex Research* (New Haven: Yale University Press, 1982), p. 316.

Chapter I: Nymphomania in the Body

1. Hor and Sprague [no first names], "Case of Nymphomania," *Boston Medical and Surgical Journal* 25 (1841): 61–62.

2. The discussion that follows draws on the work of James H. Cassedy, *Medicine in America: A Short History* (Baltimore: Johns Hopkins Press, 1991); John Duffy, *From Humors to Medical Science: A History of American Medicine*, 2d ed. (Urbana: University of Illinois Press, 1993); Deborah Kuhn McGregor, *From Midwives to Medicine: The Birth of American Gynecology* (New Brunswick: Rutgers University Press, 1998); Regina Morantz-Sanchez, *Conduct Unbecoming a Woman: Medicine on Trial in Turn-of-the-Century Brooklyn* (New York: Oxford University Press, 1999); Ornella Moscucci, *The Science of Woman: Gynaecology and Gender in England, 1800–1929* (Cambridge: Cambridge University Press, 1990); Charles E. Rosen-

berg, "The Therapeutic Revolution: Medicine, Meaning and Social Change in Nineteenth-Century America," in *The Therapeutic Revolution: Essays in the Social History of America*, ed. Morris J. Vogel and Charles E. Rosenberg (Philadelphia: University of Pennsylvania Press, 1979), pp. 3–25; Cynthia Eagle Russett, *Sexual Science: The Victorian Construction of Womanhood* (Cambridge, MA: Harvard University Press, 1989); Edward Shorter, *From Paralysis to Fatigue: A History of Psychosomatic Illness in the Modern Era* (New York: Free Press, 1992); Carroll Smith-Rosenberg and Charles Rosenberg, "The Female Animal: Medical and Biological Views of Woman and Her Role in Nineteenth-Century America," *Journal of American History* 60 (1973): 332–56; and Nancy Theriot, "Women's Voices in Nineteenth-Century Medical Discourse: A Step Toward Deconstructing Science," *Signs: Journal of Women in Culture and Society* 19 (1993): 1–31.

3. Rosenberg, "The Therapeutic Revolution," p. 5.

4. For a full-length study published later in the century, see Horatio R. Storer, *The Causation, Course and Treatment of Reflex Insanity in Women* (Boston: Lea & Shepard, 1871); McGregor, *From Midwives to Medicine*, pp. 137, 143, 155; Morantz-Sanchez, *Conduct Unbecoming*, p. 117; Mary Poovey, "'Scenes of an Indelicate Character': The Medical 'Treatment' of Victorian Women," in *The Making of the Modern Body*, ed. Catherine Gallagher and Thomas Laqueur (Berkeley: University of California Press, 1987), p. 145.

5. For example, see the cases described in John Charles Bucknill and Daniel H. Tuke, *A Manual of Psychological Medicine* (New York: Hafner Publishing Co., 1858), the first modern textbook of psychological medicine, written in England and widely read in America in reprints in the *American Journal of Insanity* and other publications.

6. Ann E. Goldberg, "A Social Analysis of Insanity in Nineteenth-Century Germany: Sexuality, Delinquency, and Anti-Semitism in the Records of the Eberbach Asylum," Ph.D. diss., University of California at Los Angeles, 1992, chap. 2: "Nymphomania: The Medical Setting," pp. 56–138.

7. In addition, hereditary or constitutional weakness was thought to predispose certain women to nervous and mental conditions. Some doctors also looked to social causes, such as overcrowding and the stresses of urban life. A few even commented on the social constrictions which society placed on women as contributing factors to what they perceived to be a rise in these illnesses.

8. M. D. T. Bienville, *Nymphomania, or a Dissertation Concerning the Furor Uterinus*, trans. Edward Sloane Wilmot (London: J. Bew, 1775), p. 51. See Michael Mason, *The Making of Victorian Sexuality* (New York: Oxford University Press, 1994), p. 194: "Even the moralism of nineteenth-century medicine, which might strike the modern observer as thoroughly disagreeable, had its consoling aspects."

For example, for many couples it might have been a relief to believe that they were virtuously restraining their sexual behavior by having intercourse once a week, or less often.

9. "Analytic Reviews," and "On the Pathology and Characteristics of Insanity," *Journal of Psychological Medicine and Mental Pathology* 2 (1849): 19–30 and 534–54; "Case of Apoplexy in the Cerebellum," *Lancet* 1 (1849): 319–20; "Case of Hysteria and Hysteromania," *American Journal of Insanity* 17 (1860–61): 126–52; "Report on Insanity," *Transactions of the American Medical Association* 19 (1868): 161–88; David Ferrier, *Functions of the Brain* (London: Smith, Elder, 1876), p. 122; Michael Shortland, "Courting the Cerebellum: Early Organological and Phrenological Views of Sexuality," *British Journal for the History of Science* 20 (1987): 173–99; Theriot, "Women's Voices," pp. 4–10.

10. See, e.g., M. Magendie, "Lectures on the Physiology of the Nervous System," *Lancet* 2 (1836–37): 463–65, 505.

11. Cassedy, *Medicine in America*, p. 74; Duffy, *From Humors to Medical Science*, pp. 71–74; Theriot, "Women's Voices," pp. 4–7.

12. "On the Pathology," *Journal of Psychological Medicine*, 539; R. Dunn, "Case of Apoplexy in the Cerebellum," *Lancet* 1 (1849): 321; Shortland, "Courting the Cerebellum," 182–89.

13. Thomas Laycock, *A Treatise on the Nervous Diseases of Women* (London: Longman, Orme, 1840), pp. 176–77; Samuel Ashwell, *A Practical Treatise on the Diseases Peculiar to Women*, 3rd ed. (Philadelphia: Blanchard & Lea, 1848), p. 703; Charles D. Meigs, *Woman: Her Diseases and Remedies* (Philadelphia: Blanchard & Lea, 1859 [1848]), pp. 151–52; Fleetwood Churchill, *On the Diseases of Women* (Philadelphia: Blanchard & Lea, 1857), pp. 70–73, 402; Hugh L. Hodge, *On the Diseases Peculiar to Women* (Philadelphia: Blanchard & Lea, 1860), p. 101; S. E. D. Shortt, *Victorian Lunacy: Richard M. Bucke and the Practice of Late Nineteenth-Century Psychiatry* (Cambridge: Cambridge University Press, 1986); Smith-Rosenberg and Rosenberg, "The Female Animal."

14. Harvey Graham, *Eternal Eve: The Mysteries of Birth and the Customs That Surround It* (London: Hutchinson, 1960), p. 257; Duffy, *From Humors to Medical Science*, p. 180. Charles Rosenberg and Carroll Smith-Rosenberg, *The Male Midwife and the Female Doctor: The Gynecology Controversy in Nineteenth-Century America* (New York: Arno Press, 1974), includes reprints of important documents in the debate.

15. Marshall Hall, "On a New and Lamentable Form of Hysteria," *Lancet* 1 (1850): 660–61; see also McGregor, *From Midwives to Medicine*, p. 49; Moscucci, *The Science of Woman*, p. 116; Charles Rosenberg, "The Practice of Medicine in New York a Century Ago," *Bulletin of the History of Medicine* 41 (1967): 241.

16. Theriot, "Women's Voices," pp. 17–21.

17. Homer Bostwick, *A Treatise on the Nature and Treatment of Seminal Diseases, Impotency and Other Kindred Affections*, 8th ed. (New York: Stringer & Townsend, 1855), pp. 208–11.

18. *Ibid.*, p. 209.

19. *Ibid.*, pp. 210–11.

20. William Hammond, *A Treatise on Insanity in Its Medical Relations* (New York: Appleton, 1883), p. 552; Frank Lydston, "Sexual Perversion, Satyriasis and Nymphomania," *Medical and Surgical Reporter* 61 (1889): 283; Max Huhner, *Disorders of the Sexual Function in the Male and Female* (Philadelphia: F. A. Davis, 1920 [1916]), 159.

21. Henry Maudsley, *The Pathology of Mind* (London: Julian Friedmann, 1867), p. 388; see also Bucknill and Tuke, *A Manual of Psychological Medicine*, p. 524.

22. F. H. Hamilton, "Varicocele and Extirpation of the Testes, with Remarks upon the Radical Treatment of Varicocele," *Boston Medical and Surgical Journal* 25 (1841): 153–59; H. J. Bigelow, "Castration as a Means of Cure for Satyriasis," *Boston Medical and Surgical Journal* 61 (1859): 165–66; George T. Welch, "Satyriasis Caused by Varicocele, and Ceasing After Successful Operation for the Latter," *Medical Record* 36 (1889): 181. Surgical and pharmacological methods in the treatment of excessive male sexuality, usually masturbation, were widespread in the second half of the nineteenth century, including blistering the prepuce (foreskin), placing a silver ring through the prepuce, and infibulation. See E. H. Hare, "Masturbatory Insanity: The History of an Idea," *Journal of Mental Science* 108 (1962): 10–11.

23. Dr. Field quoted in "Obstinate Erotomania," *American Journal of Obstetrics and Diseases of Women and Children* (hereafter cited as *AJO*) 1 (1869): 423–24.

24. Horatio R. Storer, "Cases of Nymphomania," *American Journal of Medical Science* 32 (1856): 378–87. The following references are from this case.

25. John Tompkins Walton, "Case of Nymphomania Successfully Treated," *American Journal of Medical Science* 33 (1857): 47–50. The following references are from this case.

26. See Henry Maudsley, *Body and Mind* (London: Macmillan, 1873), p. 76; Richard von Krafft-Ebing, *Psychopathia Sexualis* (New York: G. P. Putnam's Sons, 1965 [1886]), pp. 400–408.

27. Andrew Scull and Diane Favreau, "The Clitoridectomy Craze," *Social Research* 53 (1986): 243–60; Moscucci, *The Science of Woman*, pp. 108–09, 131–32; Shorter, *From Paralysis to Fatigue*, pp. 77–80. The medical historian Nancy Tomes, "Historical Perspectives on Women and Mental Illness," in *Women, Health and Medicine in America*, ed. Rima D. Apple (New York: Garland, 1990), pp. 159–60, offers

the following cautionary note to simplistic theories of male doctors' motivations: "The majority of gynecological surgery performed by neurologists aimed simply at repairing the common injuries of childbirth, while asylum doctors rarely did gynecological exams, much less surgery."

28. William Goodell, "Discussion: 'Oophorectomy' by Thomas Savage," in *Transactions of the International Medical Congress, Seventh Session* (London: J.W. Kolckmann, 1881), p. 295, cited in Lawrence D. Longo, "The Rise and Fall of Battey's Operation: A Fashion in Surgery," in *Women and Health in America: Historical Readings*, ed. Judith Leavitt (Madison: University of Wisconsin Press, 1984), p. 283.

29. Longo, "The Rise and Fall," p. 271. According to Longo, p. 275, the operation was "performed widely by urban as well as rural physicians, not only for various neuralgias, severe dysmenorrhea, but for epilepsy, nymphomania and insanity."

30. Moscucci, *The Science of Woman*, p. 102.

31. Graham Barker-Benfield, *The Horrors of the Half-Known Life* (New York: Harper & Row, 1976), pp. 80–90; Longo, "The Rise and Fall," p. 274; Scull and Favreau, "The Clitoridectomy Craze," 251; see Shorter, *From Paralysis to Fatigue*, pp. 77–80, for a discussion of how many operations were performed. According to a story told by Walter Alvarez of the Mayo Clinic, and retold by Shorter, women in small-town America in the 1920s and 1930s believed that clitoridectomies would relieve inordinate sexual hunger.

32. A. J. Block, "Sexual Perversion in the Female," *New Orleans Medical and Surgical Journal* 22 (1894): 1–6. See also J. A. Sutcliffe, "Excision of the Clitoris in a Child for Nymphomania," *Indiana Medical Journal* 8 (1889): 64–65.

33. T. Spencer Wells, Alfred Hegar, and Robert Battey, "Castration in Nervous Diseases: A Symposium," *American Journal of Medical Science* 92 (1886): 470.

34. William Pawson Chunn, "A Case of Nymphomania," *Maryland Medical Journal* 17 (1887): 121; Robert Lawson Tait, "Note on the Influence of the Removal of the Uterus and Its Appendages on the Sexual Appetite," *British Gynaecological Journal* 4 (1888): 315; A. Laptham Smith, "A Case in Which Sex Feeling First Appeared After Removal of Both Ovaries," *AJO* 42 (1900): 839–42; Moscucci, *The Science of Woman*, p. 127.

35. Charles K. Mills, "A Case of Nymphomania with Hystero-Epilepsy and Peculiar Mental Perversions—the Results of Clitoridectomy and Oophorectomy—The Patient's History as Told by Herself," *Philadelphia Medical Times* 15 (1885): 534–40.

36. I have considerably condensed the case.

37. For a discussion of the role of women patients in the creation of the meaning of disease, see Theriot, "Women's Voices," 16–24.

38. Mills, "A Case of Nymphomania," 538.

39. *Ibid.*, 539.

40. *Ibid.*, 536.

41. *Ibid.*

42. C. H. F. Routh, "On the Etiology and Diagnosis Considered Specially from a Medico-Legal Point of View for Those Cases of Nymphomania Which Lead Women to Make False Charges Against Their Medical Attendants," *British Gynaecological Journal* 2 (1887): 485–511, quote at 486; see also Frank Lydston, "Sexual Perversion, Satyriasis and Nymphomania," *Medical and Surgical Reporter* 61 (1889): 281–85, and Howe, *Excessive Venery*, pp. 108–09.

43. Routh, "On the Etiology," 489–90.

44. Howe, *Excessive Venery*, pp. 109–10.

45. J. Milne Chapman, "On Masturbation as an Etiological Factor in the Production of Gynic Diseases," *AJO* 16 (1883): 450–58, 578–98, quote at 595; see also F. S. Sharpe, "Hairpin in the Female Bladder," *American Journal of Medical Sciences* 68 (1874): 577–78; S. E. McCully, "Letter to the Editor: Masturbation in the Female," *AJO* 16 (1883): 844–46; Lydston, "Sexual Perversion," 282; Block, "Sexual Perversion," 5.

46. See, e.g., James Jager Hillary, "Behavior of the Uterus During Orgasm," *AJO* 16 (1883): 1170–71; McCully, "Letter," 844–45. John Rutledge Martin, in his "Sex and Science: Victorian and Post-Scientific Ideas in Sexuality," Ph.D. diss., Duke University, 1978, pp. 102–17, reviewed Victorian medical opinion about female sexuality and concluded that most physicians recognized that women experienced both sexual desire and pleasure in intercourse, although male sexual desire was understood to be stronger. See also Mason, *The Making of Victorian Sexuality*, pp. 200–04, in which he points out that the oft-quoted remark by the mid-century physician, William Acton—"The majority of women . . . are not very much troubled with sexual feelings of any kind"—was an attempt by Acton to reassure anxious men that female sexuality was not something to be afraid of and that it was also "unparalleled in the sexual literature of the day."

47. R. L. Payne, "A Case of Nymphomania," *Medical Journal of North Carolina* 2 (1859): 569–70.

48. Chapman, "On Masturbation," 458; see also Poovey, "Scenes of an 'Indelicate Character,'" 137–68.

49. Krafft-Ebing, *Psychopathia Sexualis*

50. Krafft-Ebing, *Psychopathia Sexualis*, pp. 402–03; A. von Schrenk-Notzing, *Therapeutic Suggestions in Psychopathia Sexualis*, trans. Charles Gilbert Chaddock (Philadelphia: F. S. Davis, 1895), p. 32; Lydston, "Sexual Perversion," 316; A. Forel, *The Sexual Question: A Scientific, Psychological, Hygienic and Sociological Study*

(NewYork: Physicians and Surgeons, 1924 [1906]), p. 252; Max Huhner, *Disorders of the Sexual Function in the Male and Female* (Philadelphia: F. A. Davis, 1920 [1916]), p. 164; Sander Gilman, *Sexuality: An Illustrated History* (NewYork: Wiley, 1989), p. 299.

51. Carlton Frederick, "Nymphomania as a Cause of Excessive Venery," *AJO* 56 (1907): 810.

52. George Chauncey, "From Sexual Inversion to Homosexuality: Medicine and the Changing Conceptualization of Female Deviance," *Salmagundi* 58–59 (1983): 124–25; David Greenberg, *The Construction of Homosexuality* (Chicago: University of Chicago, 1988), p. 427; Nancy Sahli, "Smashing: Women's Relationships Before the Fall," *Chrysalis* (1979): 18–27.

53. L. M. Phillips, "Nymphomania: Reply to Questions," *Cincinnati Medical Journal* 10 (1895): 467–71.

54. *Ibid.*, 469.

55. *Ibid.*

56. *Ibid.*

57. *Ibid.*, 471

Chapter 2: Nymphomania's New Guises

1. Judge Ben Lindsey, "Wisdom for Parents," in *Sex in Civilization*, ed. V. F. Calverton and S. D. Schmalhausen (Garden City, NY: Garden City Publishing Co., 1929), p. 188; Beatrice Forbes-Robinson Hale, "Women in Transition," in *Sex in Civilization*, pp. 68-9.

2. John D'Emilio and Estelle B. Freedman, *Intimate Matters: A History of Sexuality in America* (NewYork: Harper & Row, 1988), pp. xv–xvi.

3. Barbara Epstein, "Family, Sexual Morality, and Popular Movements in Turn-of-the-Century America," in *Powers of Desire: The Politics of Sexuality*, ed. Ann Snitow, Christine Stansell, and Sharon Thompson (New York: Monthly Review Press, 1983), pp. 117–30; Kathy Peiss, *Cheap Amusements: Working Women and Leisure in Turn-of-the-Century New York* (Philadelphia: Temple University Press, 1986); Joanne Meyerowitz, *Women Adrift: Independent Wage Earners in Chicago, 1880–1930* (Chicago: University of Chicago Press, 1988).

4. D'Emilio and Freedman, *Intimate Matters*, p. 174.

5. Theodore Van de Velde, *Ideal Marriage* (NewYork: Random House, 1930), p. 157. This book went through over fifty printings between 1926 and 1968.

6. See, e.g., Karen Lystra, *Searching the Heart: Women, Men, and Romantic Love in Nineteenth-Century America* (NewYork: Oxford University Press, 1989).

7. Christina Simmons, "Companionate Marriage and the Lesbian Threat,"

Frontiers: A Journal of Women's Studies 4 (1979): 54–59; Carol Bacchi, "Feminism and the Eroticization of the Middle-Class Woman: The Intersection of Class and Gender Attitudes," *Women's Studies International* 2 (1988): 43–53.

8. Havelock Ellis, *Studies in the Psychology of Sex,* 2 vols. (New York: Random House, 1936 [1906]), vol. 1:part 2, p. 203. Ellis cited percentages of frigid women given by leading sexologists, such as Shufeldt, 75%; Hegar, 50%; Furbringer, over 50%; Effertz, 10%; Moll, 10–66%.

9. Sigmund Freud, *Three Essays on the Theory of Sexuality,* trans. and ed. James Strachey (New York: Basic Books, 1962 [1905]), pp. 86–87; see also Sigmund Freud, "Some Psychical Consequences of the Anatomical Distinction Between the Sexes," *Collected Papers,* vol. 5, trans. and ed. James Strachey (London: Hogarth Press, 1950 [1925]), p. 194; Sigmund Freud, "Femininity," *New Introductory Lectures on Psychoanalysis,* trans. and ed. James Strachey (New York: Norton, 1965 [1933]), pp. 146–47, 157–58. Freud understood the clitoris to act as a transmitter of sexual excitation; however, he ignored this insight in his argument that mature sexual experience for women meant solely a vaginal orgasm. See Elisabeth Young-Bruehl, *Freud on Women: A Reader* (New York: Norton, 1990), p. 23.

10. Margaret Sanger, *Happiness in Marriage* (New York: Brentano, 1926), p. 21; Joseph Collins, *The Doctor Looks at Love and Life* (New York: George H. Doran Co., 1926), p. 32.

11. Wilhelm Stekel, *Frigidity in Women in Relation to Her Love Life,* trans. James S. Van Teslaar, vol. 2 (New York: Grove Press, 1962 [1926]), p. 15. For a different Freudian perspective, see Karen Horney, "The Flight from Womanhood: The Masculinity-Complex in Women as Viewed by Men and Women," *International Journal of Psychoanalysis* 7 (1926): 324–39; see also Carol Groneman, "Nymphomania and the Freudians," *Psychohistory Review* 23 (1995): 125–42.

12. The Freudians were not the first to argue that nymphomaniacs were frigid. Although some earlier authorities also made this connection, they did not assume that frigidity consisted of a failure to achieve a vaginal orgasm.

13. Otto Fenichel, "Outline of Clinical Psychoanalysis," *Psychoanalytic Quarterly* 2 (1933): 567.

14. Fenichel, "Outline," 563–68.

15. Ibid., 567–68.

16. Bernard S. Talmey, *Woman: A Treatise on the Normal and Pathological Emotions of Feminine Love,* 7th enlarged ed. (New York: Practitioners' Publishing Co., 1912), pp. 78, 104–05.

17. Masturbation had been blamed in the past for various problems, including decreasing the desire for intercourse in both men and women. Interest in female masturbation took on particular resonance in the early twentieth century

because of the concern that sexual satisfaction in marriage required women to have vaginal orgasms.

18. Walter Gallichan, *Sexual Antipathy and Coldness in Women* (Boston: Stratford Co., 1930), pp. 29–30; see also Shirley Jeffreys, *The Spinster and Her Enemies* (London: Pandora, 1985), pp. 166–78.

19. Ellis, *Studies*, vol. 1: part 2, p. 241.

20. Talmey, *Woman*, pp. 102–03.

21. *Ibid.*, pp. 105–06.

22. *Ibid.*, pp. 106–07.

23. Van de Velde, *Ideal Marrige*, pp. 221–25.

24. William Healy, *The Individual Delinquent* (Boston: Little, Brown, 1924), p. 248.

25. Elizabeth Lunbeck, "'A New Generation of Women': Progressive Psychiatrists and the Hypersexual Female," *Feminist Studies* 13 (1987): 513–43; Gerald Grob, *The Mad Among Us: A History of the Care of America's Mentally Ill* (New York: Free Press, 1994), pp. 149–51.

26. Quoted in Lunbeck, "A New Generation," p. 513; Kathy Peiss, "'Charity Girls' and City Pleasures: Historical Notes on Working-Class Sexuality, 1880–1920," in *Passion and Power: Sexuality in History*, ed. Kathy Peiss and Christina Simmons (Philadelphia: Temple University Press, 1989), pp. 57–69.

27. Ruth M. Alexander, *The "Girl Problem": Female Sexual Delinquents in New York, 1900–30* (Ithaca, NY: Cornell University Press, 1995).

28. Quoted in Peiss, "'Charity Girls,'" p. 64.

29. Quoted in Lunbeck, "'A New Generation,'" 535, from the case records of the Boston Psychopathic Hospital, which according to the author was one of the most highly regarded of American mental hospitals in this period.

30. Phyllis Blanchard, *The Adolescent Girl: A Study from the Psychoanalytic Point of View*, rev. ed. (New York: Dodd, Mead, 1930 [1920]), p. 169; Alexander, *The "Girl Problem*," pp. 59–65; Regina G. Kunzel, *Fallen Women, Problem Girls: Unmarried Mothers and the Professionalization of Social Work* (New Haven: Yale University Press, 1993) pp. 36–64.

31. See Mary E. Odem and Steven Schlossman, "Guardians of Virtue: The Juvenile Court and Female Delinquency in Early Twentieth Century Los Angeles," *Crime and Delinquency* 37 (1991): 186–203.

32. Many mental health professionals wrote about these issues. See, e.g., Ernest B. Hoag and Edward H. Williams, *Crime, Abnormal Minds and the Law* (Indianapolis: Bobbs-Merrill, 1923).

33. Sophonisba Breckenridge and Edith Abbott, *The Delinquent Child and the Home* (New York: Charities Publication Committee, 1912), pp. 37–38. For a his-

torical overview, see Steven Schlossman and Stephanie Wallach, "The Crime of Precocious Sexuality: Female Juvenile Delinquency in the Progressive Era," *Harvard Educational Review* 48 (1978): 63–94. For the continuing power of the paradigm, see Meda Chesney-Lind, "Juvenile Delinquency: The Sexualization of Female Crime," *Psychology Today* 8 (1974): 43–46.

34. William Healy, *The Individual Delinquent* (Boston: Little, Brown, 1924), pp. 249, 255, 403.

35. William I. Thomas, *The Unadjusted Girl, Supplement to the Journal of the American Institute of Criminal Law and Criminology* (Boston: Little, Brown, 1925), p. 109; E. E. Southard and Mary C. Jarrett, *The Kingdom of Evils: Psychiatric Social Work Presented in One Hundred Case Histories* (New York: Macmillan, 1922), p. 51.

36. The case is discussed in Southard and Jarrett, *The Kingdom of Evils*, pp. 51, 52; see also Grob, *The Mad Among Us*, pp. 150–51.

37. Southard and Jarrett, *The Kingdom of Evils*, p. 52. For a study of the Boston Psychopathic Hospital, see Elizabeth Lunbeck, *The Psychiatric Persuasion* (Princeton: Princeton University Press, 1994).

38. Southard and Jarrett, *The Kingdom of Evils*, pp. 53–54.

39. *Ibid.*, p. 56.

40. *Ibid.*, p. 55; see also George Robb, "The Way of All Flesh: Degeneration, Eugenics and the Gospel of Free Love," *Journal of the History of Sexuality* 6 (1996): 589–604.

41. Southard and Jarrett, *The Kingdom of Evils*, pp. 57–61.

42. Peter L. Tyor, "'Denied the Power to Choose the Good': Sexuality and Mental Defect in American Medical Practice, 1850–1920," *Journal of Social History* 10 (1977): 481.

43. Ernest Hoag, for example, recorded the following difference in the percentages of feebleminded boys and girls: 14% of boys and 34% of girls in the Los Angeles Juvenile Court, and 49% of boys and 79% of girls in the Honolulu Juvenile Court. See Hoag and Williams, *Crime*, pp. 139–40.

44. Alexander, *The "Girl Problem*," p. 179; Hoag and Williams, *Crime*, p. 6.

45. Carrie Weaver Smith, "What the Clinic Reveals," in *Woman's Coming of Age: A Symposium*, ed. Samuel Schmalhausen and V. F. Calverton (New York: Liveright, 1931), pp. 190–205; Emily Lamb, "Study of Thirty-Five Delinquent Girls," *Journal of Delinquency* 4 (1919): 85.

46. Healy, *The Individual Delinquent*, pp. 245–50; Max Huhner, *A Practical Treatise on Disorders of the Sexual Function in the Male and Female* (Philadelphia: F. A. Davis, 1920), p. 163; Hoag and Williams, *Crime* p. 149; Lamb, "Study," 84.

47. Healy, *The Individual Delinquent*, pp. 189–91.

48. *Ibid.*, pp. 190–91.

49. The case is cited in Thomas, *The Unadjusted Girl*, pp. 172–94.

50. *Ibid.*, p. 172.

51. *Ibid.*, pp. 182–88.

52. *Ibid.*, p. 189.

53. *Ibid.*, p. 191.

54. *Ibid.*, p. 192.

55. See Regina G. Kunzel, "White Neurosis, Black Pathology," in *Not June Cleaver: Women and Gender in Postwar America, 1945–1960*, ed. Joanne Meyerowitz (Philadelphia: Temple University Press, 1994), p. 316: "Indeed, in the early twentieth century, when illegitimacy among working-class white women came under such intense scrutiny, their African American counterparts seemed hardly worthy of notice." See also Grob, *The Mad Among Us*, p. 151: "Hypersexual activity in white females [at Boston Psychopathic Hospital] was taken as evidence of psychopathy to the staff; similar behavior by black women was regarded as expression of an ingrained natural immorality of the race."

56. For a readable examination of these theories, see Cynthia Russett, *Sexual Science: The Victorian Construction of Womanhood* (Cambridge, MA: Harvard University Press, 1989).

57. Cases like Esther's, which were multiplied by thousands in criminal courts and juvenile institutions, together with economic and political fears of immigrants, led to the first major immigration restriction in the nation's history in the 1920s.

58. See Carroll Smith-Rosenberg, "The New Woman as Androgyne: Social Disorder and Gender Crisis," in *Disorderly Conduct: Visions of Gender in Victorian America*, ed. Carroll Smith-Rosenberg (New York: Knopf, 1985), pp. 245–96; Daniel J. Walkowitz, *Working With Class: Social Workers and the Politics of Middle-Class Identity* (Chapel Hill: University of North Carolina Press, 1999), pp. 87–111.

59. John F. W. Meagher, "Homosexuality: Its Psychobiological and Psychopathological Significance," *Urologic and Cutaneous Review*, 23 (1929): 509, 511.

60. Quoted disapprovingly in Florence Guy Seabury, "Stereotypes," in *Our Changing Morality: A Symposium*, ed. Freda Kirchwey (New York: Albert & Charles Boni, 1924), p. 226.

61. William J. Robinson, "Book Reviews," *New York Medical Journal* 112 (1920): 470; Ellis, *Studies* vol. 1: part 2, p. 241.

62. On the importance of Havelock Ellis's work, see Paul Robinson, *The Modernization of Sex* (New York: Harper & Row, 1976), pp. 1–42.

63. Alice Beals Parson, "Man-Made Illusions About Women," in *Woman's Coming of Age*, ed. Schmalhausen and Calverton, pp. 27–29.

64. See Peter Gay, *The Bourgeois Experience, Victoria to Freud*, vol. I: *Education of*

the Senses (New York: Oxford University Press, 1984), pp. 164–68.

65. Ernest Jones, "The Early Development of Female Sexuality," *International Journal of Psycho-Analysis* 8 (1927): 467.

66. Quoted in Elaine Showalter, ed., *These Modern Women: Autobiographical Essays from the Twenties* (New York: Feminist Press, 1979), p. 16.

67. Smith-Rosenberg, "The New Woman," p. 266.

68. Katherine B. Davis, *Factors in the Sex Life of Twenty-Two Hundred Women* (New York: Harper & Bros., 1929), quoted in Simmons, "Companionate Marriage," p. 54; Nancy Sahli, "Smashing: Women's Relationships Before the Fall," *Chrysalis* 8 (1979): 18–27.

69. Collins, *The Doctor*, p. 101.

70. Ellis, *Studies*, vol. 1: part 4, p. 250; see also George Chauncey, "From Sexual Inversion to Homosexuality: Medicine and the Changing Conceptualization of Female Deviance," Salmagundi 58–59 (1983): 114–46.

Chapter 3: The Sex Experts

1. Nelly Oudshoorn, "Endocrinologists and the Conceptualization of Sex, 1920–1940," *Journal of the History of Biology* 23 (1990): 163–86, quote at 168.

2. Nelly Oudshoorn, "Endocrinologists," 167–68. The Swiss drug company, Ciba, marketed ovarian extract in 1913; see Gail Vines, *Raging Hormones* (Berkeley: University of California Press), 1993, p. 15. Earlier doctors had experimented with monkey or goat gland transplants in their private patients.

3. Merriley Borell, "Organotherapy and the Emergence of Reproductive Endocrinology," *Journal of the History of Biology* 18. (1985): 1–30.

4. Robert B. Greenblatt, Frank Mortara, and Richard Torpin, "Sexual Libido in the Female," *American Journal of Obstetrics and Gynecology* 44 (1942): 658–63, quote at 663.

5. Oudshoorn, "Endocrinologists," 168.

6. Barbara Ehrenreich and Diedre English, *For Her Own Good: 150 Years of the Experts' Advice to Women* (Garden City, N.Y.: Anchor Press/Doubleday, 1978), p. 248; Oudshoorn, "Endocrinologists," 184; see also Diana Long Hall, "Biology, Sex Hormones and Sexism in the 1920s," in *Women and Philosophy: Toward a Theory of Liberation*, ed. Carol Gould (New York: G. P. Putnam's Sons, 1976).

7. William H. Perloff, "Role of the Hormones in Human Sexuality," *Psychosomatic Medicine* 11 (1949): 136.

8. Vines, *Raging Hormones*, pp. 18–19; Nelly Oudshoorn, *Beyond the Natural Body: An Archaeology of Sex Hormones* (London: Routledge, 1994), pp. 15–42.

9. Greenblatt, et al., "Sexual Libido," 663.

10. S. Leon Israel, "Premenstrual Tension," *Journal of the American Medical Association* 110 (1938): 1721–22.

11. One study on the "physiology of nymphomania in dairy cattle," which did define nymphomania, attributed it to an upset in the endocrine functions, specifically, to ovarian cysts. Nymphomania in cows was characterized by the development of "masculinity"—that is, bellowing in a deep, bull-like voice and assuming the menacing attitude of a bull. Interestingly, nymphomania in cows could lead either to an excess of libido or to its complete lack. Oliver Wayman, "A Study of the Physiology of Nymphomania in Dairy Cattle," Ph.D. diss., Cornell University, 1951.

12. Greenblatt, et al., "Sexual Libido," 660.

13. In keeping with contemporary notions of what was appropriate femininity, one 1935 study (reported on the front page of *The New York Times*, Oct. 28, 1935) described adrenal gland surgery, which was recommended for women suffering from "abnormal personalities," including "aversion to marital relationship, despondency, suicidal tendency and a general drift away from feminine toward decidedly masculine traits."

14. Greenblatt, et al., "Sexual Libido," 662. This article contains a review of other similar studies at 659–60. See also Udall J. Salmon and Samuel H. Geist, "Effect of Androgens Upon Libido in Women," *Journal of Clinical Endocrinology* 3 (1943): 235–38.

15. H. S. Rubinstein, H. D. Shapiro, and Walter Freeman, "The Treatment of Morbid Sex Craving with the Aid of Testosterone Propionate," *American Journal of Psychiatry* 97 (1940): 703–10. The cases that follow are described in this study.

16. *Ibid.,* 705–06.

17. *Ibid.,* 706–07.

18. *Ibid.,* 704.

19. A. R. Abarbanel, "Percutaneous Administration of Testosterone Propionate for Dysmenorrhea," *Endocrinology* 26 (1940): 765–73.

20. *Ibid.,* 770.

21. Perloff, "Role of the Hormones," 134.

22. Anne C. Carter, E. J. Cohen, and E. Shorr, "The Use of Androgens in Women," *Vitamins and Hormones* 5 (1947): 317–91. This article reviews other studies on hormones and libido.

23. *The Over-Sexed Woman: Relief and Control Under Bromide Sedation* (St. Louis: Dios Chemical Co., 1951). The quotes that follow come from the brochure, which can be found at the Kinsey Institute for Research in Sex, Gender, and Reproduction, Bloomington, Indiana.

24. See Nathan Flaxman, "Nymphomania—A Symptom, Part II," *Medical*

Trial Technique Quarterly 19 (1973): 308. Flaxman comments that bromides, when used repeatedly over a number of years, can cause bromism and an acute psychosis.

25. Allen Churchill, "Psychiatry Looks at the Oversexed Girl," *Point* 2 (1955): 48–52, quote at 49.

26. Few yet called attention to what later would be considered a factor in hypersexuality, that is, having been sexually abused as a child.

27. John Burnham, "The Influence of Psychoanalysis Upon American Culture," in *American Psychoanalysis: Origins and Development*, ed. Jacques M. Quen and Eric T. Carlson (New York: Brunner Mazel, 1978); Vern L. Bullough, *Science in the Bedroom: A History of Sex Research* (New York: Basic Books, 1994), pp. 61, 148; Miriam Lewin, *In the Shadow of the Past: Psychology Portrays the Sexes* (New York: Columbia University Press, 1984), p. 189; Regina G. Kunzel, "White Neurosis, Black Pathology: Constructing Out-of-Wedlock Pregnancy in Wartime and Postwar U.S.," in *Not June Cleaver: Women and Gender in Postwar America, 1945–60*, ed. Joanne Meyerowitz (Philadelphia: Temple University Press, 1994), p. 311.

28. Louise Fox Connell, *Reader's Digest* (July 1943), pp. 92–95.

29. See, e.g., William G. Niederland, M.D., "'Masculine' Women Are Cheating at Love," *Coronet* (May 1953), pp. 41–44; "Gladys Denny Shultz, "Letters to Joan," *Ladies' Home Journal* (April 1947), pp. 31, 216–17; Amram Scheinfeld, "'Cold' Women—and Why," *Reader's Digest* (August 1948), pp. 124–26.

30. Niederland, "'Masculine' Women," 44; Connell, "Women's Responsibility," 93.

31. Quoted in Ehrenreich, *For Her Own Good*, p. 279.

32. Diana Scully and Pauline Bart, "A Funny Thing Happened on the Way to the Orifice: Women in Gynecology Textbooks," *American Journal of Sociology* 78 (1973): 1047. See, e.g., J. P. Greenhill, *Office Gynecology*, 9th rev. ed. (Chicago: Year Book Medical Publishers, 1971); Edward Weiss and O. Spurgeon English, *Psychosomatic Medicine*, 2nd ed. (Philadelphia: W. B. Saunders Co., 1943).

33. William S. Kroger and S. Charles Freed, *Psychosomatic Gynecology* (Philadelphia: W. B. Saunders Co., 1951), p. 407.

34. *Ibid.*, p. 409.

35. *Ibid.*, p. 407.

36. According to Ehrenreich and English, *For Her Own Good*, p. 277, only about 5% of gynecologists at the time were women.

37. "Medicine: The Cold Women," *Time*, June 26, 1950, pp. 80–81.

38. Elaine Tyler May, *Homeward Bound: American Families in the Cold War Era* (New York: Basic Books, 1988), p. 76. May comments that three-quarters of women who had been employed in war industries were still employed in 1946,

but 90% of them were earning less than they had during the war.

39. Joanne Meyerowitz, "Beyond the Feminine Mystique: A Reassessment of Postwar Mass Culture, 1946–58," in *Not June Cleaver*, ed. Myerowitz, p. 231.

40. Greenhill, *Office Gynecology*, p. 120; Weiss and English, *Psychosomatic Medicine*, p. 571.

41. Edmund Bergler, *Neurotic Counterfeit-Sex: Homosexuality, Impotence, Frigidity* (New York: Grune & Stratton, 1951); Frank Caprio, *Female Homosexuality* (New York: Citadel Press, 1953); A. M. Krich, *The Homosexuals: As Seen by Themselves and Thirty Authorities* (New York: Citadel Press, 1954); Donna Penn, "The Sexualized Woman: The Lesbian, the Prostitute, and the Containment of Female Sexuality in Postwar America," in *Not June Cleaver*, ed. Meyerowitz, pp. 358–81.

42. Caprio, *Female Homosexuality*, p. 306.

43. *Ibid.*

44. Victor Eisenstein, *Neurotic Interaction in Marriage* (New York: Basic Books, 1956), pp. 107, 112–14; Caprio, too, believed that married couples who engaged in "certain sexual preferences, namely fellatio, cunnilingus, coitus per anum and various positions such as the wife who prefers to lie on top, and assume the active role," exhibited latent homosexuality. See *Female Homosexuality*, p. 306.

45. Allen Churchill and Pierre Rube, "Nymphos Have No Fun," *Esquire* (August 1954), pp. 21, 104–05.

46. *Ibid.*, p. 104.

47. Anonymous, "My Bride Was a Nymphomaniac," *MR.* (December 1956), pp. 6, 67–68.

48. Roy Walcott Van Horn, "Promiscuous Women Can Be Cured," *Coronet* (October 1955), pp. 77–80.

49. Alfred C. Kinsey, Wardell B. Pomeroy, and Clyde E. Martin, *Sexual Behavior in the Human Male* (Philadelphia: W. B. Saunders Co., 1948). Kinsey hoped to compile 100,000 individual sex histories. He did not include black men in the first volume because "the Negro sample, while of some size [approximately 1,000], is not yet sufficient for making analyses comparable to those made here for the white male" (p. 6). See also Donald Porter Geddes, ed., *An Analysis of the Kinsey Reports* (New York: Dutton, 1954). For more recent analyses, see Janice M. Irvine, *Disorders of Desire* (Philadelphia: Temple University Press, 1990), pp. 45–51; James H. Jones, *Alfred C. Kinsey: A Public/Private Life* (New York: Norton, 1997); Paul Robinson, *The Modernization of Sex: Havelock Ellis, Alfred Kinsey, William Masters and Virginia Johnson* (New York: Harper & Row, 1976), pp. 42–119; and Leonore Tiefer, *Sex Is Not a Natural Act and Other Essays* (Boulder, CO: Westview Press, 1995), pp. 20–21.

50. Wardell B. Pomeroy, *Dr. Kinsey and the Institute for Sex Research* (New

Haven: Yale University Press, 1982), p. 342, cites *This Week Magazine* for the title, "The Great Kinsey Hullabaloo."

51. *Time* quote cited in Geddes, *An Analysis*, p. 289; see also Pomeroy, *Dr. Kinsey*, pp. 342–67.

52. Alfred C. Kinsey, Wardell B. Pomeroy, Clyde E. Martin, and Paul H. Gebhard, *Sexual Behavior in the Human Female* (Philadelphia: W. B. Saunders Co., 1953). The total number of women in the sample was 7,789. Because the sexual histories of the white women who had served prison sentences (915) differed as a group from the other females, and because the non-white sample (934) was not large enough, the analyses excluded both groups.

53. *Ibid.* These statistics can be found on pp. 416, 286, 375, 528, 529, respectively.

54. *Ibid.*, p. 14.

55. Quoted in Geddes, *An Analysis*, p. 364.

56. Kinsey, et al., *Sexual Behavior in the Human Female*, p. 12.

57. *Ibid.*, p. 346.

58. *Ibid.*, pp. 134–35; 142; 446–50.

59. *Ibid.*, pp. 510–11; Irvine, *Disorders of Desire*, pp. 46–47.

60. Kinsey, Pomeroy, and Martin, *Sexual Behavior in the Human Male*, p. 199.

61. *Ibid.*

62. *Ibid.*, pp. 201–02.

63. Quoted in Pomeroy, *Dr. Kinsey*, p. 316.

64. Kinsey, et al., *Sexual Behavior in the Human Female*, pp. 582–84.

65. Edmund Bergler and William S. Kroger, *Kinsey's Myth of Female Sexuality* (New York: Grune & Stratton, 1952), pp. 36, 82; Robinson, *Modernization of Sex*, p. 115; Irvine, *Disorders of Desire*, p. 59.

66. Kinsey, Pomeroy, and Martin, *Sexual Behavior in the Human Male*, p. 8; Robinson, *The Modernization of Sex*, pp. 42–119.

67. Kinsey, et al., *Sexual Behavior in the Human Female*, pp. 510–11; Irvine, *Disorders of Desire*, pp. 46–47.

Chapter 4: Nymphomania in the Courts

1. *People* v. *Bastian*, 330 Mich 457, 47 N.W. 2d 692 (1951).

2. Vivian Berger, "Man's Trial, Woman's Tribulation: Rape Cases in the Courtroom," *Columbia Law Review* 77 (1977): 23; see also Susan Brownmiller, *Against Our Will: Men, Women and Rape* (New York: Bantam Books, 1975), and Leon Letwin, "'Unchaste Character,' Ideology, and the California Rape Evidence Laws," *Southern California Law Review* 54 (1980): 35–89.

3. *People* v. *Cowles*, 246 Mich 429, 431, 432, 224 N.W. 387 (1929). In this case, the appeals court admitted testimony from the two medical experts who had observed the complainant in the courtroom. After observing the prosecutrix, the experts testified that in their opinion she was a "pathological falsifier, a nymphomaniac, and a sexual pervert."

4. *People* v. *Bastian*, p. 463, citing *People* v. *Cowles*, p. 429.

5. Annotation, "Necessity and Admissibility of Expert Testimony as to Credibility of Witnesses," *American Law Reports* 3d, 20 (1968): 688.

6. Roger B. Dworkin, "The Resistance Standard in Rape Legislation," *Stanford Law Review* 18 (1966): 683; for additional examples, see John M. MacDonald, *Rape Offenders and Their Victims*, 2d ed. (Springfield, IL: Charles C. Thomas, 1975), p. 202: "Repressed erotic wishes or fantasies may be converted into beliefs and the girl may be convinced of the reality of her claim of rape despite convincing evidence to the contrary."

7. Note, *Columbia Law Review*, 67 (1967): 1138.

8. Roscoe N. Gray, *Attorneys' Textbook of Medicine*, 3rd ed. (New York: M. Bender, 1950), p. 940.

9. Ralph Slovenko, "A Panoramic Overview: Sexual Behavior and the Law," pp. 52–53, in *Sexual Behavior and the Law*, ed. Ralph Slovenko (Springfield, IL: Charles C. Thomas, 1965), quoted in Dworkin, "The Resistance Standard," 682.

10. John Henry Wigmore, *Evidence in Trials at Common Law*, rev. James H. Chadbourn, 10 vols. (New York: Little, Brown, 1970). Wigmore began his work with the publication of a four-volume edition of *Evidence* in 1904–05. He published a revised five-volume edition in 1923 and a supplement in 1934. The definitive expanded and revised ten-volume edition was completed before his death at the age of eighty in 1943. See "J. H. Wigmore, Scholar and Reformer," *Criminal Law, Criminology and Police Science* 53 (1962): 277–300. For a critical analysis of Wigmore, which focuses particularly on his discussion of incest and sexual abuse of young girls, see Leigh B. Bienen, "A Question of Credibility: John Henry Wigmore's Use of Scientific Authority in Section 924a of the *Treatise on Evidence*," *California Western Law Review* 19 (1983): 235–68.

11. According to Berger, "Man's Trial," 27: "Because of his academic stature, Wigmore's ideas on proper proof in rape proceedings have carried disproportionate weight."

12. Wigmore, *Evidence*, vol. 3, sect. 924a, p. 736.

13. *Ibid.*, sect. 934a, pp. 767–70. Although some of the text was revised, it appears to have been an editorial decision in the first major revision in 1970 to retain much of the original text. For the most recent edition, see Arthur Best, *1999 Supplement to Wigmore on Evidence* (Aspen, CO: Aspen Law and Business, 1999), p.

398, which retains the section on "Abnormal mentality of women complainants: nymphomania."

14. Wigmore, *Evidence*, vol. 3, sect. 924a, p. 736.

15. *Ibid.*, p. 737.

16. Cited in *ibid.*, p. 744. Menninger later changed his view and concluded that over 75% of the young women in his clinic had been sexually abused.

17. Cited in *ibid.*, pp. 745–46.

18. Matthew Hale, *History of the Pleas of the Crown*, vol. I (Philadelphia: R. H. Small, 1847), p. 634. Proof of actual physical resistance by the woman and substantial force by the man was necessary to prove non-consent. In the 1950s and 1960s, the "utmost resistance" standard was generally replaced by a "reasonable resistance" standard. Feminists criticized this standard on many grounds, including the question of who determines what is "reasonable," and why lack of resistance should be considered evidence of consent in rape when it plays no role in determining guilt or innocence in other crimes.

19. The actual frequency of false rape reports is estimated to be about the same percentage as for other crimes. See Susan Estrich, *Real Rape* (Cambridge, MA: Harvard University Press, 1987), p. 15.

20. Treatises that combined medicine and the law focused on women's sexual delusions even though men's brains were also thought to be subject to sexual delusions and hallucinations. See, e.g., Francis Wharton, *Medical Jurisprudence*, 4th ed. (Philadelphia: Kay & Brother, 1882–84), sect. 518. In *State of Washington* v. *Pryor*, 74 Wash 121, 132 P. 874 (1913), a criminal abortion case, the appeals court ruled that evidence that the prosecutrix suffered "delusions, hallucinations and illusions" should have been admitted to counter her testimony that the physician aborted her fetus.

21. For an example of Freud's influence, see *People of California* v. *Sigal*, 235 Cal.App.2d 449, 48 Cal.Rptr. 481 (1965), in which the judge commented: "A world of psychological knowledge has been revealed to us by giants like Freud. . . ." See also the often-quoted Note, "Forcible and Statutory Rape: An Explanation of the Operation and Objective of the Consent Standard," *Yale Law Journal* 62 (December 1952): 66: "Many women, for example, require as a part of preliminary 'love play' aggressive overtures by the man. . . . And the tangible signs of struggle may survive to support a subsequent accusation by the woman." See Bienen, "A Question of Credibility," 240, for a discussion of how Freud greatly influenced Wigmore and the many legal theorists who referred to Wigmore's work; Brownmiller, *Against Our Will*, pp. 343–62.

22. Sigmund Freud, *Collected Papers*, trans. Joan Riviere, vol. 4 (London: Hogarth Press and the Institute of Psychoanalysis, 1950), p. 145; Estrich, *Real Rape*,

p. 38. Many texts could be cited. See, e.g., Manfred S. Guttmacher and Henry Weihofen, *Psychiatry and the Law* (New York: Norton, 1952), p. 375: "Women frequently have fantasies of being raped"; Winfred Overholser, *The Psychiatrist and the Law* (New York: Harcourt, Brace, 1953), p. 53, who comments on the importance of Freud and the unconscious in understanding that "false accusations of sexual offenses . . . [occur as] a result of fantasy"; and Morris Ploscowe, *Sex and the Law* (New York: Prentice Hall, 1951), pp. 189–90: "The rule that a man can be convicted on the uncorroborated testimony of the female complainant alone places any man at the mercy of revengeful, spiteful, blackmailing, or psychopathic complainants."

23. Helene Deutsch, *The Psychology of Women, a Psychoanalytic Interpretation*, vol. 2 (New York: Greene & Stratton, 1944–45), pp. 79–81. Deutsch raised the issue of the terrible penalties black men faced as a result of white women's false rape accusations caused by their supposed masochistic yearnings and rape fantasies. This was the right criticism for the wrong reason. See also Brownmiller, *Against Our Will*, pp. 251–52.

24. Berger, "Man's Trial," 25–28.

25. *People* v. *Bastian*, p. 462.

26. L. Bender and A. Blau, "The Reaction of Children to Sexual Relations with Adults," *American Journal of Orthopsychiatry* 7 (1937): 500–18, cited in Judith Herman and Lisa Hirschman, "Father-Daughter Incest," *Signs: A Journal of Women in Culture and Society* 2 (1977): 738. See also Erna Olafson, David L. Corwin, and Roland C. Summit, "Modern History of Child Sexual Abuse Awareness: Cycles of Discovery and Suppression," *Child Abuse and Neglect* 17 (1993): 14, in which the authors cite an "influential 1955 state-sponsored study of child abuse victims, most of whom were female, at San Francisco's Langley Porter Clinic [which] described the majority of the victims as 'seductive,' 'flirtatious,' and 'sexually precocious.'" See also Bienen, "A Question of Credibility," 235: "Prior to the movement of the mid-1970s to reform the rape laws . . . the law, as expressed in statutes, reported appellate opinions, and legal commentaries, typically expressed denial, suspicion, and disbelief when confronted with allegations of incest or sexual abuse of young girls."

27. Alfred M. Freedman, Harold I. Kaplan, and Benjamin J. Sadock, *Comprehensive Textbook of Psychiatry-II*, 2d ed. (Baltimore: Williams & Wilkins, 1975), p. 1536.

28. Joseph Weiss, et al., "A Study of Girl Sex Victims," *Psychiatric Quarterly Supplement* 29 (1955): 24. This study was part of the Langley Porter research mentioned in note 26.

29. The controversy over "recovered memories" vs. "false memory syn-

drome," especially in several sensational 1990s cases of children who accused child-care workers of sexual abuse, is related but tangential. For a Pulitzer Prize–winning critical analysis, see Richard Ofshe and Ethan Watters, *Making Monsters: False Memories, Psychotherapy, and Sexual Hysteria* (New York: Charles Scribner's Sons, 1994).

30. Comment, "Psychiatric Evaluation of the Mentally Abnormal Witness," *Yale Law Journal* 59 (1950): 1325; S. J. Machtinger, "Psychiatric Testimony for the Impeachment of Witnesses in Sex Cases," *Journal of Criminal Law and Criminology* 39 (1949): 750–54.

31. Annotation, "Necessity or Permissibility of Mental Examination to Determine Competency or Credibility of Complainant in Sexual Offense Prosecution," *American Law Reports* 4th, 45 (1986): 310–72.

32. *People v. Russel*, 70 Cal Rept 210, 443 P. 2d 794, 796–97 (1968).

33. *Ibid.*, p. 797.

34. *Ibid.*, p. 798.

35. *Ibid.*

36. *Ibid.*, p. 797.

37. *Ibid.*, p. 802.

38. Young boys also experienced incestuous sexual assaults, which were blamed on their sexual precociousness, but these accounts were much less frequent in the literature. See, e.g., Leo L. Orenstien, "Examination of the Complaining Witness in a Criminal Court," *American Journal of Psychiatry* 107 (1951): 686, in which the author described a case of a thirty-five-year-old white male who is accused of sodomizing his nine-year-old son. The boy is described as "effeminate in appearance and mannerisms, [who] undoubtedly welcomed the father's behavior."

39. See Estrich, *Real Rape*, for a lucid discussion of why "simple" rape—in which an unarmed man rapes a woman he knows—has been so difficult for society to recognize as "real" rape.

40. *Giles, et al. v. Maryland*, 386 U.S. 66, 87 S.Ct. 793 (1966).

41. See A. Robert Smith and James V. Giles, *An American Tragedy: A True Account of the Giles-Johnson Case* (Washington, DC: New Republic Book Co., 1975); see also MacDonald, *Rape*, pp. 253–58.

42. Hubert Feild and Leigh Bienen, *Jurors and Rape: A Study in Psychology and the Law* (Lexington, MA: Lexington Books, 1980), pp. 116, 118, found that the race of the defendant affects jurors and "distorts the outcome of rape prosecution to the same degree as the victim's prior sexual history, albeit in the opposite direction." Quoted in Charles Alan Wright and Kenneth W. Graham, Jr., *Federal Practice and Procedure*: Evidence Sect. 5382, 1997 Supplement (St. Paul, MN: West Publishing Co., 1997), p. 171.

43. *State of Maryland* v. *Giles and Giles*, 239 MD 458, 474, 212 A. 2d 101 (1965).

44. Smith and Giles, *An American Tragedy*, pp. 231–33.

45. *Giles, et al.* v. *State of Maryland*, p. 798, n. 6, citing the *dissenting* judges in the Court of Appeals.

46. *Ibid.*, p. 795.

47. *Ibid.*, p. 811. Justices Black, Clark, Harlan, and Stewart dissented.

48. Joseph Johnson was pardoned by Governor Agnew in 1967.

49. GA. Code. Ann., Sect. 24-9-67 (1995) cites *Jones* v. *State of Georgia*, 232 Ga 762, 208 S.E. 2d 850 (1974). But see *Ohio* v. *Buerger*, WL 10062 (Ohio App, 1981), an incest case in which defendant tried to prove that his daughter was a nymphomaniac and not credible. The court ruled that the "disease" in the Ohio statute did not contemplate emotional ailments such as nymphomania, but rather referred to physical ailments such as gonorrhea.

50. See, e.g., *Iowa* v. *Myers*, 382 N.W. 2d 91 (1986); *Hampton* v. *Wisconsin*, 92 Wis 2d 450, 285 N.W. 2d 868 (1979); *Porter* v. *Nevada*, 94 Nev 142, 576 P2d 275 (1978).

51. As of mid-April 1999, there were no changes in this provision of the Georgia Statutes. See GA. Code. Ann., Sect. 24-9-67 (1995, Supp. 1999).

52. Jackson Rannells, "Loving Vibes at the End of the Line," *San Francisco Chronicle*, April 22, 1970, p. 1.

53. *Ibid.*

54. Merla Zellerbach, "An Investigator in the Nymphomania Case," *San Francisco Chronicle*, April 30, 1970, p. 41.

55. Rannells, "Loving Vibes," p. 1.

56. Jackson Rannells, "Jury Deliberates Case of the Cable Car Blonde," *San Francisco Chronicle*, April 29, 1970, p. 3; see also "Medical Testimony in a Case of Trauma and Nymphomania (AKA, San Francisco Cable Car Case), Showing the Cross-Examination of the Defendant's Neuropsychiatrist by the Plaintiff's Lawyer," *Medical Trial Technique Quarterly* 19, part I (1972): 110. This is a transcript of selected medical testimony from the trial, which was provided by the plaintiff's lawyer.

57. "Medical Testimony," *Medical Trial Technique Quarterly*, part II (1972): 231–33.

58. "Final Day of Cable Car Testimony," *San Francisco Chronicle*, April 25, 1970, p. 5.

59. "Medical Testimony," *Medical Trial Technique Quarterly*, part I, p. 97.

60. Rannells, "Jury Deliberates," p. 3; "Cable Car Blonde Awarded $50,000," *San Francisco Chronicle*, April 30, 1970, pp. 1, 26.

61. For an overview, see Leigh Bienen's three articles on rape in *Women's Rights Law Reporter* 3 (1976): 45–57; 3 (1977): 90–137; 6 (1980): 171–212.

62. Julie A. Allison and Lawrence S. Wrightsman, *Rape: The Misunderstood Crime* (Newbury Park, CA: Sage Publications, 1993), pp. 209, 216–18. See also Estrich, *Real Rape*; Gary LaFree, *Rape and Criminal Justice: The Social Construction of Sexual Assault* (Belmont, CA: Wadsworth Publishing Co., 1989); Patricia Searles and Ronald J. Berger, eds., *Rape and Society: Readings on the Problem of Sexual Assault* (Boulder, CO: Westview Press, 1995); Cassia Spohn and Julie Horney, *Rape Law Reform: A Grassroots Revolution and Its Impact* (New York: Plenum Press, 1992). Hawaii, Iowa, North Carolina, and Florida have subsequently rescinded rape shield laws.

63. According to Ronald J. Berger, Patricia Searles, and W. L. Neuman, "Rape Law Reform: Its Nature, Origin, and Impact," in *Rape and Society*, ed. Searles and Berger, p. 228: "Studies have generally found little change that could be directly attributed to law reform in the number of crimes that citizens report to the police, in police arrest and clearance rates, and in conviction rates." Allison and Wrightman, *Rape*, p. 216: "The efforts to assess the effects of these reforms empirically have led to conflicting conclusions." See also Spohn and Horney, *Rape Law Reform*, p. 173: "Like many others who have studied reforms aimed at the court system, [we have found] that the rape law reforms placed few constraints on the tremendous discretion exercised by decision makers in the criminal justice system."

64. Reformed rape laws continue to allow the defendant to introduce evidence of the complainant's past sexual conduct under certain circumstances, in particular, sexual activity with the accused. In addition, despite the fact there is no evidence which proves that sexually active women are more likely to lie, many jurisdictions allow a defendant to challenge a victim's credibility by presenting evidence such as the following. When a woman alleges rape after going home from a bar with a man she just met there, many judges would admit testimony about her past sexual conduct with other men she had also taken home from the bar. Finally, racist assumptions about African American women's promiscuity—an ugly holdover from a period when white men used this rationalization to justify their sexual access to slave women—hides the fact that black women are much more likely to be victims of rape than are white women. See Jennifer Wiggins, "Rape, Racism, and the Law," in *Rape and Society*, ed. Searles and Berger, pp. 212–22.

65. Wright and Graham, *Federal Practice and Procedure*: Evidence Sect. 5385 (1980), pp. 556–57. The authors document that courts were often reluctant to relinquish to expert witnesses the jury's right to determine credibility. In many cases, such as *New Mexico* v. *Romero*, the court ruled that the victim did not have to submit to a psychiatric examination. On the other hand, other courts continue to

emphasize the power to order such examinations. See also *ibid.*, Evidence Sect. 5385 (1997 Supp.), p. 200.

66. *Ibid.*, Evidence Sect. 5385 (1980), p. 557.

67. According to Edward J. Imwinkelreid, *Exculpatory Evidence: The Accused's Constitutional Right to Introduce Favorable Evidence* (Charlottesville, VA: Michie Co., 1990), p. 201, several courts have allowed the accused "to introduce evidence of the complainant's sexual conduct when it is relevant to show the complainant's bias or motive." See also Wright and Graham, *Federal Practice and Procedure*: Evidence Sect. 5385 (1980), p. 556, and Evidence Sect. 5387 (1994 Supp.), p. 178, citing *State* v. *Clarke*, 343 N.W.2d 158, 162 (Iowa 1984): "State conceded that evidence of prior sexual acts would be admissible as basis for psychiatric opinion that charged crime was fantasized, but court notes disagreement of writers on this point."

68. *Missouri* v. *Jones*, 716 S.W. 2d 799, 803 (1986).

69. Imwinkelreid, *Exculpatory Evidence*, p. 229. He suggests that "while no court [to date] has adopted Judge Blackmar's argument . . . the accused might be better advised to contend alternatively that the evidence [of nymphomania] shows her motive for lying." Thus, the accused's constitutional right to employ the theory that the accuser was biased can override rape shield laws. See also Wright and Graham, *Federal Practice and Procedure*: Evidence Sect. 5387 (1994 Supp.), p. 169, citing *People* v. *Hackett*, 421 Mich. 338, 365 N.W. 2d 120, 124 (1984): "Evidence of victim's prior sexual conduct for the narrow purpose of showing bias would almost always be constitutionally required to be admitted."

70. According to Wright and Graham, *Federal Practice and Procedure*: Evidence Sect. 5387, p. 579, there is "much reason to suspect that the literature on 'pathological lying' by women is simply old-fashioned sexist assumptions dressed up in pseudo-scientific jargon." They remind the reader that "much of this literature was generated by a study of girls from lower-class homes and involved charges of incest. The falsity of the charges is assumed based on the denial of stepfathers or institutional custodians."

71. *Missouri* v. *Jones*, p. 803.

72. *Chew* v. *Texas*, 804 S.W. 2d 633 (Tex. App—San Antonio, 1991); see also "Victim Returns to Testify After Collapse," UPI, Regional News, January 26, 1989, and *Texas Lawyer*, December 3, 1990, for coverage of the original trial.

73. "Victim Returns to Testify," UPI, p. 14.

74. *Chew* v. *Texas*, p. 634.

75. *Ibid.*, although technically the rules of evidence that shield a complaining witness in a rape case generally cover only "prior sexual conduct" or "past sexual behavior," not sexual behavior after the alleged rape.

76. *Ibid.*, p. 638.

77. *Ibid.*, p. 635.

78. *Ibid.*, pp. 641, 643. Justice Peeples was also calling attention to the distinction the rules of evidence make between the use of reputation and opinion vs. specific acts of conduct to prove character.

79. The Texas statute, which allows proof of promiscuity of statutory rape victims, was criticized but applied in *Hernandez* v. *State*, Tex. App., 754 S.W. 2d 321, 324 (1988).

80. Appellate opinions are the basic texts used in law schools to teach the law.

81. See Wright and Graham, *Federal Practice and Procedure*: Evidence Sect. 5382, pp. 496–97: "The fact that the prosecution has no appeal means that instances of abuse of the victim that led to an acquittal do not appear in the appellate reports."

82. The 1997 Supplement to Federal Practice and Procedure (p. 139) reviews the revised text of Rule 412, the federal rule of evidence concerning the relevance of victims' past behavior in sex offense cases, and cites the need for "safeguarding the victim against stereotypical thinking." In light of the tenacity of such prejudices, the newly revised rules proposed stricter guidelines regarding the admissibility of evidence relevant to the victim's past sexual behavior. See also Wright and Graham, Federal Practice and Procedure: Evidence Sect. 5385 (1999 Supp.), p. 317: the category "nymphomaniac" is still included. The case cited, *In Interest of Doe,* App. 1995, 918 P.2d 254, 263, 81 Hawai'i 447, is a case in which the "expert's opinion that the victim was a 'mental defective' incapable of consenting was based on her prior sexual conduct, defendant was entitled to introduce that conduct on cross-examination."

Chapter 5: The Sexual Revolution

1. William H. Masters and Virginia Johnson, *Human Sexual Response* (Boston: Little, Brown, 1966), p. 216.

2. *Ibid.*, p. 149.

3. Masters and Johnson, "The *Playboy* Interview," *Playboy* (May 1968), p. 158.

4. Mary Jane Sherfey, *The Nature and Evolution of Female Sexuality* (New York: Random House, 1966), pp. 110, 122, 134, 141; first published in *Journal of the American Psychoanalytic Association* 14 (1966); excerpted in Robin Morgan, ed., *Sisterhood Is Powerful* (New York: Random House, 1970), pp. 220–230, one of the first anthologies of the new women's liberation movement; and popularized in Barbara Seaman, *Free and Female: The Sex Life of the Contemporary Woman* (New York: Coward, McCann & Geoghegan, 1972).

5. Sherfey, *The Nature and Evolution of Female Sexuality*, pp. 134–38.

6. Masters and Johnson, *Human Sexual Response*, pp. 3–8. The following discussion of Masters and Johnson's work draws on the analyses of Janice Irvine, *Disorders of Desire: Sex and Gender in Modern American Sexology* (Philadelphia: Temple University Press, 1990), pp. 86–87; Paul Robinson, *The Modernization of Sex* (Ithaca, NY: Cornell University Press, 1989), pp. 120–90; Lynne Segal, *Straight Sex: Rethinking the Politics of Pleasure* (Berkeley: University of California Press, 1994), p. 93; Carol Tavris, *The Mismeasure of Women* (New York: Simon & Schuster, 1992), pp. 210–11; and Leonore Tiefer, *Sex Is Not a Natural Act and Other Essays* (Boulder, CO: Westview Press, 1995), pp. 41–58.

7. "The Second Sexual Revolution," *Time*, January 24, 1964, p. 54.

8. The following discussion of the sexual revolution and the women's movement draws on six analyses: Stephanie Coontz, *The Way We Never Were: American Families and the Nostalgia Trap* (New York: Basic Books, 1992); John D'Emilio and Estelle B. Freedman, *Intimate Matters: A History of Sexuality in America* (New York: Harper & Row, 1988); Alice Echols, *Daring to Be Bad, 1967–1975* (Minneapolis: University of Minnesota, 1989); Barbara Ehrenreich, *Re-Making Love: The Feminization of Sex* (Garden City, NY: Anchor Press/Doubleday, 1986); Lillian Rubin, *Erotic Wars: What Happened to the Sexual Revolution?* (New York: Harper & Row, 1990); and Segal, *Straight Sex*. Two studies of the women's movement appeared too late to be included: Susan Brownmiller, *In Our Time: Memoir of a Revolution* (New York: Dial Press, 1999), and Ruth Rosen, *The World Split Open: How the Modern Women's Movement Changed America* (New York: Viking, 2000).

9. According to Coontz, *The Way We Never Were*, p. 198: "In the 1970s, there was a huge surge in the proportion of single girls having had coitus and a comparable shift in attitudes accepting of this behavior." See also Irvine, *Disorders of Desire*, pp. 105–33; I. David Welch, ed., *Humanistic Psychology: A Source Book* (Buffalo: Prometheus Books), 1978.

10. Betty Friedan, *The Feminine Mystique* (New York: Norton, 1963); Helen Gurley Brown, *Sex and the Single Girl* (New York: B. Geis Associates, 1962).

11. Alex Comfort, *The Joy of Sex* (New York: Simon & Schuster, 1972); Boston Women's Health Collective, *Our Bodies, Ourselves* (New York: Simon & Schuster, 1973); Nancy Friday, *My Secret Garden: Women's Sexual Fantasies* (New York: Trident Press, 1973); Marabell Morgan, *The Total Woman* (Old Tappan, NJ: F. H. Revell, 1973).

12. Masters and Johnson, *Human Sexual Response*, pp. 21–22.

13. Anne Koedt, *The Myth of the Vaginal Orgasm* (Boston: New England Free Press, 1969), p. 1.

14. Alix Kates Shulman, "Organs and Orgasms," in *Woman in Sexist Society:*

Studies in Power and Powerlessness, ed. Vivian Gornick and Barbara K. Moran (New York: Basic Books, 1971), pp. 203, 205. See also Shere Hite, *The Hite Report: A Nationwide Study of Female Sexuality* (New York: Dell, 1976). For a history of the clitoris, see Thomas P. Lowry, ed., *The Clitoris* (St. Louis: Warren Gren, 1976).

15. Koedt, *The Myth of the Vaginal Orgasm*, p. 5.

16. Eugene E. Levitt, "Nymphomania," *Sexual Behavior* 3 (1973): 15. Levitt coauthored the 1989 "update" of the *Kinsey Report*, Albert D. Klassen, Colin J. Williams, and Eugene Levitt, *Sexual Morality in the U.S.* (Middletown, CT: Wesleyan University, 1989); see also his entry on nymphomania in the *Encyclopedia of Psychology*, ed. Raymond J. Corsini, 2d ed. (New York: Wiley, 1994 [1984]), vol. 2, p. 498.

17. Levitt, "Nymphomania," 13; see also Joshua S. Golden, "What Is Sexual Promiscuity?", *Medical Aspects of Human Sexuality* (hereafter cited as *MAHS*) 2 (1968): 47–53; Jim Orford, "Hypersexuality: Implications for a Theory of Dependence," *British Journal of Addiction* 73 (1978): 299–310.

18. Levitt, "Nymphomania," 16.

19. *Ibid.*, 17.

20. Donald W. Hastings, *Impotence and Frigidity* (Boston: Little, Brown, 1963), p. 15; William Fry, "Psychodynamics of Sexual Humor: Nymphomania," *MAHS* 12 (1978): 119, although Fry added that this too is a stereotype of male sexuality.

21. Eustace Chesser, *Strange Loves: The Human Aspects of Sexual Deviation* (New York: Morrow, 1971), p. 180; see also Clifford Allen, *A Textbook of Psychosexual Disorders*, 2d ed. (London: Oxford University Press, 1969), p. 355.

22. Chesser, *Strange Loves*, pp. 179–80.

23. See, e.g., Golden, "What Is Sexual Promiscuity?", 47–53; Jerry M. Lewis, "Promiscuous Women," *Sexual Behavior* 1 (1971): 74–80; Joseph LoPiccolo and Julia Heiman, "Cultural Values and the Therapeutic Definition of Sexual Function and Dysfunction," *Journal of Social Issues* 33 (1977): 166–83; Ira Reiss, "Sexual Renaissance in America: A Summary and Analysis," *Journal of Social Issues* 22 (1966): 123–37.

24. Alfred Auerbach, "Nymphomania," *MAHS* 6 (1972): 9; see also Auerback's article, "Satyriasis and Nymphomania," *MAHS* 2 (1968): 39–41, 44–45.

25. "The Don Juan," *Sexual Behavior* (December 1972), pp. 4–9; James L. McCary, *Human Sexuality*, 2d ed. (New York: Van Nostrand Reinhold, 1973), p. 304. My thanks to Leonore Tiefer, who told me that McCary's text was one of the few available for her to use in teaching one of the first college-level courses on human sexuality in 1972. See also Eugene Pumpian-Mindlin, "Nymphomania and Satyriasis," in Charles Wahl, ed., *Sexual Problems, Diagnosis and Treatment in Medical Practice* (New York: Free Press, 1967), pp. 163–71.

26. Auerback, "Satyriasis and Nymphomania," 41, 44; see also, Marcus Mc-Broom, "A Clinical Appraisal of Some Sexually Promiscuous Females," *Journal of the National Medical Association* 55 (1963): 290–94.

27. Stanley E. Willis, "Sexual Promiscuity as a Symptom of Personal and Cultural Anxiety," *MAHS* 1 (1967): 22, 16. A similar article was included in Wahl, *Sexual Problems*, pp. 173–91.

28. Willis, "Sexual Promiscuity," 20, 21.

29. *Ibid.*, 22.

30. Albert Ellis and Edward Sagarin, *Nymphomania: A Study of the Oversexed Woman* (New York: Gramercy Publishing Co., 1964), p. 29.

31. *Ibid.*, pp. 26–29.

32. *Ibid.*, p. 70.

33. *Ibid.*, pp. 15–16.

34. *Ibid.*, pp. 19–20.

35. According to Thomas Laqueur, *Making Sex: Body and Gender from the Greeks to Freud* (Cambridge, MA: Harvard University Press, 1990), pp. 3–4: "The commonplace of much contemporary psychology—that men want sex while women want relationships—is the precise inversion of pre-Enlightenment notions that, extending back to antiquity, equated friendship with men and fleshiness with women."

36. Donald W. Burnap and Joshua S. Golden, "Sexual Problems in Medical Practice," *Journal of Medical Education and Practice* 42 (1967): 50; James McCary, *Sex Myths and Fallacies* (New York: Van Nostrand Reinhold, 1971), p. 122.

37. In addition to those discussed below, a few of the many titles published during the period are Rey Anthony, *The Housewives' Handbook in Selective Promiscuity* (New York: Documentary Books, 1962); Adelaide Bry, *The Sexually Aggressive Woman* (New York: New American Library, 1975); Robert Bledsoe, *Female Sexual Deviations and Bizarre Practices* (Los Angeles: Sherburne Press, 1964); David O. Cauldwell, ed., *Unusual Female Sexual Practices* (Inglewood, CA: Banner Books, 1966); Franklin S. Klaf and Bernhardt J. Hurwood, *Nymphomania: A Psychiatrist's View* (New York: Lancer Books, 1964); Benjamin Morse, *The Sexually Promiscuous Female* (New York: Monarch, 1963); and Nathan Shiff, *Diary of a Nymph* (New York: Lancer Books, 1961).

38. According to John Oliven, *Clinical Sexuality: A Manual for the Physician and the Professions* (Philadelphia: J. B. Lippincott, 1974), p. 430: "Because of modern principles of treatment, the massive sexual excesses of hospitalized female schizophrenics are no longer seen." On the other hand, Jerome Goodman, "Nymphomania and Satyriasis," in *Behavior in Excess*, ed. S. Joseph Mule (New York: Free Press, 1981), p. 249, states: "It is usual to find excessive sexual stimulation ac-

companied by flagrant social behavior on the wards of psychiatric hospitals. . . ."
See also Ivor Feldstein, "Nymphomania II," *British Journal of Sexual Medicine* (August 1982): 35–36.

39. Thomas P. Detre and Jonathan M. Himmelhoch, "Hyperlibido," *MAHS* 7 (1973): 72, 77, 80, 85, reviews the various conditions associated with increases in sexual desire, including mania, schizophrenia, sociopathy, and those associated with apparent increases, including depressive disorders, and organic brain syndromes. But see Ming T. Tsuang, "Hypersexuality in Manic Patients," *MAHS* 9 (1975): 83, 86, 89, in which he contends that while hypersexuality is often the first sign of manic illness, there might be a double standard at work for women that allows less activity in female sexual behavior before labeling it hypersexual than would be the case for males. F. Kraupe Taylor, *Psychopathology: Its Cause and Symptoms*, rev. ed. (Baltimore: Johns Hopkins University Press, 1979 [1966]), pp. 162–63, discusses nymphomania, along with dypsomania and kleptomania but not satyriasis, under the category of obsessive-compulsive neuroses. On the other hand, Harold I. Kaplan and Benjamin J. Sadock, *Modern Synopsis of Comprehensive Testbook of Psychiatry / III*, 3d ed. (Baltimore: Williams & Wilkins, 1981 [1972]), p. 265, includes nymphomania, kleptomania, pyromania, and dypsomania in a category of compulsive acts, not usually connected with obsessive-compulsive neurosis.

40. J. Henry Rusk, *Insatiable Women, Unfaithful Wives* (San Diego: Greenleaf Classics, 1972).

41. Edward Podolsky and Carlson Wade, *Nymphomania*, Sexual Behavior Series, no. 3 (New York: Epic Publishing Co., 1961), pp. 18, 20.

42. Victoria Morhaim, *Casebook: Nymphomania* (New York: Dell, 1964).

43. *Ibid.*, p. 7. Ellis also claimed that these cases of frigid nymphomaniacs were fairly typical, even though he criticized the notion that nymphomaniacs were frigid in his own book, *Nymphomania: A Case Study*.

44. American Psychiatric Association, *Diagnostic and Statistical Manual of Mental Disorders* (Washington, DC: APA, 1952), pp. 98, 121.

45. Herb Kutchins and Stuart A. Kirk, *Making Us Crazy. DSM: The Psychiatric Bible and the Creation of Mental Disorders* (New York: Free Press, 1997), p. 11.

46. Reflecting changing cultural notions about sexuality, *DSM-III* cast the spotlight on too little—rather than too much—sex. Since sex was now perceived as critical to health and well-being, not wanting to have sex, or not enjoying it when you did, became the more important disorder. See Janice Irvine, "Regulating Passion: The Invention of Inhibited Sexual Desire and Sex Addiction," in *Deviant Bodies*, ed. Jennifer Terry and Jacqueline Urla (Bloomington: Indiana University Press, 1995), pp. 314–37.

47. *DSM-III* (Washington, DC: APA, 1980), p. 283.

48. Stephen B. Levine, "A Modern Perspective on Nymphomania," *Journal of Sex and Marital Therapy* 8 (1982): 316.

49. *DSM-III-R* (Washington, DC: APA, 1987), p. 296.

50. *DSM-IV* (Washington, DC: APA, 1994), p. 538. The category "Sexual Disorder Not Otherwise Specified" now stated: "Distress about a pattern of repeated sexual relationships involving a succession of lovers who are experienced by the individual only as things to be used."

51. Recent surveys and studies indicate that men outnumber women among child molesters by very large percentages. See Erna Olafson, David L. Corwin, and Roland C. Summit, "Modern History of Child Sexual Abuse Awareness: Cycles of Discovery and Suppression," *Child Abuse and Neglect* 17 (1993): 16.

52. David Finkelhor, *A Sourcebook on Child Sexual Abuse* (Beverly Hills, CA: Sage Publications, 1986), p. 15. The number of child sexual abuse cases reported rose from 7,559 in 1976 to 71,961 in 1983. Child sexual abuse covers a broader range of offenses than incest, which *Webster's Dictionary* defines as "sexual intercourse between persons so closely related that they are forbidden by law to marry." Today, especially with the increase in modern "blended" families, "incest" may also include stepfathers.

53. Finkelhor, *Sourcebook*, p. 67. According to Finkelhor, although empirical studies show a strong association between class and child abuse, "most representative surveys have been unable to find any relationship" between class and child *sexual* abuse.

54. Louise Armstrong, *Kiss Daddy Goodnight: A Speak Out on Incest* (New York: Pocket Books, 1978); see also Florence Rush, *The Best Kept Secret: Sexual Abuse of Children* (Englewood Cliffs, NJ: Prentice Hall, 1980); Toni A.H. McNaron and Yarrow Morgan, eds., *Voices in the Night: Women Speaking Out About Incest* (Pittsburgh: Cleis, 1982); and Janet Liebman Jacobs, *Victimized Daughters: Incest and the Development of the Female Self* (New York: Routledge, 1994). As Jacobs points out (p. 42), the victim experiences a "complicated psychological process of self blame which allows the child to preserve the image of the idealized parent" and also to restore an illusion of control.

55. See Jacobs, *Victimized Daughters*, p. 48; Christine Courtois, "The Incest Experience and Its Aftermath," *Victimology: An International Journal* 4 (1979): 337–47; Mary deYoung, *The Sexual Victimization of Children* (Jefferson, NC: McFarland & Co., 1982); Linda Gordon, *Heroes of Their Own Lives: The Politics and History of Family Violence* (New York: Viking Penguin, 1988); Judith Herman and Lisa Hirschman, "Father-Daughter Incest," *Signs: Journal of Women in Culture and Society* 2 (1977): 735–56; Judith Herman, *Father-Daughter Incest* (Cambridge, MA: Harvard University Press, 1981).

56. Joseph H. Beitchman, et al. "A Review of the Short-Term Effects of Child Sexual Abuse," *Child Abuse and Neglect* 15 (1991), 537–56; Beitchman et al., "A Review of the Long-Term Effects of Child Sexual Abuse," *Child Sexual Abuse and Neglect* 16 (1992), 101–18.

57. Robert M. Goldenson, *The Encyclopedia of Human Behavior: Psychology, Psychiatry and Mental Health*, vol. 2 (New York: Doubleday, 1970), pp. 882–84; Jerome Goodman, "Nymphomania," *MAHS* 16 (1982): 64–65, 70; Natalie Shainess, "Nymphomania, Hostile Sex and Superego Development," in *Sexual Dynamics of Anti-Social Behavior*, ed. Louise B. Schlesinger and Eugene Revitch (Springfield, IL: Charles Thomas Publisher, 1983), p. 52.

58. Beitchman, "Review of the Long-Term Effects," 115. This authoritative study concluded: "In comparison with women not reporting a history of CSA (child sexual abuse), women who do report a history of CSA more commonly: show evidence of sexual disturbance or dysfunction." This included fear of sex, less sexual interest, less sexual pleasure, promiscuity, or confused sexual orientation. See also "Maltreated Children," *Annual Review of Psychology*, ed. Janet T. Spence, John M. Darley, and Donald J. Foss, 48 (Palo Alto, CA: Annual Reviews, 1997), p. 422: "The most consistent finding reflected in the sexual abuse literature has been that sexual abuse is associated with some degree of sexual maladjustment often characterized by sexual precocities, promiscuity, or sexual aggression."

59. James Leslie McCary, "My Most Unusual Sexual Case: Nymphomania," *MAHS* 13 (1979): 74–75. McCary wrote about the same case in a 1972 article in the same journal: "Nymphomania: A Case Study," 6 (1972): 192, 197–98, 202, 210.

60. McCary, "My Most Unusual Sexual Case," 74.

61. *Ibid.*, 75.

62. Louise Armstrong, *Rocking the Cradle of Sexual Politics: What Happened When Women Said Incest* (New York: Addison-Wesley, 1994), p. 123, argues that a backlash against the mothers who accused their husbands of sexually abusing their children has occurred and that some courts treat the raising of sexual abuse as merely a ploy by the wives to win custody of the children. A lawyer and expert in child custody cases, Mary Ann Mason, makes a similar argument; see her book, *The Custody Wars* (New York: Basic Books, 1999), pp. 144–45, 165–73. See also Helen Daniels, "Truth, Community, and the Politics of Memory: Narratives of Child Sexual Abuse," in *Bad Girls, Good Girls: Women, Sex, and Power in the Nineties*, ed. Nan Bauer Maglin and Donna Perry (New Brunswick, NJ: Rutgers University Press, 1996), pp. 150–63.

63. Mason, *The Custody Wars*, pp. 144–45, 165–73.

64. Joan Jacobs Brumberg, *The Body Project: An Intimate History of American Girls* (New York: Random House, 1997).

65. "Inside Story: Baby Beauty Queens," Arts and Entertainment Channel, May 18, 1998

Chapter 6: Happy Nymphos and Sexual Addicts

1. *New York Times Sunday Magazine*, November 21, 1993, p. 69; Dinitia Smith, "Eartha Kitt, Living Her Nine Lives to the Fullest," *New York Times*, March 2, 1999.

2. *Jenny Jones*, "Three Women Whose Hobby Is Sex," March 10, 1992, and "Sexual Promiscuity Without Apology," May 16, 1994.

3. Marion Winik, "Confessions of a Serious Nymphomaniac," *Cosmopolitan* (June 1995), pp. 160, 164–65.

4. Kathryn McMahon, "The *Cosmopolitan* Ideology and the Management of Desire," *Journal of Sex Research* 27 (1980): 382.

5. Carol Tavris and Susan Sadd, *The Redbook Report on Female Sexuality* (New York: Delacorte Press, 1975), p. 3.

6. Judith Coburn, "Thinking of Having a Fling?" *Mademoiselle* (May 1979), pp. 182–83, 250, 252.

7. Lewis Burkes Frumkes, "One Night Stands: Risky or Fun?" *Harper's Bazaar* (February 1980), pp. 107, 151, 154.

8. David Givens, "Sexcess and Excess: Are You a Nymphomaniac?", *Harper's Bazaar* (April 1986), pp. 72–73.

9. Sheila Moramarco, "Women's Confidential Guide to Better Sex," *Harper's Bazaar* (October 1983), pp. 206–07, 248.

10. Sue Mitthenthal, "New Sexual Attitudes," *Glamour* (September 1985), pp. 338–39, 425, 427.

11. Kiki Olson, "Sex with a Stranger," *Glamour* (October 1985), pp. 168, 172–73.

12. Bonnie Allen, "The Sexual Revolution," *Essence* (February 1983), p. 61.

13. Robert Staples, "The Sexual Revolution and the Black Middle Class," *Ebony* (August 1987), pp. 56–58.

14. Allen, "The Sexual Revolution," 62.

15. Bebe Moore Campbell, "Sexual Freedom and the 'Now' Woman," *Ebony* (August 1982), p. 58.

16. McMahon, "The *Cosmopolitan* Ideology," p. 382; Ellen McCracken, *Decoding Women's Magazines from Mademoiselle to Ms.* (New York: Macmillan, 1993), pp. 158–62; Ellen McCracken, "Demystifying *Cosmopolitan*: Five Critical Methods," *Journal of Popular Culture* 16 (1982): 30–42.

17. Winik, "Confessions," 164.

18. *Ibid.*, 165.

19. *Ibid.*, 160. Lillian Rubin, *Erotic Wars: What Happened to the Sexual Revolution?* (New York: Harper & Row, 1990), p. 116, states that women often understate their sexual experience because they believe that their boyfriends would not approve if they revealed the real extent of their experience.

20. "Ask E. Jean," *Elle* (February 1995), p. 78.

21. Blanche Vernon, "Sex Questions Guys Are Too Embarrassed To Ask You," *Mademoiselle* (November 1996), pp. 148–50.

22. "Dr. Ruth," *Los Angeles Times*, February 28, 1988.

23. The discussion of porn films and videos that follows draws on the analyses of Linda Williams, *Hard Core: Power, Pleasure and the "Frenzy of the Visible"* (Berkeley: University of California Press, 1989); Feminist Anti-Censorship Task Force (FACT), *Caught Looking: Feminism, Pornography, and Censorship* (East Haven, CT: Long River Books, 1992); Laura Kipnis, *Bound and Gagged: Pornography and the Politics of Fantasy in America* (New York: Grove Press, 1996); Robert H. Rimmer and Patrick Riley, *The X-Rated Videotape Guide IV* (Buffalo: Prometheus Books, 1994); and Robert Stoller, *Porn: Myths for the Twentieth Century* (New Haven: Yale University Press, 1991). The term "happy nympho" is mine.

24. Williams, *Hard Core*, pp. 112–13. For a different point of view, see Susan Lurie, "Pornography and the Dread of Women," in *Take Back the Night: Women on Pornography*, ed. Laura Lederer (New York: Morrow, 1980), pp. 159–73. Linda "Lovelace" Marchiano later joined the anti-pornography movement and testified at the 1983 Minneapolis hearings that she had been held captive and forced to perform in porn movies. See Catherine A. MacKinnon and Andrea Dworkin, *In Harm's Way: The Pornography Civil Rights Hearings* (Cambridge, MA: Harvard University Press, 1997), pp. 60–66.

25. John Hubner, *Bottom Feeders from Free Love to Hard Core* (New York: Doubleday, 1993), pp. 172, 203.

26. *Time*, March 30, 1987, p. 63.

27. Williams, *Hard Core*, pp. 175–79.

28. Candida Royale, "Porn in the USA," *Social Text* 37 (1993): 23–32; Linda Williams, "A Provoking Agent: The Pornography and Performance Art of Annie Sprinkle," *Social Text* 37 (1993): 117–33; Kegan Doyle and Dany Lacombe, "Porn Power: Sex, Violence, and the Meaning of Images in 1980s Feminism," in *Bad Girls, Good Girls: Women, Sex, and Power in the Nineties*, ed. Nan Bauer Maglin and Donna Perry (New Brunswick: Rutgers University Press, 1996), pp. 188–204.

29. The discussion of the anti-porn struggle draws on the following studies: Gail Dines, Robert Jensen, and Ann Russo, *Pornography: The Production and Con-

sumption of Inequality (New York: Routledge, 1998); Andrea Dworkin, *Pornography: Men Possessing Women* (G. P. Putnam's Sons, 1979); Carole S. Vance, ed., *Pleasure and Danger: Exploring Female Sexuality* (Boston: Routledge & Kegan Paul, 1984); FACT, *Caught Looking*; Kipnis, *Bound and Gagged*; Lederer, ed., *Take Back the Night*; MacKinnon and Dworkin, *In Harm's Way*; Lisa Palac, *The Edge of the Bed: How Dirty Pictures Changed My Life* (Boston: Little, Brown, 1998); Lynne Segal and Mary McIntosh, *Sex Exposed: Sexuality and the Pornography Debates* (New Brunswick: Rutgers University Press, 1993); and Ellen Willis, *No More Nice Girls: Countercultural Essays* (Hanover, NH: University Press, 1992).

30. Attorney General's Commission on Pornography, *Final Report* (Nashville, TN: Rutledge Hill Press, 1986).

31. Susan Brownmiller, "Let's Put Pornography Back in the Closet," in *Take Back the Night*, ed. Lederer, p. 254.

32. Andrea Dworkin, *Woman Hating* (New York: Harper & Row, 1974); Dworkin, "Why So-Called Radical Men Love and Need Pornography," in *Take Back the Night*, ed. Lederer, p. 152.

33. MacKinnon and Dworkin, *In Harm's Way*, pp. 269–70.

34. Ellen Willis, "Feminism, Moralism, and Pornography," in FACT, *Caught Looking*, p. 56.

35. Dave Kehr, "Friday's Guide to Movies and Music," *Chicago Tribune*, March 20, 1992.

36. *Basic Instinct*—description on the video box cover.

37. Yvonne Tasker, *Working Girls: Gender and Sexuality in Popular Culture* (London: Routledge, 1998), pp. 124–25. See also Mary Ann Doane, *Femmes Fatales: Feminism, Film Theory, Psychoanalysis* (New York: Routledge, 1991), p. 238; and Andrea Weiss, *Vampires and Violets: Lesbians in Film* (New York: Penguin, 1993).

38. John Lahr, "The Big Picture: Call Her Voracious," *New Yorker*, March 25, 1996, pp. 72–79.

39. Center for the Study of Southern Culture, *The Encyclopedia of Southern Culture* (Chapel Hill: University of North Carolina Press, 1989), p. 662.

40. CNN *Showbiz Today*, transcript #769, segment #6, April 6, 1995.

41. Kevin Smith, Screenplay of *Chasing Amy*, pp. 97, 102.

42. John Hughes, Screenplay for *The Breakfast Club*, pp. 97, 102. My thanks to my research assistant, Kathy Feeley, for bringing this scene to my attention.

43. Quoted in the film. My thanks to my colleague Norma Manatu-Rupert for her discussion of this film. See her Ph.D. dissertation, "A Comparison of the Sexual Imagery of Black Women in Contemporary American Films by Black and White Filmmakers," New York University, 1998; Jacquie Jones, "The Construction of Black Sexuality: Towards Normalizing the Black Cinematic Experience," in

Black American Cinema, ed. Manthia Diawara (New York: Routledge, 1993), pp. 247–56; bell hooks, "whose pussy is this? A feminist comment," in *reel to reel: race, sex, and class at the movies*, ed. hooks (New York: Routledge, 1995); pp. 227–35; Michele Wallace, "Films," *The Nation*, June 4, 1988, pp. 800–01.

44. Quoted in the film *She's Gotta Have It*.

45. Quoted in the film *Everyone Says I Love You*; Joel and Ethan Coen, Screenplay for *The Big Lebowski*, pp. 50, 52–53.

46. Molly Haskell, *From Reverence to Rape*, 2d ed. (Chicago: University of Chicago Press, 1987), p. 388.

47. *Atlanta Constitution*, September 9, 1991; *Chicago Tribune*, September 20, 1991; *The Guardian*, January 10, 1992; *Los Angeles Times*, September 10, 1991; *Newsday*, December 15, 1991; *New York Times*, August 1, 1991; *People* Magazine, September 23, 1991; *St. Petersburg Times*, August 11, September 11, and November 1, 1991; *Times Picayune*, September 13, 1991; *Toronto Star*, September 5, 1992; *USA Today*, September 4 and October 31, 1991; *Washington Post*, July 23, August 28, September 11, 1991; and on Reuters Wire Service on September 13 and 26, 1991, and UPI, July 30, 1991.

48. Ellis Rubin as told to Richard Smitten, *Kathy: A Case of Nymphomania* (Hollywood, FL: Lifetime Books, 1993), p. 157.

49. *Geraldo*, February 10, 1992.

50. Rubin, *Kathy*, pp. 25–28; Reuters Wire Service, July 26, 1991.

51. *Larry King Live*, November 8, 1991.

52. *St. Petersburg Times*, September 11, 1991.

53. *Larry King Live*, November 8, 1991.

54. *Ibid.*

55. *Geraldo*, January 10, 1994.

56. *Ibid.*, February 10, 1992.

57. *Maury Povich*, April 16, 1996.

58. *USA Today*, September 4, 1991.

59. *Oprah Winfrey*, May 14, 1999.

60. Patrick Carnes, one of the founders of the movement, stated that onethird of his groups are women. See Daniel Goleman, "Some Sexual Behavior Viewed as an Addiction," *New York Times*, October 16, 1984. Statistics from the National Association of Sexual Addiction Problems cited on *Oprah Winfrey*; see also Eileen P. Gunn, "Addicted to Sex," *Fortune*, May 10, 1999, pp. 66–80. The problem of too much sex has captured the public imagination. Despite that fact, according to the psychologist and sex therapist Sandra Leiblum, who commented on a paper I gave on nymphomania to the Keen's Seminar on Sexuality in 1991, female patients most often complain to therapists today about *low* sexual desire (the

too-tired-to-have-sex refrain), not about being oversexed. See Janice Irvine, "Regulated Passions: The Invention of Inhibited Sexual Desire and Sexual Addiction," in *Deviant Bodies*, ed. Jennifer Terry and Jacqueline Urla (Bloomington: Indiana University Press, 1995), pp. 314–37.

61. See, e.g., "Dear Abby," "Says She's Addicted to Sex," *New York Post*, December 26, 1983; Carol Saline, "To the Addict, Sex Is Like the Junkie's Needle, or the Alcoholic's Next Martini," *Daily News*, February 24, 1985; Ann Landers, "The Double Life of the Sex Addict," *Los Angeles Times*, April 26, 1988; "Sexual Binging Won't Bring You Happiness," *USA Today*, August 5, 1986; Barbara Dolan, "Do People Get Hooked on Sex?" *Time*, June 4, 1990, p. 72; and Jean Seligman, "Taking Life One Night at a Time," *Newsweek*, July 20, 1987. One of the earliest medical articles was by Jim Orford, "Hypersexuality: Implications for a Theory of Dependence," *British Journal of Addiction* 73 (1978): 299–310.

62. The section on sexual addiction draws on the work of: Janice Irvine, "Reinventing Perversion: Sexual Addiction and Cultural Anxiety," *Journal of the History of Sexuality* (1995): 429–50; Patrick Carnes, *The Sexual Addiction* (Minneapolis: CompCare Publications, 1983); Tana Dineen, *Manufacturing Victims: What the Psychology Industry Is Doing to People* (Montreal: Robert Davies, 1996); Charlotte Kasl, *Women, Sex, and Addiction: A Search for Love and Power* (New York: Harper & Row, 1989); Wendy Kaminer, *I'm Dysfunctional, You're Dysfunctional* (Reading, MA: Addison-Wesley, 1991); Robin Norwood, *Women Who Love Too Much* (Los Angeles: Jeremy P. Tarcher, 1985); and Stanton Peele, *Diseasing of America: Addiction Treatment Out of Control* (Lexington, MA: Lexington Books, 1989).

63. Emotional neglect or psychological abuse is defined very broadly, and includes the effects of divorce, death, accidents, war, early hospitalization, isolation, as well as willful abuse.

64. As Janice Irvine points out in "Regulated Passions," pp. 314–17, "Inhibited Sexual Desire" and "Sex Addiction" were both invented as diagnostic categories at the same time.

65. Stephen Arterburn, *Addicted to "Love": Understanding Dependence of the Heart: Romance Relationships and Sex* (Ann Arbor, MI: Vine Books, 1996).

66. See the Web site of the National Council on Sexual Addiction and Compulsivity (NCSAC) at www.ncsac.org.

67. Norwood, *Women Who Love Too Much*. In AA, "co-dependent" originally meant the partner, usually the wife, of an alcoholic whose behavior "enabled" the husband to keep drinking.

68. Kasl, *Women, Sex, and Addiction*, p. 43. See also Charlotte Kasl, *Many Roads, One Journey* (New York: Harper Perennial, 1992), p. 96; Anne McBean, "Assessment and Treatment of Sexually Compulsive Women: A Guide Through the

Labyrinth," paper presented at the National Conference on Sexual Compulsivity/Addiction, sponsored by the University of Minnesota's Program in Human Sexuality, May 19–21, 1991. My thanks to Tim Smith for supplying me with audio tapes of the conference.

69. "Position Paper: Women Sex Addicts," NCSAC Web site.

70. Rebecca Chalker, "Updating the Model of Female Sexuality," SIECUS Report 22 (1994): 1–6, quoted in Peter B. Anderson and Cindy Struckman-Johnson, *Sexually Aggressive Women* (New York: Guilford Press, 1998), p. 30.

71. For a sampling of programs, see "What Sexual Addiction Is and How It Can Be Overcome," Christian Broadcasting Network's *The 700 Club*, April 28, 1998; "Three Women Recovering from Sexual Addiction Discuss Their Therapy," CNBC's *Real Personal*, June 26, 1995; "My Wife Can't Get Enough Sex," *Geraldo*, January 10, 1994; "Do People Really Suffer From Sexual Addiction?" *Doctor Dean*, September 4, 1992; "Sex Addicts," *Jenny Jones*, November 21, 1991.

72. *Oprah Winfrey*, May 14, 1999.

73. There are many versions of these questionnaires; see NCSAC Web site for examples. See also Alan J. Smith, "Development of the Neismith Sexual/Romantic Addiction Questionnaire," Ph.D. diss., University of Nebraska, 1990.

74. In *Women, Sex, and Addiction*, p. xi, for example, Kasl states that "childhood abuse, along with poverty and oppression, underlie numerous addictions." But only the influences of childhood abuse are examined throughout the book. For an additional critique, see Martin P. Levine and Richard R. Troiden, "The Myth of Sexual Compulsivity," *Journal of Sex Research* 25 (1988): 347–63.

75. *Oprah Winfrey*, May 14, 1999.

Afterword

1. See Natalie Angier, *Woman: An Intimate Geography* (New York: Houghton Mifflin, 1999), p. 334, for a critique of the newest theories in evolutionary psychology, which support the traditional notion that women have lower sex drives than men. Angier asks how women would know what their potential sexual desires might be: unlike men, for whom "the diagnosis of 'nymphomaniac' is never made," women are universally punished if they display evidence of strong desire, "if they disobey their 'natural' inclination toward a stifled libido."

index

225